WORKING FOR THE BRAND

Josh Bornstein is an award-winning Australian lawyer, specialising in employment and labour-relations law, and writer. In his day job, he has sued a lot of badly behaved corporations and acted for employees who were sacked for expressing controversial views. He is a member of the board of the progressive think tank The Australia Institute and the advisory board of the Centre for Employment and Labour Relations Law at the University of Melbourne. He is also a member of a sports disciplinary tribunal.

WORKING FOR THE BRAND

how corporations are destroying free speech

Josh Bornstein

SCRIBE
Melbourne | London | Minneapolis

Scribe Publications
18–20 Edward St, Brunswick, Victoria 3056, Australia
2 John St, Clerkenwell, London, WC1N 2ES, United Kingdom
3754 Pleasant Ave, Suite 100, Minneapolis, Minnesota 55409, USA

Published by Scribe 2024

Copyright © Josh Bornstein 2024

All rights reserved. Without limiting the rights under copyright reserved above, no part of this publication may be reproduced, stored in or introduced into a retrieval system, or transmitted, in any form or by any means (electronic, mechanical, photocopying, recording or otherwise) without the prior written permission of the publishers of this book.

The moral rights of the author have been asserted.

Typeset in 12/17 pt Adobe Garamond Pro by J&M Typesetting

Printed and bound in Australia by Griffin Press

Scribe is committed to the sustainable use of natural resources and the use of paper products made responsibly from those resources.

Scribe acknowledges Australia's First Nations peoples as the traditional owners and custodians of this country, and we pay our respects to their elders, past and present.

978 1 761381 04 1 (paperback edition)
978 1 761385 79 7 (ebook)

A catalogue record for this book is available from the National Library of Australia.

scribepublications.com.au
scribepublications.co.uk
scribepublications.com

CONTENTS

Introduction		1
ONE	Rage and Revenge	7
TWO	Flexible Control	31
THREE	Do Corporations Have Feelings?	61
FOUR	The Ethically Washed Brand	93
FIVE	A Festival of Hypocrisy: free speech and cancel culture	123
SIX	Academic Freedom and the University Brand	157
SEVEN	The Journalism Paradox	193
EIGHT	Consensual Sex and Work	225
NINE	The Battle to Democratise Economic Power	251
Acknowledgements		*277*
Notes		*279*

Because if you in name have a democracy, but in your day-to-day life you're treated like a serf in your economic transactions, that's really going to undermine people's day-to-day experience of whether they're free.
    –Lina Khan, chair of the US Federal Trade Commission

Introduction

When I was five years old, I discovered that a lawyer got paid to argue. I liked to argue. I announced my decision then and there: I would become a lawyer when I grew up. Other than for a short period in my early teens, when I flirted with the idea of becoming a jockey, I remained steadfast. My parents were utopian socialists who surrounded me with Marxist texts and instilled in me a visceral attachment to defending the underdog. I struggled with the nuances of dialectical materialism, but sticking up for the underdog has never left me. It guaranteed a lot of schoolyard conflict because there was always someone to stick up for. I worked out pretty quickly that I was better with words than with my fists. When my parents suddenly removed me from the state school system and sent me to an elite private school, I was severely outnumbered by rabid anti-Semites and conservatives. For a time, I became the underdog. Thankfully, I still enjoyed arguing.

My career as a trade union lawyer started in the late 1980s, just as the neoliberal era was taking hold and trade unions were finding themselves increasingly under attack. For years, I worked with them to try to stem the relentless flow of union-busting by Australian big businesses. Despite some strong resistance and momentous legal victories, we lost the war. Union membership collapsed catastrophically to the point where, by 2023, only 8 per cent of private sector employees in Australia were union members. In post-bargaining workplaces, employee wages and conditions are determined by unilateral managerial decree.

As the labour market was de-unionised, I increasingly took on cases for individual employees and witnessed up close the traumatic impact of losing a job or of a career being derailed. Along the way, I developed niche areas of legal practice. I cornered the market in sacked rabbis and academics facing disciplinary proceedings. I worked with women in media and the arts. In the wake of #MeToo, I have represented a growing cohort of women pursuing sexual harassment claims against judges in different Australian courts.

I am no mechanic, but my job has given me an extraordinary opportunity to look under the bonnet of organisations when things go awry. I have peered inside the operations of major mining and financial-services corporations, religious institutions, media and sporting empires, universities, courts, and political parties. In the process, I have been struck by the gulf between corporate brands and the reality of their business models and workplace culture. In the 21st century, major corporations are more powerful than ever. As they have accrued wealth, status, and political influence, they have become more ruthless at fending off anything that might challenge their extraordinary power—whether it comes in the form of taxation, regulation, or unionisation.

Corporations now invest more than ever in their brands, which proclaim that they care, are imbued with commendable purposes, and are activists for social betterment. In reality, the corporate-brand industry is a form of ethics-washing. When threatened, the brand is unforgiving and ruthless. And as social media use has reduced our attention span to 45-second increments and upended our lives and culture, it has also threatened the brand. The broken democracy of social media has fomented a culture of shaming, punishment, bullying, and Colosseum justice. It is replete with bad-faith actors who seek to punish their foes by depriving them of income. This is done by the simple device of linking an individual's speech to their corporate employer, pressuring the corporation to take action. It has allowed anyone to criticise, satirise, or try to smear a corporation online.

As the online revolution has unfolded, I have found myself acting for employees who have been shamed online and then sacked by their employer — ostensibly to protect the corporate brand. Usually, their sin was to say or do something in their personal lives that attracted the online mob: a controversial or dissident view, or even a bad joke. The mob would not only try to shame the individual target, but would also pressure their employer to sack them. It has become a commonplace, grim ritual. Each time the shaming and sacking ritual unfolds, the message sent to workers is chilling.

It wasn't always this way.

On 20 July 1935, Hubert O'Donnell, a junior porter employed by the Department of Railways in Sydney, was arrested and charged with manslaughter. The criminal charge alleged that he had assisted in the procurement of an illegal abortion, after which the woman he was assisting had died.

He immediately reported the situation to his employer and advised that he would need several days off work. He then asked to take a period of absence as annual leave. His request was refused. Instead, the head of the traffic branch suspended O'Donnell from work without pay for alleged misconduct, based on the charge that he faced. His suspension without pay continued for the next six months.

Ultimately, O'Donnell was acquitted of the criminal charge. He then sued his employer to recover the wages he had lost during his suspension, arguing that both the suspension and the deprivation of his wages were illegal. The case went all the way up to Australia's highest court, where O'Donnell was vindicated. The High Court reasoned that the disciplinary action taken against him was for his conduct outside the workplace and that such conduct had no bearing on his work as a junior porter. The disciplinary action was therefore unlawful. The court found that there was a crucial distinction to be drawn between 'misconduct as a citizen' and 'misconduct as an employee'. Accordingly, the Department of Railways had no legitimate right to punish O'Donnell for his conduct as a citizen.

Would Hubert O'Donnell have survived in the labour market of the 21st century, in which the online revolution has eliminated the divide between our work and personal lives, and in which an errant tweet or a Facebook 'like' can bring a career undone? He would be caught in the crossfire of a social media frenzy and the dictates of contemporary brand-management. The situation would generate an organisational 'crisis' that would be mediated by the CEO, together with human resources managers, in-house counsel, and brand managers. There would be catastrophising about an online culture war; a possible consumer boycott by the pro-life lobby; and predictions of irreparable brand damage.

All paths would inexorably lead to its inevitable denouement. A decision would be taken to 'liberate' the employee's career opportunities, to be communicated on a Friday afternoon at a meeting with People and Culture, accompanied by a direction to leave the building immediately. The employee would be accompanied by a security officer to gather up their belongings, with a reminder that the services of the Employee Assistance Program would be available for two weeks post-termination. And as the shell-shocked employee left the building, the press release invoking the company's values would be on its way.

Work brings people together. We spend more time at work than we do with our family and friends. We meet, bond, befriend, fall out; we collaborate, experiment, fail, and learn. We gather to share our experiences, knowledge, and perspectives on work and everything else. We discover people with widely divergent views, and we scrutinise and debate them. Work is an endless source of theatre—comic, tragic, or absurdist. How else to explain the demand from Karl in Finance for HR to urgently investigate his allegations that Jeff from IT is deliberately leaving defecation stains on the sides of the toilet bowl as part of a bullying campaign against him? *Deliberately*.

Work is also where civic discourse occurs, a key component of citizenship and democracy. The issues confronted in the workplace invariably bleed into the major political and social issues of the day. When workers employed by a major corporation band together to seek to establish improvements in labour standards, their activism has far-reaching impacts—both in other workplaces and in the polity. Those improvements can moderate the power of corporations, including by redistributing wealth. A workplace that is characterised by discussion, debate, and dissent feeds into the democracy we strive for when we are not at work. The weakening of trade unions and collective bargaining in the labour market is reflected more broadly in the weakening of other institutions that moderate the excesses of corporate power.

The essential nature of the employment relationship involves a gross disparity in power. As corporations have been de-unionised and freed of important regulation, the scandalous mistreatment of vulnerable workers, including migrant and young workers, has become an almost banal feature of the labour market. In the decades since the 1980s, elaborate business models have been built to exploit employees, generating increasing economic inequality and political instability in many developed economies. Wages have been suppressed to shore up record profits. In de-unionised workplaces, employees work up to 80 hours a week or are offered zero-hours contracts. Wage theft and fake internships are rife. That part of the labour market in which workers compete for piecework — a regression to pre-Industrial Revolution exploitation — has been rebadged and glamourised as 'the gig economy'.

In the 21st-century labour markets of diminished liberal democracies, including Australia, the UK, and the US, the power imbalance between major corporations and their employees has become so repressive that each time an employee starts a new job, they not only sell their labour to the company, but they trade away critical parts of their citizenship. They are forced to promise that in their life they will not say or do anything to disturb the corporate brand, particularly on social media. They cannot be sure what that promise entails, and the corporation can't either. An employee whose sexuality is provocative or controversial is a risk to the brand. So, too, is the political dissident, climate activist, religious fundamentalist, or inconvenient truth-teller. Jesus was fortunate to be a self-employed carpenter and to live in the pre-Twitter age.

The corporation requires that an employee be highly engaged, productive, and resilient at work, and after hours live a quiet, uneventful, and uncontroversial life — a life as a brand ambassador.

CHAPTER ONE

Rage and Revenge

Jim Schembri is a journalist, critic, and author. His website showcases his articles, film reviews, and interviews with comedians, and is replete with denunciations of cancel culture and wokeism. Sometime in the 1980s, we met at the screening of a John Waters film at the Valhalla Cinema in Richmond. The Valhalla specialised in cult movies, and engendered a loyal following of aficionados of *The Blues Brothers* and *The Rocky Horror Picture Show*. Schembri, a pop-culture enthusiast and aspiring film critic, was among a group of friends and friends of friends. He was witty and eccentric.

Schembri worked his way up from humble beginnings in the newspaper industry to become a prominent film critic for *The Age* newspaper in Melbourne. His film criticism divided readers. He took aim at 'the Cinemafia'—those responsible for 'an oppressive orthodoxy' who demanded that 'while certain films and directors must be reviled, others are supposed to command instant critical respect, automatic adulation and, in some cases, virgin sacrifice'.[1]

Over time, a loud anti-Schembri camp emerged. The anti-Schembrists deplored his love of popular lowbrow fare, including his passion for Tom Cruise films and his brand of right-wing politics. From time to time, his columns provoked a particularly strong response, such as when he complained that there were too many gay characters in *Outland*, a US sitcom about a group of gay science-fiction fans, and when he panned the movie *Brokeback Mountain*. In the 2000s, anti-Schembrists began to appear more regularly on emerging social media platforms such as Facebook and Twitter.

Schembri wrote about the difficulties of the job, and proposed a ten-step guide for aspiring critics. Step 2 was 'Grow a thick skin. You'll need it.' But maybe Schembri's own skin wasn't thick enough. He was easily angered by his critics, and he retaliated by trying to get them sacked. He corresponded with their bosses, suggesting that their employees were discrediting them, and implying that legal action was imminent. His correspondence was deliberately ambiguous, suggesting that he might be writing on behalf of *The Age* newspaper.

One of the critics, Matt Michalowski, had lambasted Schembri on Twitter. Michalowski's Twitter account made no mention of his employer, but that didn't matter to Schembri. The following day, Schembri tracked down Michalowski's employer to 'lodge a formal complaint'. His bemused manager passed on Schembri's contact details and asked Michalowski to sort it out. Schembri pursued the same approach in corresponding with Vapormedia, a company that employed another anti-Schembrist, Chris Mayer. Schembri wrote:

> I am working on an idea for a story about social media policy in the workplace and am hoping you can help. Do you have somebody named Chris Mayer in your company? If so, is this his Twitter feed? https://twitter.com/#!/chrismayer
> Thanking you.
> Yours
> Jim Schembri

Schembri then spoke with a Vapormedia manager and asked how he felt about Mayer's personal Twitter account reflecting on the company. Once again, the company manager refused to take the bait. He recognised that Mayer's criticisms of Schembri had nothing to do with their business or Mayer's job. There were other such tangles, including a robust exchange between Schembri and a satirical Twitter account purporting to be that of an intern at the ABC.

Then Schembri was exposed. On 2 March 2012, *Crikey* reported that '*Age* film critic Jim Schembri has repeatedly contacted the employers of Twitter critics — in some cases issuing them with veiled legal threats — in an apparent attempt to shut down dissent on the social networking site.' Schembri was shamed for trying to get his critics sacked. He had also wrongly implied that he had been authorised by his employer to threaten legal action against them. The news story prompted others, including a group of comedians, to publicise their stories of Schembri's penchant for vengeance.

In response to the *Crikey* exposé, *The Age* announced that Schembri was going on leave. This was followed shortly after by another announcement that Schembri no longer worked at the newspaper. To this day, it remains unclear whether he was sacked or was forced to resign. What was clear was that, in order to try to achieve his punitive objectives, he had tried to link each company to its employee's behaviour. In the absence of any rational link, Schembri would attempt a form of guilt by association. The attempt to shame each company failed miserably, and ultimately cost Schembri his career as a newspaper critic. He paid a very high price: a 28-year career at the newspaper was unceremoniously brought to an end.

Schembri's actions occurred at a juncture in the 21st century in which social media had not completely reshaped our culture. In a sense, Schembri experienced the precursor to a social media pile-on, albeit a modest pile-on. His preferred methods of retaliation—including email and telephone calls—now appear quaint and old-fashioned.

There are echoes of Jim Schembri's demise in the story of Bret Stephens. An anti-Trump conservative, Stephens is a senior journalist at *The New York Times*, a former editor of *The Jerusalem Post*, and a winner of the Pulitzer Prize for Commentary. Stephens is also a self-proclaimed 'champion' of the First Amendment. He attributes his commitment to free speech in the US to 'a longstanding cultural bias in favour of the gadfly, the muckraker, the contrarian, the social nuisance'. Stephens has written that 'Free speech—at least speech that is truly free—is always a scandal to someone or other.'

He has been heavily criticised for his climate-change scepticism (which views he has since renounced), and has been accused of racism—including after describing anti-Semitism as the 'disease of the Arab mind' and referring to Palestinians as 'mosquitoes' in a 2013 column for *The Wall Street Journal*. Nevertheless, Stephens claimed that he was 'sufficiently immunized to the way social media works', acknowledging that platforms such as Twitter allow more people than ever before to express their views.[2]

Then, in August 2019, Dave Karpf, a media and communications academic at George Washington University, jokingly referred to Stephens as a 'bedbug'. Karpf had seen an earlier tweet from a *New York Times* staffer complaining that there were bedbugs in the newsroom. Karpf was one of many who tried to respond humorously to the staffer when he posted, 'The bedbugs are a metaphor. The bedbugs are Bret Stephens.' Karpf's tweet was underappreciated: it received a mere nine likes. Later that day, Karpf was surprised to receive an email from Stephens, which was cc'd to the provost of George Washington University. The subject line read 'From Bret Stephens, New York Times':

Dear Dr. Karpf,

Someone just pointed out a tweet you wrote about me, calling me a 'bedbug.' I'm often amazed about the things supposedly decent people are prepared to say about other people—people they've never met—on Twitter. I think you've set a new standard.

I would welcome the opportunity for you to come to my home, meet my wife and kids, talk to us for a few minutes, and then call me a 'bedbug' to my face. That would take some genuine courage and intellectual integrity on your part. I promise to be courteous no matter what you have to say.

Maybe it will make you feel better about yourself.

Please consider this a standing invitation. You are more than welcome to bring your significant other.

Cordially,

Bret Stephens[3]

Why include Karpf's employer in such a communication? The email implicitly invited the university to discipline or sack Karpf, but the university didn't take the bait. In fact, the provost, Forrest Maltzman, took a commendable approach. Maltzman wrote to Stephens that, 'As you know, as an academic, Professor Karpf speaks for himself and does not take direction from me. His opinions are his own.' He invited Stephens onto campus to speak 'about civil discourse in the digital age'.

Karpf was not done. He posted the email sent to him and his boss by Stephens on Twitter. This time, his tweet garnered 48,500 likes and 7,500 retweets. Stephens' hypocrisy was mercilessly pilloried by an array of online critics. He was publicly shamed, and it hurt. He responded by announcing his departure from Twitter. 'Twitter is a sewer. It brings out the worst in humanity. I sincerely apologise for any part I've played in making it worse, and to anyone

I've ever hurt ... I'm deactivating this account,' Stephens explained.[4] His career remained otherwise intact.

In the seven years that separated the experiences of Schembri and Stephens, the impact of social media platforms escalated dramatically. The major platforms appeared in the early 2000s with the utopian promise of strengthening social bonds, democratising the distribution of information, and spreading hope for greater democracy. On 21 March 2006, Jack Dorsey sent the first tweet which read "just setting up my twttr". By 2008, Facebook had established its global dominance, commanding 100 million users.

In 2009, Facebook introduced a 'like' function, allowing users to publicly show their appreciation for a post. Twitter one-upped Facebook by launching a retweet function in the same year, allowing users to endorse and share the posts of others with their followers. By 2012, Facebook had introduced a 'share' button for iPhones to similar effect.

The innovations became crucial to the financial success of the Big Tech companies that were under growing pressure from their investors to generate profits. Maximising user engagement with their platforms enabled them to harness the data generated by the users and sell it to advertisers and others. The equation was simple: more rage equalled more engagement, equalled more data, equalled more sales, equalled more profits for the social media giants. Those who posted content that generated outrage were rewarded with greater internet virality—likes, retweets, more followers, fame, and, sometimes, fortune. The platforms sought to further monetise the anger by developing algorithms that drove more outrage-inducing content to the users who responded to it, and the cycle continued. In March 2016, Twitter replaced its chronological timeline (tweets ordered by time) with an algorithmic timeline in which tweets that were popular were given much greater prominence.

Jim Schembri's and Bret Stephens' attempts to exact revenge on their adversaries rebounded on them with disastrous consequences. While both were publicly shamed for seeking to exact revenge on their critics, shaming became a key weapon as social media developed, used by vengeful online mobs to deprive their targets of their jobs.

The anger business
Stoking rage for profit has been an enduring media business model since at least the late-19th century, when tabloid media outlets containing 'yellow journalism', including the *New York Journal* and the *New York World*, came to prominence in the US. In recent decades, the model has been adopted by media organisations across television, radio, newspapers, and social media. In the US, the abolition of 'the fairness doctrine' in 1987 — a requirement that holders of broadcast licences present issues of public importance in a manner that fairly reflects differing viewpoints — unleashed new anger-generating businesses. Rage-filled talkback radio became a lucrative commodity, attracting many more consumers than did its mild-mannered, rational competitors. Since Rupert Murdoch's Fox News emerged in 1996, it has been generating revenue by pumping out disinformation as well as stoking rage.

This model is aped in other parts of the world. Australia's version of Fox is Sky News, which, together with a large stable of Murdoch newspaper journalists, exploits the same methods. The list of hate targets generated by the Murdoch spear-throwers is daunting. It includes leftists, feminists, Muslims, environmentalists, atheists, climate scientists, the unemployed, trade unions, and a catch-all category, the woke generation. When the Australian continent was ravaged by catastrophic bushfires in the Black Summer of

2019–20, Miranda Devine took to Sky News to claim that 'Green ideology, not climate change, is to blame for Australia's bushfire catastrophe — truer today than it was a decade ago.' The following year, Devine was successfully sued for defamation by Quaden Bayles, a nine-year old Indigenous boy with dwarfism, after alleging that the child had falsely claimed to have been bullied in an online video. Devine was forced to settle the case, and apologised. It's not clear whether the many perverse opinions trucked by people such as Devine are genuinely held or contrived to provoke rage and clicks.

The business model has moved seamlessly into the online world. Hateful and fury-inducing content can be generated by anyone — including trolls and bots — at any time. It can be spread at lightning speed across the globe, and the more it spreads, the more money can be made. In 2019, actor Sacha Baron Cohen echoed many critics in a remarkable speech to the Anti-Defamation League, stating, 'The algorithms these platforms depend on deliberately amplify the type of content that keeps users engaged — stories that appeal to our baser instincts and that trigger outrage and fear.'[5] He described social media as the 'greatest propaganda machine of all time', and called for a fundamental rethinking of its propensity to spread hate, conspiracies, and lies. However, it is evident that the business model will prevail unless its profitability is undermined. That can only happen if major legal changes make the big platforms liable for the harm they cause.

Anyone wanting to target an opponent can use social media to encourage a mob to unleash rage and revenge. A prominent politician or journalist with a significant social media following can unleash an emotive barrage against a target, and the ensuing spectacle sometimes resembles a digital Lord of the Flies. The target may be a dissident, a contrarian, or an activist — or a scientist, truck driver, journalist, or comedian. A similar result can be triggered by posting genuine criticism with no intention for it to be echoed by thousands of others.

British journalist Jon Ronson has eloquently documented how social media has unleashed 'a great renaissance of public shaming' and a 'democratization of justice' with devastating consequences for those targeted. In his 2015 book, *So You've Been Publicly Shamed*, Ronson explores the pain and destruction caused by online mobbing.[6] Ronson was an early enthusiast for online shaming, instigating such attacks and participating in others before reconsidering and then ultimately abandoning them. He recognised the thrill of righteous indignation and the appeal of delivering swift justice, but over time was repelled by the brutality of this exercise of power and the disproportionality of the punishments meted out.

Ronson recounts the story of Justine Sacco. In December 2013, Sacco was a public relations executive for InterActiveCorp, the owner of an online dating service and other businesses, including Vimeo. Sacco was about to board a flight to South Africa when she tweeted, 'Going to Africa. Hope I don't get Aids. Just kidding, I'm white.' While she was in the air, she could not access the internet. Her tweet went viral, attracting universal condemnation as 'racist' and reeking of 'white privilege'.

By the time she landed, the online mob tracked down her employer and pressured the company to sack her. One online vigilante boasted that, 'We are about to watch this @JustineSacco bitch get fired. In REAL time.'

Sacco deleted her tweet and issued an apology for 'being insensitive to this crisis — which does not discriminate by race, gender or sexual orientation, but which terrifies us all uniformly — and to the millions of people living with the virus, I am ashamed.'

She was then very publicly sacked by InterActiveCorp, which issued the following statement:

> The offensive comment does not reflect the views and values of IAC. We take this issue very seriously, and we have parted ways with the employee in question. There is no excuse for the hateful statements that have been made and we condemn them unequivocally. We hope, however, that time and action, and the forgiving human spirit, will not result in the wholesale condemnation of an individual who we have otherwise known to be a decent person at core.[7]

Sacco hailed from a white South African family who were supporters of the African National Congress. When it was all over, she explained that her tweet was an attempt at a satirical jibe at the insularity of Americans.

> To me it was so insane of a comment for anyone to make … I thought there was no way that anyone could possibly think it was literal … To put it simply, I wasn't trying to raise awareness of AIDS or piss off the world or ruin my life. Living in America puts us in a bit of a bubble when it comes to what is going on in the third world. I was making fun of that bubble.

Prior to sending that fateful tweet, Sacco had satirically tweeted about another passenger with bad body odour. Then, while in transit at Heathrow airport, she tweeted, 'Chilly—cucumber sandwiches—bad teeth. Back in London!'

Sacco was eviscerated for making a joke. A joke that was edgy, dark, and offensive—but a joke nevertheless. Had she recounted the joke at a comedy festival, it might have been received as an act of genius or an act of stupidity; or, quite possibly, both. Sacco's experience is testament to the golden rule that many of us have repeatedly broken: don't do satire online. Even email satire is dangerous. Her joke, decontextualised and flung around the world by an angry mob, led to her vilification and the loss of her job. Such misunderstanding; such a ridiculous punishment. But in the online world, it's not just misunderstood jokes that unleash the beast.

Her life would have been different had InterActiveCorp not succumbed. It had a choice. Like Vapormedia or George Washington University, it could have chosen to reject the demands to sack Sacco. After all, there is the culture spread by the online mob, but the cancellation is in the hands of the corporation. It chose to sack her, and, by doing so, it chose to feed the beast.

Anatomy of a pile-on

The first time I confronted corporate cancel culture was when I encountered Scott McIntyre, an Australian journalist and football commentator who worked for the Special Broadcasting Service (SBS). SBS is a hybrid-funded Australian public broadcasting radio, online, and television network. McIntyre joined SBS in 2003, and worked as a sports reporter for the network, with a focus on soccer, from 2008 to 2015.

Before falling into journalism, McIntyre had studied Asian history and Japanese at the University of Sydney. As a student, he had been fascinated by Allan Clifton's 1951 memoir, *Time of Fallen Blossoms*. Clifton was an Australian intelligence officer who was based near Hiroshima in Japan with the British Commonwealth Occupation Force (BCOF) after the end of World War II. Between 1945 and 1952, 16,000 Australians formed part of the BCOF, which sought to demilitarise Japan and promote democracy. Clifton's memoir detailed accounts of rapes, extra-judicial killings, thefts, and assaults by the occupying Australian soldiers. He wrote:

> I stood beside a bed in hospital. On it lay a girl, unconscious, her long, black hair in wild tumult on the pillow. A doctor and two

nurses were working to revive her. An hour before she had been raped by 20 soldiers. We found her where they had left her, on a piece of wasteland. The hospital was in Hiroshima. The girl was Japanese. The soldiers were Australians.[8]

McIntyre was struck by the contrast of accounts such as this with what he had learned at school about Australia's military history. He came to believe that, by shrouding its military in an unhealthy mythology, Australia, like other countries, had failed to confront the reality that its soldiers committed their own share of wartime atrocities. McIntyre had travelled extensively throughout Asia and Europe, spending a year working in Japan. In 2004, he met Naoko Tsuchiya, a Japanese woman who was studying in Sydney. They married in 2007, and had two children.

On Anzac Day 2015, McIntyre was, like most Australians, enjoying the public holiday. He took his two young children for a morning stroll in the inner west of Sydney. They walked past a familiar Anzac Day sight: people in pubs getting drunk, garrulous, and rowdy. He strongly disapproved of the glorification of war and the drunken expressions of patriotism.

That evening, McIntyre took to Twitter to criticise the behaviour of some Australian soldiers in war zones, the atomic bombings of Hiroshima and Nagasaki, and the celebration of Anzac Day. 'The cultification of an imperialist invasion of a foreign nation that Australia had no quarrel with is against all ideals of modern society', he tweeted, adding, 'Wonder if the poorly-read, largely white, nationalist drinkers and gamblers pause today to consider the horror that all mankind suffered.'

In another post, he wrote, 'Remembering the summary execution, widespread rape and theft committed by these "brave" Anzacs in Egypt, Palestine and Japan.' A further post read, 'Not forgetting that the largest single-day terrorist attacks in history were committed by this nation & their allies in Hiroshima & Nagasaki.'

Finally, he posted a chilling image of concrete steps with the words, 'Innocent children, on the way to school, murdered. Their shadows seared into the concrete of Hiroshima.'

McIntyre's words echoed Alan Seymour's 1958 play *The One Day of the Year*, which condemned Anzac Day as a day of 'bloody wastefulness', and foreshadowed what historian Carolyn Holbrook in 2017 called a 'screaming tribe of great, stupid, drunken, vicious, bigoted no-hopers'.[9] In the late 1960s and early 1970s, in the wake of Australia's involvement in the Vietnam War, protests were routinely held on Anzac Day in opposition to that war. Protesters also targeted conscription and, in later years, Australia's military involvement in general, as well as highlighting the female victims of rape in all wars.

As a student at Melbourne University in the late 1980s, I remember watching an evening news report of a feminist protest against rape by soldiers on Anzac Day. The report showed several protesters, including an academic whom I recognised, being arrested by police. She was back at work next day leading my history tutorial.

However, over the following decades, Anzac Day evolved to become a key celebration of patriotism and Australian identity. Crowds attending Anzac Day services swelled, more Australians travelled to Gallipoli, and more cars sported Australian flags.

By 2015, anti-war statements such as McIntyre's profoundly challenged the popular perception of Australia's soldiers and the commemoration of Anzac Day. In other words, they were an affront to a certain nationalist ideal of Australian identity. So it came to pass that, in response to McIntyre's tweets, a combination of Murdoch media journalists and conservative politicians unleashed an online campaign to have him sacked from his job. The frenzied attack was documented by journalist Wendy Bacon.[10] Less than an hour after he posted his tweets, Rita Panahi, a Murdoch tabloid journalist with a large social media following, tweeted: 'Your taxpayer dollars at work'.

In response to Panahi, Mark Textor, a conservative campaigner and director of lobbying group Crosby Textor, followed suit with a tweet tagging Panahi and SBS: '@RitaPanahi this man is happy to take a wage from the taxpayers he insults. How brave. @SBS'.

A federal government minister, Jamie Briggs, followed suit with, 'I wonder is [sic] @SBS agrees with this from a publicly funded journalist? This is disgraceful and shouldn't be tolerated.' (Briggs was forced to resign from parliament a few months later, after allegations of sexual harassment were made against him.)

Others joined the fray, seeking intervention from the minister for communications, Malcolm Turnbull. At that time, Turnbull was an aspirant for the leadership of the federal Liberal Party.

Sir Tony of Coogee chimed in with, 'Complete filth you are. When is @TurnbullMalcolm going to reign in SBS & ABC journos?' Benjamin Hearn, responding to Panahi and Kenny, added that 'this bloke needs to be taken outside and given a flogging! What a fucking muppet!'

Then Sky News presenter Chris Kenny weighed in. A former political adviser, including a stint as chief of staff to Turnbull, Kenny wielded his Twitter account like a set of nunchuks. He had a penchant for targeting the employers of his ideological enemies to pressure them to take action against them. Kenny retweeted his colleague Rita Panahi, adding his own invective together with a demand for his old boss to take action against SBS: 'SBS presenter proudly flaunts his weapon grade stupidity. Ungrateful, disrespectful tool. Please look at this creep's timeline @mcintinhos and get him off public payroll. Disgrace @SBS @TurnbullMalcolm @JasonClareMP @RSL_Auspol'.

A few minutes later, he tried again: 'Please read this timeline @

mcintinhos Contact @sbs He lives off your taxes/dishonours you. Also try @TurnbullMalcolm @JasonClareMP #'

The demand on Turnbull to act worked. At about 9.00 pm, Turnbull spoke by telephone with Michael Ebeid, the-then CEO of SBS. Although the contents of the conversation have not been released, Turnbull denies demanding that Ebeid sack McIntyre. Ebeid claims that he assured Turnbull that an investigation would be conducted by SBS. Nevertheless, within minutes and without waiting for any investigation, Ebeid took to Twitter.

At 9.07 pm, Ebeid tweeted, 'Comments from @mcintinhos are his own, disrespectful and not at all the views of @SBS. We remember and commemorate our ANZACs.'

Shortly after Ebeid's intervention, Turnbull retweeted Ebeid and then, referring to McIntyre's tweet about children who had died during the bombing of Hiroshima, added his own condemnation, which read: 'Difficult to think of more offensive or inappropriate comments than those by @mcintinhos. Despicable remarks which deserve to be condemned.'

Chris Kenny continued to agitate for McIntyre to be sacked: '@michaelebeid @mcintinhos @SBS don't think a little tweet quite cuts it ... if he said that about Turks you'd sack him @TurnbullMalcolm'

As the evening wore on, Kenny continued predicting that McIntyre would be sacked, before adding, 'the scumbag hates Australians but sucks a living from them'. A year before this bout of online vigilantism, Kenny had written in support of relaxing laws against racial vilification, arguing that, 'Free speech is important. It is the most fundamental right; forming the very foundation of the democratic society that underpins all the freedom and prosperity we enjoy.'

The next morning, SBS sacked Scott McIntyre. If the broadcaster had conducted an investigation, it had broken all land-speed records.

Manager Ken Shipton spoke with McIntyre to advise him of the decision, and then confirmed it in an email that read:

> As discussed, because of your actions, your employment with SBS has been terminated effective immediately. The decision has been made because you refused reasonable directions asking you to delete the offensive tweets you posted on Anzac Day and refusal to issue an apology which has brought SBS and yourself into disrepute. Refusing a reasonable direction from your manager is a summary dismissable offence.
>
> Additionally you have breached the SBS Code of Conduct, SBS's Corporate Values and the SBS Social Media Guidelines which has resulted in your role being untenable because the community and our audiences have lost confidence and faith in you as a member of our on air team.[11]

Like virtually all employees in the labour market, McIntyre had been required by his employment contract to abide by a code of conduct, the company's values, and the company's workplace policies, including its social media policy.

The SBS code of conduct stated:

> SBS employees must not engage in any act, including using new or social media in a personal or SBS capacity, which may compromise the reputation and integrity of SBS.
>
> This includes:
>
> … Being careful not to engage in activities in their private life that could adversely affect the reputation and integrity of SBS.

The SBS social media policy contained a set of key principles that were said to apply, whether for 'personal or work use':

- Engage with the community—social media empowers employees to connect with SBS's audiences, enhance communication and encourage debate. Use social media channels to add value for audiences and SBS.
- Be authentic, truthful and transparent subject to your responsibilities under the SBS Code of Conduct.
- Treat everyone with honesty, respect, fairness, courtesy and sensitivity.
- Always communicate in line with SBS's values.

SBS's social media protocols stated that:

While SBS employees have a right to make public comment and to enter into public debate in their personal capacity, it is important to ensure that SBS is not brought into disrepute. Individuals should consider how their posts will be perceived by the community, taking into account the standards which apply to their work.

What are the parameters that must be navigated to ensure that SBS's reputation and integrity is not impugned? No one knows. Employees are left to try to guess. Perhaps engaging in criminal conduct by robbing a bank is out. Then again, what has that got to do with SBS? The broadcaster is committed to multiculturalism, and so loudly arguing in favour of white supremacy would be out. Similarly, so would be announcing one's candidature for election on behalf of the racist political party One Nation. Criticising SBS content or other journalists? Possibly. Misrepresenting that you are authorised to speak on behalf of SBS could certainly qualify. Does that mean a producer cannot attend an anti-abortion rally or support same-sex marriage?

In the US, legislation that is vague and incapable of proper definition is struck down as unconstitutional. A statute may be deemed to be impermissibly vague when a citizen cannot determine what conduct is prohibited: it is a violation of the vagueness doctrine. In the words of Justice Gorsuch:

> Vague laws invite arbitrary power. Before the Revolution, the crime of treason in English law was so capriciously construed that the mere expression of disfavoured opinions could invite transportation or death. The founders cited the crown's abuse of 'pretended' crimes like this as one of their reasons for revolution. See Declaration of Independence. Today's vague laws may not be as invidious, but they can invite the exercise of arbitrary power all the same—by leaving the people in the dark about what the law demands and allowing prosecutors and courts to make it up.[12]

The vagueness doctrine does not extend to dealings between private parties; its focus is on the relationship of the state with its citizens. Nevertheless, it is closely related to the legal notions of due process and natural justice, which dictate that before an adverse decision can be made, a person affected by it must be able to understand the allegations against them.

SBS's rules about speech—and other rules like them across the labour market—are impossibly unclear. The rules also set impossibly high standards of behaviour and values. No one is able to be authentic, truthful, transparent, honest, respectful, fair, courteous, and sensitive at all times. Not priests. Not judges. And definitely not politicians. Jesus wasn't, and couldn't. Nelson Mandela, ditto. Mother Theresa, I'm afraid not.

Indeed, there are obvious tensions between these qualities such that it is impossible to simultaneously comply with them. Hopefully, as we move from childhood into our teenage years, we learn that to be authentic, truthful, transparent, and honest at all times can be hurtful and even destructive. Children are often given leeway to express themselves with honesty and authenticity. 'Why is that man walking like that?', a child may ask her parent.

McIntyre was sacked for bringing both himself and SBS into disrepute. And yet the rules of his employment stated that he had a right to enter public debate in his personal capacity. That is what he did. There was no suggestion that McIntyre was expressing opinions on behalf of his employer. He was a sports journalist; his views about Anzac Day bore no rational connection with his employment.

McIntyre had engaged in the same conduct before without any adverse consequences. He had tweeted similar sentiments on Anzac Day in prior years. On these occasions there was no controversy, and he was not disciplined or sacked by SBS. He was entitled to have concluded that he was not jeopardising his employment by exercising a right most of us take for granted: the right to express our deep political convictions.

But Anzac Day 2015 was different because McIntyre was targeted by right-wing journalists and politicians. On this occasion, his words attracted the vigilantism of an angry mob. He had no way of knowing that in repeating views that he had previously communicated online, this time would be different.

Just as university provost Forrest Maltzman rebuffed Bret Stephens' invitation to discipline Dave Karpf, SBS should have rejected the vigilantes. It wouldn't have been that hard to do. SBS could have put out a statement containing two simple messages: an acknowledgement that McIntyre's views were controversial and did not represent his employer; and that he was entitled to hold and express those views because he was a citizen in a democracy. Instead, SBS wilted under pressure.

If employees are required by their employment contract to

never express views privately — or, at least, outside their working environment — that might offend anyone or result in a controversy, they have forfeited important democratic and human rights. They have forfeited a crucial part of their citizenship.

Australian employees' right to hold a political opinion is protected by the Fair Work Act. Specifically, employees cannot be sacked by reason of their 'political opinion'. The laws arguably override the terms of an employment contract. For example, a term of a contract that stated 'You are not allowed to vote Labor' would likely breach anti-discrimination laws and would have no legal effect. Any attempt to enforce it could be successfully resisted.

Shortly after his sacking, I agreed to represent McIntyre on a pro bono basis. I assembled a team of highly regarded barristers who also agreed to act pro bono, including Michael Lee SC (later Justice Lee of the Federal Court) and Noel Hutley QC. We argued that SBS had illegally sacked McIntyre because he had expressed a 'political opinion' in contravention of the Fair Work Act.

The case was not straightforward. For decades, conservative Australian judges have interpreted many laws designed to protect employees very narrowly. As a result, the protections of anti-discrimination laws are much diminished. The word 'political' has been construed to bear on 'the form, role, structure, feature, purpose, obligations, duties, or some other aspect of government'. In several previous decisions about the meaning of 'political opinion', judges had read down the expression by limiting the meaning to opinions about elections or government policy. SBS argued that McIntyre's views on the commemoration of Anzac Day and military history were far removed from the expression of 'political opinion'. After much legal skirmishing, the case was settled on confidential terms in April 2016, a year after the sacking. The parties issued a joint statement, which read:

SBS acknowledges that Mr McIntyre was a well-respected sports reporter with SBS for a period spanning over a decade, and SBS is disappointed that it was unable to continue with his services following his Tweets …

Mr McIntyre acknowledges that the views expressed in his Tweets on 25 April 2015 were his views and that they were contentious. Mr McIntyre regrets any attribution of his views to SBS and acknowledges that SBS was drawn into controversy following the expression of his views.[13]

The shaming and sacking of Scott McIntyre unleashed a domino effect. McIntyre and his family received many death threats. He lived under immense pressure. The very public nature of his sacking and the threats that accompanied the campaign against him meant that he was unlikely to find another job as a journalist in a hurry — not that the field of soccer journalism is large anyway.

His wife, Naoko Tsuchiya, found the situation enormously upsetting, humiliating, and frightening. She had been on a short holiday in New Zealand when the controversy erupted. She struggled to understand why her husband had provoked the controversy, and was angry with him for upending their quiet lives. She returned home to Sydney immediately, but, as the threats continued, became anxious about her safety and that of the children. She started to think about fleeing Australia.

Within weeks, Tsuchiya decided to return to Japan with the two children, Hinata, aged six, and Harugo, aged four, to stay with her parents in Tokyo. She told McIntyre to come and join them once he could do so. McIntyre wanted her to stay and support him, but reluctantly accepted her decision. While he stayed in Australia pursuing redress for his sacking, McIntyre spoke on Skype with his family regularly.

Naoko ultimately rented a Tokyo apartment and waited for McIntyre to join her. When he finally did so, the relationship resumed, but it was clear that Tsuchiya had not forgiven him. She remained angry. For several years, the relationship was strained. After struggling to reboot his career, McIntyre undertook most of the childcare while Tuschiya worked full time.

In May 2019, McIntyre came home to the apartment to find that Tsuchiya and the two children were gone. She had removed the children from school, changed her phone number, and disappeared with them. He discovered that the abduction had been planned for some time and that his daughter's hair had been cut to disguise her. His desperate attempts to find his children resulted in his arrest for trespass and incarceration for six weeks.

Child abduction in Japan is an industry, the by-product of its brutal family law system. A raft of professionals advise parents on the planning, execution, and defence of such abductions. Perversely, the legal system rewards the parent who abducts the child. The police do not investigate or prosecute claims, and they actively impede the parent who is trying to reconnect with their child. McIntyre threw himself into advocating reform to the Japanese legal system, joining many other affected parents in what has become a powerful international campaign. In February 2019, the United Nations Committee on the Rights of the Child recommended that Japan introduce laws that permit joint custody after divorce to 'ensure that the right of the child to maintain personal relations and direct contact' with both parents. (In March 2024, legislation was introduced into the Japanese parliament giving courts the power to grant joint custody if there is a dispute).

One year to the day after McIntyre's ordeal began, on Anzac Day in April 2016, Yassmin Abdel-Magied, an engineer, author, Muslim activist, and ABC presenter, posted seven words on her Twitter account:

'Lest. We. Forget. (Manus, Nauru, Syria, Palestine.)' The references to Manus and Nauru were a protest against successive Australian governments' policies of the mandatory offshore detention of refugees. Within minutes of posting the comment, Abdel-Magied apologised 'unreservedly' and deleted the reference to the four locations.

In the ensuing months, Abdel-Magied was relentlessly pilloried, condemned, and tormented by conservative politicians, Murdoch media journalists, and online mobs. A huge amount of column space was deployed to humiliate and torment her. Typical of the conservative campaign was a front-page attack in *The Daily Telegraph* headlined by 'ABC host's ultimate insult to Anzac legend' and opening with 'Un-Australian Broadcasting Corporation backs activist who demeans our war heroes.' Politicians and Murdoch journalists piled on, calling for her deportation. One Murdoch troll, who referred to Abdel-Mageid as a 'flea', fantasised about the temptation to run her over with a car. The obligatory death and rape threats and videos of beheadings ensued.

Abdel-Magied hosted a weekly show called *Australia Wide* on ABC TV. The show highlighted the stories of different parts of the community, including young people and those living in rural areas. Initially, the ABC rejected any suggestion that Abdel-Magied should be disciplined or censored, stating that, 'Her views and opinions ... are her own and don't represent those of the ABC.' It was not to last. Ultimately, the ABC succumbed to the political and public pressure, and quietly sacked Abdel-Magied after 'counselling' her. Corporate gigs suddenly stopped. She also lost her employment at Shell.

A traumatised Abdel-Magied sought the assistance of a psychologist. She had to move house and change her phone number. That wasn't enough. In order to escape the vilification and to protect her safety and health, Abdel-Magied fled Australia and now lives in London.

Like SBS, the ABC sacked Abdel-Magied in order to placate a right-wing mob. The ferocity of the mob was, at least in part, a bigoted and racist reaction to Abdel-Magied's skin colour and religion.

In the same year that Abdel-Mageid posted her contentious Anzac Day tweet, the Australian Defence Force commissioned an inquiry into allegations of misconduct by its forces during the Afghan war. In 2020, the inquiry conducted by Major General Justice Paul Brereton found 'credible evidence' that Australian elite soldiers had unlawfully killed 39 people during the Afghan war. Junior soldiers had been ordered to get their first kill by shooting prisoners, in a practice known as 'blooding'. Weapons were planted near Afghan bodies to cover up crimes. The inquiry recommended that 19 current or ex-special forces soldiers should be investigated by police over the killings of 'prisoners, farmers or civilians' in 2009–13.

Australia's most decorated living soldier is Ben Roberts-Smith. In June 2023, a Federal Court judge made damning findings against Roberts-Smith after he failed in a defamation suit against Nine newspapers. In what has been described as 'a landmark moment in Australian military history', the court found that, upon the balance of probabilities, he was complicit in four unlawful murders during his service in Afghanistan, including the cold-blooded killing of an elderly man and another disabled man whose prosthetic leg was souvenired.

In contrast to the treatment meted out to McIntyre and Abdel-Magied in response to their tweets, Murdoch media journalists continued to fawn over Roberts-Smith even after the findings against him. Typical was Peta Credlin of Sky News, who argued that any war crimes were the responsibility of 'risk-averse governments and military hierarchies' who 'expected too much of the SAS and the commandos'. In the nihilistic culture wars of the 21st century, an anti-nationalist tweet is far more heinous a sin than a war crime.

CHAPTER TWO

Flexible Control

It's difficult to conceive of a democratic nation-state possessing anything resembling the powers that corporations now have over their employees. Where on Earth, even in autocratic states, can citizens be compelled to undertake random drug tests, have the duration of their toilet breaks limited, and be monitored by a digital tracking device? Is there a nation that punishes citizens who fail to meet diet and fitness standards, or fail to comply with dress-code regulations? Or that instals GPS technology in all vehicles to track all drivers' movements? Democracies don't block their citizens from accessing the legal system to pursue redress against the state in open court, or instead compel them to take any dispute with it to a private umpire. But large corporations often do so.

US philosopher Elizabeth Anderson is one of the few commentators to publicly critique the extraordinary reach of corporate control over the lives of workers. In her 2017 book, *Private Government: how employers rule our lives (and why we don't talk about it)*,[1] she argues that most people in the United States and other liberal societies spend their working lives under a form of subordination and control that resembles a dictatorship. Anderson has coined the term 'private government' to describe the 21st-century labour market in which the corporation is a 'government that has arbitrary, unaccountable power over those it governs', even after hours.

Anderson highlights the paradox that, in a country in which a health edict requiring masks to be worn during a lethal pandemic provoked nationwide protests, violent confrontations, and civil disobedience, all in the name of personal freedom, the coercive surveillance and control exercised by American companies over the lives of their workers is almost universally and meekly accepted. And while the US has set the pace for repressive workplace control, corporations in other developed countries, including the UK and Australia, have followed a similar path.

There is no shortage of dystopian material for Anderson to work with. The unchecked power of corporations, combined with new technology, has elevated the intensity and pace of work, squeezing every ounce of downtime out of workers' days. There has a been a rapid growth in the development of worker-data surveillance systems, which are now used by almost two-thirds of medium-to-large companies in the US. The systems 'do everything from monitoring email and web browsing, to tracking workers' location and movement, to recording what keystrokes and eye movements they make, or when their screens go dark'.[2]

Amazon alone has produced a steady stream of labour-market abuses. As early as 2011, a report emerged of a local Amazon warehouse that had forced its employees to work in temperatures exceeding 100 degrees Fahrenheit.[3] The company had arranged for paramedics to wait outside to assist any employees who collapsed from heat exhaustion or dehydration. Its warehouse operations in the US, Australia, and the UK all rely on constant electronic monitoring so that:

As soon as one item is scanned, a solid bar on the bottom of the screen immediately starts to count down, showing how much time they have to reach their next item, which could be anywhere in the 24,000-square-metre warehouse. If an item is not scanned within the required time, the worker's 'pick rate' is marked down. At the centre in Dandenong South, pick rates are handed out to workers once or twice a day, and those falling below benchmark targets have to explain to their managers why.[4]

The company is also notorious for its prohibition of 'time theft' — a ban on employees exchanging casual remarks at work. Amazon's workers are also surveilled to monitor their speed and productivity. Workers complain of being tracked by an algorithm and of being fired for not being fast enough. An Amazon spokesperson told *The Guardian* in February 2020, 'Like most companies, we have performance expectations for every Amazonian and we measure actual performance against those expectations.'

Emily Guendelsberger, a journalist who worked undercover at an Amazon warehouse, wrote of her experience:

> I wasn't prepared for how exhausting working at Amazon would be. It took my body two weeks to adjust to the agony of walking 15 miles a day and doing hundreds of squats. But as the physical stress got more manageable, the mental stress of being held to the productivity standards of a robot became an even bigger problem.[5]

Guendelsberger's scan gun was her 'own personal digital manager', which monitored and timed her every movement.

Stephen Normandin worked for several years for Amazon Flex as a 'contract driver' delivering groceries and packages. Normandin was monitored through a system of real-time data collection and algorithmic analysis. His performance rating plummeted after a series of incidents that were out of his control: coming across inaccessible gated communities and lockers, unresponsive recipients, and unhelpful responses from the company.[6] Subsequently he received an email stating that his contract had been terminated. Stephen appealed the decision, but his appeal failed.

Access for all citizens to an open, independent, and impartial legal system is one of the hallmarks of a liberal democracy, but US corporations increasingly prohibit such access to employees in dispute with them. Instead, they force employees to engage in mandatory arbitration behind closed doors. Such requirements in the US labour market now apply to about 55 per cent of non-union private sector workers. According to a 2017 study by Alexander Colvin, about 60 million American workers can no longer go to court to seek redress for underpayment of minimum wages, or protection against discrimination or harassment.[7] Instead, they are compelled to pursue claims in a private arbitration process: a parallel, private justice system that is conducted without external scrutiny. Legal disputes involving whistleblowers, sexual harassment, bullying, or underpayment pursued in a court in the full public glare are considered to be bad for the brand. The mandatory arbitration agreements are also promoted as a strategy to block employees from participating in class actions against their employers.

The reach of such agreements sometimes crosses international borders. When David Heller, an Uber driver in Toronto, sought to participate in a class action against the company, seeking the right to be paid minimum wages and conditions, Uber tried to block him by relying on the mandatory arbitration term in his standard-form contract. The provision not only purported to stop him from participating in any class action, but also compelled him to pursue his claim through private arbitration in the Netherlands, which required an upfront fee of $14,500. In 2020, Canada's Supreme Court found the clause to be 'unconscionable', and declared the contract void based on the inequality of bargaining power between the parties and the cost of arbitration.

This repressive control doesn't end when the employment ends. Non-compete clauses, also known as restraint-of-trade clauses, severely restrict the freedom of movement of ex-employees—stopping employees from going to work for businesses in competition with their former employer, often for up to 12 months. The effect can be to stop an employee working in their chosen profession or area of expertise. As the labour market has been de-unionised in recent decades, non-competes have spread from higher-paid employees to almost all categories of worker. I have kept as a memento of sorts an Australian employment contract for a minimum-wage childcare worker employed by a suburban childcare centre. It contains a restraint-of-trade clause that states:

> In consideration of the Employee's remuneration and to protect the Employer's goodwill, the Employee undertakes not to be directly interested or concerned in (as a child care worker, child care educator, child care trainee, nominated supervisor, child care service director, independent contractor, shareholder, director, consultant, business partner or any other appointment within the Child Care Industry) a business engaged in the Child Care Industry within a 5km radius of the Centre.

The non-compete clause applied for a period of four months after the termination of her employment so as to prevent the minimum-wage childcare worker from being able to care for children at a nearby centre. The childcare industry is plagued by staff shortages.

The legality of non-competes is often in doubt, but the cost of litigation is prohibitive for most employees.

In cases in which a corporation wants to keep a highly valued employee out of circulation for longer than any non-compete obligation would allow, it may require the employee to go on what is known as 'gardening leave' for a significant period before the termination of employment. This means that the employee is essentially paid to stay at home for up to 12 months, and then ceases employment. Then the employee may be restrained for up to another 12 months from working for a competitor.

In April 2024, the US Federal Trade Commission enacted a nationwide ban on new non-compete agreements for the overwhelming majority of US employees. The FTC argued that such clauses inhibit mobility in the labour market, suppress wages, and exacerbate racial and gender pay inequality. In a statement, the FTC's chair, Lina Khan, said that, 'The freedom to change jobs is core to economic liberty and to a competitive, thriving economy.'

In Australia, Labor assistant minister Andrew Leigh was spearheading a push for the abolition of non-competes for lower-paid workers. Leigh argued that non-competes were stifling competition between businesses and were 'stopping workers from seeking out a better-paying job or from starting a new business'.[8]

A controlling history

In one way or another, oppressive workplace control has been a feature of the employment relationship since the 1800s. English labour law, which was imported into its colonies, treated the master-and-servant relationship as a personal one, like that of husband and wife. Based on the assumption that no area of a servant's life was beyond the reach of their employer's control, a master enjoyed an extensive right to control his servants—including their behaviour, dress, and moral standards.

During the Industrial Revolution, the master-and-servant relationship was superseded as companies grew to employ large numbers of workers in factories. The relationship between employer and employee came to be governed by employment contracts operating under a legal doctrine of freedom of contract. The doctrine stipulated that the parties to an employment contract were free and autonomous, and enjoyed equal bargaining power. As Professor Otto Kahn-Freund famously observed, such a doctrine obscured the 'inequality of bargaining power which is inherent and must be inherent in the employment relationship'.[9]

Until 1875, the Master and Servant Act governed the relationship between employers and employees, who were bound by a legal contract. It applied to the overwhelming majority of manual wage-workers, and allowed British employers to 'have their workmen sent to the house of correction and held at hard labour for up to three months for breaches of their labour agreements'.[10] Labour-market 'coercion'—the criminal prosecution of workers for breach of contract, with punishments including imprisonment, forced labour, whipping, and orders of specific performance—was commonplace.

In 1867, the law was reformed to reduce the most severe punishment for an employee's breach of contract. Imprisonment was replaced by the imposition of criminal fines. However, employees who absconded continued to face orders to return to their employers, and those who could not pay their fines or resisted returning to their employer faced the threat of three months' imprisonment.

Today, employment contracts continue to legitimise subordination. The subordination is baked into standard terms that impose duties of fidelity and obedience on employees. The control is autocratic, but not unlimited. Employees can't be bought and sold, or violently punished for insubordination. Nevertheless, the extent and type of control exercised by corporations over their employees' lives has periodically ebbed and flowed.

In Europe and the US, the 'welfare capitalism' movement of the late 19th and early 20th century practised a form of benevolent control, often with a view to resisting trade union recruitment efforts and government regulations. In the 1890s, the Cadbury family, who were Quakers, built a model village outside Birmingham in England. The village was named Bournville and was constructed to house the confectionery company's workforce near the factory. Bournville incorporated schools, leisure facilities, and theatres, and even employed doctors and dentists—providing the employees with amenities and conditions far superior to those suffered by many workers living in Britain at that time.

The Cadbury family advocated a moral lifestyle, discouraging drunkenness, gambling, and bad language. It promulgated a series of lifestyle rules designed to regulate the after-hours lives of the workforce, such as, 'In a truly happy home, Father or Mother will conduct worship at least once a day when the Bible should be read and a hymn sung', and 'Anger and worry will wear you out much more rapidly than hard work. Cultivate a cheerful and thankful spirit.'

In 1914, Henry Ford, one of the pioneers of welfare capitalism in the US, famously announced the Ford Motor Company's decision to increase its workers' wages to $5.00 per day, more than doubling the prevailing rate of $2.25 for a nine-hour day. The company declared that the change was 'the greatest revolution in the matter of rewards for its workers ever known to the industrial world'. Although *The Wall Street Journal* condemned Henry Ford as a 'class traitor', in many other quarters he was lauded for his courage in paying his workers a living wage, a characterisation that endures today. Less well known is that half of the daily wage offered by the company was effectively an at-risk bonus, payable only if the worker survived scrutiny by the company's Sociological Department.

The department, led by an Episcopalian minister, the Reverend Samuel S. Marquis, conducted random home inspections of the workforce to police alcohol consumption and to determine whether the worker met 'company standards for clean living'. The workers were assessed on whether they 'kept their homes clean, ate diets deemed healthy, abstained from drinking, used the bathtub appropriately, did not take in boarders, avoided spending too much on foreign relatives, and were assimilated to American cultural norms'.[11]

Moderating control

For a significant part of the 20th century, employees fought back. They obtained greater bargaining power with their employers, and a measure of industrial democracy, by joining trade unions and by pursuing political power and legislative reforms. The union movement spawned its own political parties in many industrialised countries, including in the UK and Australia.

After a period of intense, violent, and unsuccessful industrial disputation in Australia in the 1890s, unions pursued political power to further their thwarted objectives, spawning the creation of the Labor Party. A unique system of compulsory conciliation and arbitration of labour disputes was introduced in 1905, under which a federal tribunal was empowered to resolve industrial disputes by making an award: an instrument setting out terms and conditions of employment. Such awards provided a safety net of labour standards—an employer could not use employment contracts to subvert those terms and conditions.

Australian workers achieved a five-day, 40-hour week in 1947, and the post-war era was arguably the zenith of employees' struggle for dignity at work. In the decades that followed, employees in many democracies improved their working and living standards, obtaining a greater share of the economic pie, reduced working hours, and greater benefits, including longer annual-leave entitlements. The oppressive dimensions of employment contracts were moderated by collective organisation and legislation that combined to diminish the subordination inherent in the employment relationship.

In the US, labour activism was successfully suppressed until the Great Depression, when years of worker unrest prompted President Franklin Roosevelt to persuade Congress to pass the Wagner Act. Roosevelt ensured that, 'Employees shall have the right to organize and bargain collectively through representatives of their own choosing, and shall be free from the interference, restraint, or coercion of employers.' Workers were given the right to strike. A regulator, the National Labor Relations Board, was created to ensure that corporations complied. The Wagner Act drove a radical and rapid increase in union density, which leapt from 11 per cent to 34 per cent between 1934 and 1945.

Union activity and density peaked in many developed countries after Second World War II. Unions were institutionalised, through affiliations with socialist and social-democratic political parties, and through tripartite systems with government and employers.

It wasn't to last.

US corporations and Republicans seized an opportunity when multiracial unions began organising in the South, alarming segregationist Democrats. Relying on the support of these Democrats, Republicans pushed through the Taft-Hartley Act in 1947, winding back a number of employee protections. Under the law, states were permitted to pass further laws that allowed workers to 'free-ride'— to accept union-won benefits without paying union dues. Many unions continued to effectively bargain after the law was passed, but their decline took hold in the 1970s.

The birth of neoliberalism

On 23 August 1971, Lewis F. Powell Jr, who would be nominated to become a US Supreme Court justice two months later, wrote 'a counter-revolutionary call to arms' for big business. Titled 'Attack on the American Free Enterprise System', Powell's memorandum was penned for the US Chamber of Commerce, and it railed against the critics of business, including those campaigning against the tobacco industry. He wrote that, 'The most disquieting voices joining the chorus of criticism came from perfectly respectable elements of society: from the college campus, the pulpit, the media, the intellectual journals, the arts and the sciences, and from politicians.'

Powell urged America's capitalists to 'learn the lesson … that political power is necessary; that such power must be assiduously cultivated; and that when necessary, it must be used aggressively and with determination—without embarrassment and without the reluctance which has been so characteristic of American business'.[12]

Conservatives had to capture public opinion and shape culture, he argued, by exerting influence over the institutions that shape it. Powell challenged conservatives to control the political debate at its source by demanding 'balance' in textbooks, television shows, and news coverage. Philanthropists and other donors should demand a say in university hiring and curriculums, and 'press vigorously in all political arenas'. The key to victory, he predicted, was 'careful long-range planning and implementation', backed by a 'scale of financing available only through joint effort'.[13]

Powell's manifesto has been described as providing a blueprint for the corporate domination of American democracy, and is credited with inspiring the rapid growth in business power and influence that came to herald the neoliberal era. The intellectual underpinnings of neoliberalism were provided by a cadre of economists, including Mont Pelerin Society economists Friedrich Hayek, Milton Friedman,

Ludwig von Mises, and James Buchanan. In the 1970s and 1980s, as economic conditions were threatened by stagflation, their proposals for diminishing the role of the state in favour of boosting the private sector were enthusiastically embraced in the UK and US, and, to a lesser degree, in Australia. Laws moderating the power of big business, including competition laws and the regulation of banking and financial services, were weakened. Unions began to be muzzled by repressive regulation.

Since the 1980s, neoliberal policies have propelled the privatisation of public industry, the severe concentration of markets, and the deregulation of laws or policies that interfere with global trade and otherwise moderate the power of the private sector, as well as cutbacks to government services. Globalisation and the digital revolution spawned a boom era for multinational corporations. The World Bank and the International Monetary Fund (IMF) used monetary aid programs for developing countries to extract commitments to privatise public industry, allow free trade, cut social services, and allow multinational corporations access to new, lucrative markets.

As the 20th century came to a close, large multinational corporations became the single most powerful influence in our lives, able to shape culture, consumption, and politics according to their imperatives. Major institutions, including the public service, regulatory agencies, courts, and universities began to bend according to their influence. What academic and former US labor secretary Robert Reich labelled 'supercapitalism' spawned an art of rent-seeking through lobbying, political donations, the formation of influential think tanks, sponsorship, astro-turfing, and the infiltration of universities. The result, according to Reich, was 'an arms race for political influence' that overwhelmed 'the voice of the average citizen'.

Workplace flexibility

> As corporations have worked methodically to amass sweeping powers over their employees, they have held aloft the beguiling principle of individual freedom, claiming that only unregulated markets can guarantee personal liberty. Instead, operating under relatively few regulations themselves, these companies have succeeded at imposing all manner of regulation on their employees.
> –Miya Tokimitsu[14]

At the heart of the neoliberal project was the objective of transferring wealth from workers to capital. In order to succeed, big business led the charge to unwind labour laws that had encouraged trade union membership and collective bargaining, thereby impeding managerial prerogative. To mask their intent, business lobbyists and conservative politicians deployed an Orwellian vocabulary of 'liberty', 'freedom', 'flexibility', 'liberalisation', and 'choice'. Business-funded think tanks—such as the HR Nicholls Society in Australia—rejected the notion that a power imbalance existed between employers and employees, and urged a return to the doctrine of 'freedom of contract'. Trade unions and industrial relations tribunals were reframed as 'unwelcome third parties' that interfered with the freedom of employees and employers to individually tailor their working arrangements to suit their needs. This was effectively a call for a return to the primacy of the employment contract.

In Australia, business campaigns to 'liberalise' workplace laws became a defining feature of politics after the 1980s. In fact, since then, there has been a permanent campaign for 'industrial relations reform' that has relied on the rhetoric of freedom, choice, and flexibility. The relentless lobbying and campaigning has produced successive waves of new, more 'flexible' laws that that have seen trade union membership and collective bargaining collapse more rapidly than in almost any other country in the Organisation for Economic Co-operation and Development (OECD). The result has been a major redistribution of wealth — away from workers, in favour of shareholders. As in other developed countries, including the UK and the US, the share of economic growth enjoyed by business has reached record highs.

The expression 'workplace flexibility' is both attractive and highly ambiguous. It can mean different work arrangements designed to accommodate employees' needs, such as being allowed to work from home and to have flexible hours of work. And, undoubtedly, the availability of such work arrangements has been a significant gain for many employees. Women's participation in the labour market has boomed since the 1970s, buttressed by the availability of part-time and casual employment as well as flexible rosters. In 1966, women made up 30 per cent of the paid workforce in Australia. By 2022, it was 48 per cent.

At the same time, the rhetoric of 'flexibility' has been used successfully by business to suppress labour costs and to amass an extraordinary degree of control over the lives of employees. Corporations have sought to ensure that their employees can be reassigned as needed to undertake different tasks and even different jobs — which is described as 'functional flexibility'. Since the 1980s, 'flexibility' has also been deployed to allow businesses to replace secure full-time employment in favour of precarious work arrangements, including labour hire, independent contracting, and franchising. In the first decade of the new century, gig work emerged to much fanfare, promising to revolutionise the way people worked. Notwithstanding the futuristic hype, gig work was a reversion to piecework, a system that predated the Industrial Revolution. Workers were classed as micro-entrepreneurs, and got paid by the gig and nothing else. Two things quickly became apparent: the piece rates on offer were less than the minimum wage; and workers discovered that it was impossible to bargain with an app.

As corporations succeeded in winding back workers' power and statutory protections, the eight-hour day disappeared, and a culture of excessive working hours, wage theft, and unpaid overtime took hold. Initially, that culture ensnared professional managers and other white-collar staff, but, over time, longer working hours spread throughout the labour market. Hours for full-time workers increased, and continued to do so in the 1990s and 2000s. Many employees were required to work for 50–70 hours per week.

In 2005, corporate Australia got its wish list enacted when the Howard government introduced WorkChoices — far-reaching changes to workplace laws, accompanied by a slick taxpayer-funded advertising campaign. The changes gave primacy to individual agreements between employers and employees, to be formalised as Australian Workplace Agreements (AWAs). They were basically glorified employment contracts. Announcing WorkChoices, prime minister John Howard stated:

> The Government's aim is to give even greater freedom and flexibility to employers and employees to negotiate at the workplace level … Australia needs a workplace system geared to the present and the future, not to the past. Under this Government, that system will be one of high productivity, increasing real wages, choice and flexibility.[15]

The effects of the WorkChoices laws were quickly apparent. The AWAs that were registered under the new system were non-negotiable template documents foisted on employees by their employers. The supposed freedom to tailor individual employment arrangements resulted, instead, in thousands of identical documents being issued by large corporations—many of which severely disadvantaged their employees. A leaked report from the workplace regulator in 2006 showed that almost half of the new AWAs eliminated many minimum labour standards. One-third froze wages for the life of the agreement, and more than one-quarter were unlawful because they omitted mandatory minimum standards. Labour productivity nosedived. The Howard government responded by banning the public release of further reports by the regulator.

In the lead-up to the 2007 federal election, Australian unions fiercely opposed WorkChoices and the government that had foisted it on workers. Their 'Your Rights at Work' campaign sought to restore collective-bargaining rights, and was bolstered by regular media reports about individual workers who had suffered cuts to their pay packets, as well as other mistreatment. The empty rhetoric of individual choice, freedom, and flexibility was laid bare, and WorkChoices became political poison. At the election, the Howard government was thrown out of office, and John Howard even lost his seat in parliament.

The new Labor government sought to repair the damage to collective bargaining by introducing a new law, the Fair Work Act. The legislation was the product of exhaustive negotiations in which business lobby groups, including the Business Council of Australia, were heavily involved. Shortly after the Act was introduced in 2009, the big-business lobby began a campaign to try to dismantle it. Senior business leaders repeatedly appeared in the media to claim that the new laws had triggered a 'productivity crisis'. More flexibility, they claimed, was the antidote.

The Murdoch press embraced the productivity-crisis mantra, with *The Australian*'s former editor and senior journalist Paul Kelly warning in 2011 that 'the entire economic debate is shifting against the productivity deadening system [the Labor government] has installed'. The Business Council's Tony Shepherd argued that, 'Industrial relations laws are limiting the capacity of companies to lift their productivity … by making it harder for them to allocate their labour in the most productive ways'.[16]

As the campaign continued, I decided to undertake some research to try to better understand the elusive nuances of productivity. I discovered that there was no credible research—peer-reviewed or otherwise—that linked productivity growth to industrial-relations laws. In fact, in the years following the Fair Work Act, productivity had surged strongly.

In October 2012, I shared my research in a speech I gave at the annual conference of the Australian Industry Group, noting that productivity was increasing faster than it had for a decade, and describing the campaign being waged as propaganda. My speech was shared with *The Australian*, which retaliated swiftly, condemning and deploring me in over 3,000 words across four columns and an editorial. None of those 3,000 words addressed my research.

However, the Fair Work Act changes did not go far enough to address the myriad ways in which corporations had been enabled to de-unionise and de-collectivise workplaces. Collective bargaining and union membership continued to collapse. Notwithstanding this successful de-unionisation of the labour market, an unprecedented transfer of wealth in favour of capital, a declaration by the central bank of a 'low-wage crisis' in 2017, and endemic wage suppression, the business campaign for further industrial-relations deregulation continued. In August 2019, *The Australian Financial Review* reported that:

> Business leader Tony Shepherd has urged corporate executives to prosecute the need for an industrial relations overhaul to boost

worker pay and economic growth, arguing Australia must unleash a new wave of productivity reforms to insulate itself from global headwinds.

'The current industrial relations system lacks the flexibility essential in the modern business environment and the gig economy,' Mr Shepherd said.

The architecture of repressive control

As the neoliberal project decimated collective bargaining, the employment contract re-established its primacy in the Australian workplace. Employment contracts and workplace policies are creatures of fashion, shaped by company lawyers and HR managers according to prevailing wisdom. Just as phenomena such as hot-desking, 360-degree feedback, psychometric testing, and employee-engagement surveys arrive and spread like wildfire across workplaces, so too do particular terms in employment contracts. As a result, at any one time the contracts across different organisations contain terms that bear a remarkable resemblance to one another.

The fact that identical employment contracts—which are heavily skewed in favour of the employer—are signed by thousands of employees in large workplaces is testament to the enormous imbalance in bargaining power inherent in the employment relationship. Employees don't bargain about employment contracts. They sign template documents prepared by company lawyers. When collective bargaining disappears, bargaining itself disappears.

From the late 1990s, Australian companies began to promulgate detailed individual employment contracts and company policies for their managerial staff. The contracts sought to extend the boundaries of control over their employees' lives, including by normalising working long hours and corporate loyalty.[17] For example, a mining company's 1996 contract compelled employees not to exercise any rights to engage in collective industrial activity and not to 'undertake any paid or unpaid activity which is damaging to the interests of the company', noting that, 'Involvement in social, sporting, community, welfare, religious, artistic and political activities would not normally conflict with Company interests.' Over time, as the labour market was increasingly de-unionised, these employment contracts were foisted onto the rest of the workforce.

The contracts also required employees to abide by the terms of company policies and codes of conduct, as varied by the company from time to time. The employee was bound to accept such changes, having agreed to do so, sight unseen — ordinarily, when an employee signs an employment contract, they are not provided with the relevant policies and codes that they are agreeing to comply with. These are only made available after the employment begins, often on the company intranet. Although contracts ordinarily can only be changed with the consent of both parties, this formulation allows corporations to unilaterally vary the contract by varying company policies. By this means, the corporation gains the right to make unreasonable directions, including 'broad circumscriptions of the employee's conduct inside or outside of working hours, no matter how petty or patently unreasonable or unfair'.[18]

A standard employment contract contains a formulation such as this:

Policies
You are required to observe and comply with the Company's policies and procedures including but not limited to:

> Code of Conduct
> Ethics policy
> Electronic Communications policy

> Anti-Discrimination and Harassment policy
> Social Media policy
> Workplace Diversity policy
> Work Health and Safety policy
> These policies will be available on the intranet.
>
> The Company may depart from, vary, replace or withdraw its policies (including those referred to above and elsewhere in this contract) at any time …

While the combination of an employment contract, a code of conduct, and a suite of policies constitute an elaborate spider web of obligations on employees, there are usually a handful of provisions within them that pose the greatest risk to free speech and expression. The suite of documents, which are legally binding, routinely require employees to act respectfully, honestly, transparently, courteously, sensitively, authentically, fairly, and with integrity—at all times. The combination amounts to a morals clause: an obligation to act morally. Such requirements are to be found in the employment contracts used by, for example, casino operators, tobacco companies, fossil-fuel miners, banks, insurers, the major consultancies, and pharmaceutical corporations. It's difficult to reconcile morals clauses imposed on employees with the behaviour of a corporation that shifts its profits to notorious tax havens, subverts labour standards and suppresses wages, sells harmful goods or services, or falsely claims to be a carbon-neutral operation. In other words, it's difficult to reconcile morals clauses with the activities of many major corporations. In reality, they form part of an ethics-washing approach to business.

One large Australian logistics company's code of conduct requires employees to:

- demonstrate the behaviours of honesty, integrity, quality and trust at all times;
- set an example to others and recognise others around you who also demonstrate those behaviours; and
- speak out when you feel that these behaviours are threatened or compromised.

There is a radical distinction between corporations encouraging staff to behave decently and safely at work, and imposing a legal obligation on them to act morally on a 24/7 basis. Read literally, a contract such as this permits the company to surveil an employee who is engaging in an extramarital affair, and to thereby sack the employee for failing to act honestly and with integrity.

In any case, an obligation to always act honestly, with integrity, and to trust colleagues is both undesirable and impossible to fulfil. For example, an honest assessment of an incompetent colleague's work performance may be regarded as disrespectful. When refugee-turned-lawyer and human rights advocate Nyadol Nyuon once told me that all of us can be 'obnoxious arseholes' from time to time, I couldn't disagree with her.

The logistics company tasks employees with policing their colleagues by compelling them to 'speak out'. A requirement to report fraud, a safety hazard, or sexual harassment is perfectly understandable risk-management. But, even then, it may collide headlong with the hierarchical structure of many workplaces, in which junior employees usually won't report witnessing sexual harassment by a senior, more powerful figure for much the same reason that the victims of such harassment often won't speak up—fear of reprisal.

The idea of mandatory reporting of immoral conduct by colleagues also collides with the notorious history of mistreatment meted out to whistleblowers in major corporations. Whistleblowers' stories follow a similar trajectory. When they expose serious wrongdoing, they disturb the prevailing culture. The corporation moves to protect itself and instead to punish them.

While whistleblowers can bring corporations into disrepute, they also perform an important public service by alerting consumers and regulators to illegal and unethical conduct. Laws in many countries recognise their right to bring the corporation into disrepute, and in the US there is a scheme offering lucrative financial incentives for whistleblowing.

When a corporation tells its employees that, like the company itself, they must maintain the highest ethical standards, there is a critical catch: the promise is not binding on the company. Underlying the asymmetry of power and information baked into each employment contract is a standard stipulation that the company's code of conduct and policies 'are not incorporated as terms of your employment contract or are otherwise contractually binding on the Company. Nor does any failure by the Company to comply with its policies or procedures constitute a breach of any term of this Agreement ...'

In 2007, Peter Nikolich, an investment adviser with Goldman Sachs in Australia, sued the company for having failed to uphold its company policy on workplace bullying. Nikolich complained that Goldman Sachs had failed to comply with its *Working With Us* handbook. The handbook, containing policies and procedures that ranged far and wide, totalled 119 pages. Among the statements in the tome under the heading of 'Health and safety' was this: 'The Company: ... will take every practicable step to provide and maintain a safe and healthy work environment for all people.'

Nikolich, who worked in a small office in Canberra, claimed that he had been bullied by his supervisor. When he complained to an HR manager, there was a long delay before he received any meaningful response. As can often be the case, it appears that HR didn't want to pursue the allegations, presumably because the alleged bully was highly valued by the company. When Nikolich realised that the company would not help him, his health deteriorated. He sued Goldman Sachs for breaching his employment contract by failing to take 'every practicable step to provide and maintain a safe and healthy work environment' for him. The evidence of neglect was overwhelming, and Nikolich was successful in recovering substantial damages in light of the serious damage to his mental health.

This court finding proved a turning point. Companies became alarmed that policies they were using to manage their brand and to control their employees could be deployed against them. The standards being applied were impossible to meet, and a failure to do so could lead to expensive claims for compensation. Soon, law firms and consultants began sounding the alarm and spruiking their services to rewrite contracts so that an employee could never again sue a company for breaching company policies. The net result is that virtually all employment contracts in Australia provide an exemption to the employer from having to comply with its code of conduct and other workplace policies. When commerce and morality collide, there can only be one winner.

Corporate cancel culture

Unlike the Ford Motor Company in 1913 or Cadbury's in the 1890s, contemporary corporations are not interested in monitoring the private lives of their employees to assess whether their interaction with foreigners or their bathroom hygiene is problematic. Recreating Ford's Sociological Department would be too expensive, with an uncertain return on investment. Instead, corporations engage in surveillance of their employees' social media use, including their behaviours, attitudes, affiliations, and social connections—all to protect the corporate brand.

The power of 21st-century corporations to conduct out-of-hours employee surveillance is derived from the imposition of corporate policies that contain a right to monitor and regulate their employees' use of social media at all times. The policies bind employees, and render the line between private individual and employee obsolete. The divide has collapsed because corporations have accrued greater power over the personal lives of their staff. They have deployed that power through a burgeoning array of technology, with AI currently posing a new threat.

A typical company social media policy prohibits its employees and contractors from engaging 'in any activity or posting that could harm or tarnish the image, reputation, commercial interests and/or goodwill' of the company 'and/or any of its employees, customers, suppliers or officers'. The policy also states that the company conducts surveillance of its employees by camera, computer, and tracking devices for, inter alia, 'any legitimate purpose relating to the employment of its employees'. The policy requires employees not to say or do anything to harm the company's reputation or to bring the company into disrepute.

Of course, corporations can have a legitimate interest in ensuring that their staff don't publicly criticise and disparage them. In 2013, Paddy Manning, a highly respected and experienced journalist with the Fairfax media group, criticised his employer for publishing sponsored content. Manning's criticism skewered an article in *The Australian Financial Review* that had been sponsored by the Commonwealth Bank. Writing for a rival publication, *Crikey*, Manning described the interview as 'built on a fundamental contract between company and reporter: high-level access in exchange for soft coverage'. Manning was right. In its desperate search for new revenue streams, *The Australian Financial Review* sourced corporate sponsorship for articles, seminars, and interviews that gave business leaders a dubious platform — often to decry the apparently insufferable burden of red tape and company tax. Nevertheless, Manning's decision to go public with his criticisms and in a rival news outlet led to the loss of his job.

There is no shortage of employees complaining online about their jobs. Similarly, employees going rogue by taking to social media to discredit the company's product or services can and do cause commercial harm. Even then, the extent to which public criticism of a corporation by an employee should be censored is not straightforward. Whistleblowers who go public perform a public good by exposing misconduct and other harm. To varying degrees, whistleblower-protection laws license such speech, notwithstanding the commercial harm it may cause. Employees who are collectively bargaining with their union engage in public criticism as part of the bargaining process. Again, robust collective-bargaining laws may license such speech.

Undoubtedly, there are shades of grey in the extent to which a corporation has a legitimate interest in the private life of its staff. Should an employee whose out-of-hours recreational illicit drug use becomes known be disciplined or sacked? That may vary depending on whether the employee is employed in an ambassadorial or other public-facing role. How should we treat the example of a police officer moonlighting as a rabid racist under a social media pseudonym? Or an employee charged with assault after a fracas at a nightclub, or one identified as having attended a racist rally while wearing a company logo or uniform? Sometimes it is difficult to determine whether there is a rational connection between after-hours conduct and the legitimate requirements of a job.

Laws and regulations governing some professions and sporting organisations frequently oblige participants not to bring their profession or sport into disrepute. Such stipulations are intended to cover conduct that is not explicitly prohibited by specific rules. Sports disciplinary tribunals, for example, often hear cases that have nothing to do with on-field behaviour, such as criminal conduct, including violence and the use of illicit drugs.

However, the requirement to avoid bringing a company into disrepute or to comply with its values inevitably leads to a far more repressive realm: the censoring of controversial political speech. The parameters of what might bring a company into disrepute are impossible to define, as the term is vague. How is disrepute established? In practice, its often by 'the vibe'. It is typically not possible to define or understand what speech or activity is circumscribed and therefore punishable until after it happens. Similarly, requiring an employee to comply with a set of aspirational values renders the reach of corporate intrusion into private lives virtually limitless.

The net effect is that the expression is interpreted broadly to prohibit an employee from saying or doing anything that the company deems undesirable. This confers a discretionary power on the corporation that would be described as totalitarian if it was exercised by government. Graeme Orr and Alexandra Wells argue that 'the rise of concern for corporate branding, the pervasiveness of social media and the easy proliferation of employer-drafted policies have combined to bolster both the desire and ability of employers to …. seek to repress, socio-political expression'.[19] In practice, the power is triggered, usually unfairly, when bad-faith actors use social media to pressure a corporation to sack its employee, as can be seen from the earlier examples of Scott McIntyre and Justine Sacco.

In reality, corporate managers are only too aware that their employees' personal, after-hours communications don't represent their company's views. A vigorous debate in the pub about affairs in the Middle East, climate change, the Catholic hurch, or the commemoration of war is unlikely to lead to suggestions that the protagonists' views are the responsibility of their employers. Even an employee attending a swingers' party sporting nothing but a pair of green rubber underpants should be of no concern to the corporation. Not unless they are captured on an iPhone, and the video is posted online, tagging the corporation's social media account — in which case, all hell will break out. The employee will be charged with bringing the company into disrepute, and will be disciplined or sacked.

A risk-averse employee might choose to avoid any activity outside work that could attract criticism. That may mean avoiding social media, and suppressing their gender identity, their sexuality, or their political leanings.

For example, when Ruth came to see me several years ago, she relayed her experience of handing out how-to-vote material on election day at a voting booth for the Australian Labor Party. She had got into an argument with an older man handing out cards for the Liberal Party. The argument escalated and became unpleasant. Later that day, the argument moved onto Twitter, where the two exchanged insults. When she presented for work several days later, she was handed a letter suspending her, pending an investigation into whether she had breached the company code of conduct and values. Her adversary had managed to track down her employer and to complain about her insults. On this occasion, legal intervention saved her job. When she returned to work, it was made clear to her that the company actively supported the Liberal Party.

All of which goes to show that the standard employment contract is deeply oppressive and deeply anti-democratic.

Non-disclosure agreements

There is a more direct means that companies can take to silence employee criticism: an outright ban. Over one-third of employment contracts in the US contain a non-disclosure agreement (NDA) that applies from the moment the employment contract is signed. While NDAs often prohibit disclosure of unsavoury events or commercially sensitive information, many include a prohibition on criticising the corporation. A standard NDA states:

> You shall not at any time, directly or indirectly, disparage the Company, including making or publishing any statement, written, oral, electronic or digital, truthful or otherwise, which may adversely affect the business, public image, reputation or goodwill of the company, including its operations, employees, directors and its past, present or future products or services.

Similar provisions are found in UK employment contracts and, to a lesser extent, in Australian contracts, where they tend to be concentrated (ironically) in the media industry — particularly in commercial television and radio. The provisions tend to mask the sometimes brutal workplace cultures that seem to thrive in newsrooms. Recently, for example, the 7 Network was accused of procuring cocaine and prostitutes in order to gain exclusive interviews, and Nine was forced to deal with allegations that it sought to suppress the reality of a longstanding sexual harassment scandal by its use of NDAs.

The NDAs ban employees from criticising or disparaging the corporation — even long after their employment has ended. According to the *Harvard Business Review*, NDAs 'demand silence often broadly worded to protect against speaking up against corporate culture or saying anything that would portray the company and its executives in a negative light'.[20] While, in a number of cases, these NDAs have been struck down by US courts and tribunals, including by the National Labor Relations Board, most employees don't challenge them because of fear, ignorance, or the prohibitive cost of lawyering up. It's cheaper to fall into line.

An NDA is more commonly invoked in settlements of legal disputes: the quid pro quo required of an employee who obtains a financial settlement. The deal generally prevents the worker from discussing their experience and the settlement, and often extends to a ban on criticism of the company. The overwhelming consideration for businesses to demand NDAs is brand management.

NDAs have been used over many years to hide misconduct and thereby perpetuate it. The moral indignation and political activism generated by the #MeToo movement highlighted the harm caused by NDAs that had silenced women and suppressed the truth about the prevalence of workplace sexual assault and harassment. #MeToo exposed the legal and public relations machine that had protected offenders such as Harvey Weinstein for decades. Journalist Jenna Price condemned NDAs as 'a vile legal instrument that silences women and covers up the behaviour of sexual harassers at all levels and in every sector in Australia'.[21]

#MeToo also spawned a movement to ban the use of NDAs in sexual harassment cases. While there have been calls to ban NDAs in such cases in Australia, this approach has not yet been embraced. In 2020, the-then federal sex discrimination commissioner, Kate Jenkins, delivered her major report, Respect@Work, which stopped short of recommending a ban.

'The Commission heard about the benefits of NDAs in sexual harassment matters in protecting the confidentiality and privacy of victims and helping to provide closure,' Jenkins reported. 'However, there were also concerns that NDAs could be used to protect the reputation of the business or the harasser and contribute to a culture of silence.'[22] In the US in December 2022, President Joe Biden signed into law the Speak Out Act, which prohibits employers from using NDAs to block the victims of sexual harassment and assault from making their stories public. However, it contains a big carve-out: it only applies to pre-dispute NDAs, such as those included in employment contracts. Employers are still allowed to use these provisions as part of settlement agreements that resolve disputes involving sexual harassment.

In 2024, allegations about the scandalous mistreatment of employees working in Australian commercial newsrooms emerged. Multiple reports alleged that women working at Nine Entertainment had been sexually harassed and bullied over many years. The reports also alleged that the misconduct had been known to senior management for years and had been covered up by the profligate use of NDAs.

NDAs are not dead yet.

CHAPTER THREE

Do Corporations Have Feelings?

Corporations are people, my friend.
–Mitt Romney, 11 August 2011[1]

Israel Folau is Australia's answer to former American gridiron star Colin Kaepernick. Both took a stand and paid a terrible price for it. But, unlike Kaepernick, Folau's activism was far from heroic. On 10 April 2019, in response to the Tasmanian government allowing gender to be changed on birth certificates, Folau, a highly acclaimed professional rugby league footballer and a fundamentalist Christian, took to Facebook. His posts included a screenshot of a meme based on Corinthians 6:9–10 that stated, 'WARNING Drunks, Homosexuals, Adulterers, Liars, Fornicators, Thieves, Atheists, Idolaters HELL AWAITS YOU. REPENT! ONLY JESUS SAVES'.

The internet combusted with indignation and condemnation. Folau was widely criticised by politicians, journalists, members of the queer community, identity activists, and other rugby champions. It was not the first time that Folau had courted controversy by spouting his homophobic religious views. In September 2017, he announced his opposition to a change of law to recognise same-sex marriage. In April 2018, he was asked on Instagram what God's 'plan for homosexuals' was. He replied, 'Hell ... unless they repent of their sins and turn to God.'

Folau's employer, Rugby Australia Ltd, slammed his homophobia and made it clear that it was an inclusive organisation. Its CEO, Raelene Castle, stated, 'Whilst Israel is entitled to his religious beliefs, the way in which he has expressed those beliefs is inconsistent with the values of the sport.' Presumably, Castle's reference to the way in which Folau had expressed his beliefs was a reference to him posting his views on social media.

Like all employees of Rugby Australia, Folau had signed a template employment contract that required him to abide by its code of conduct. The code outlined the company's core values, 'including a safe, fair and inclusive environment for all', and provided that its employees had to 'use social media appropriately'. What did that mean?

Predictably, Folau's case unleashed a fierce culture war, pitting liberals and progressives against religious conservatives in a highly polarised and hypocritical debate. Progressives who had previously condemned the sackings of employees for expressing dissident left-wing views demanded that he be sacked for breaching his employment contract. Conservatives who had previously campaigned for the sacking of the same left-wing dissidents discovered a new commitment to human rights discourse, and condemned corporate overreach.

Folau remained unrepentant. 'Jesus Christ is what comes first', he explained.

After an internal disciplinary board hearing determined that Folau had contravened his employment contract, Rugby Australia sacked him. Raelene Castle explained that, 'At its core, this is an issue of responsibilities an employee owes to their employer and the commitments they make to their employer to abide by their employer's policies and procedures and adhere to their employer's values.'[2]

The Folau controversy raised complex moral, philosophical, and legal questions. It presented a clash of competing freedoms. Folau is of Tongan ancestry. Christian missionaries have had a profound impact on the Pacific Islander culture, and Folau's views were shared by other rugby players of Pacific Island descent. 'Might as well sack me and all the other Pacific Island rugby players around the world because we share the same Christian beliefs,' one player, Taniela Tupou, wrote on his Facebook page.[3] Folau and others were free, like many religious fundamentalists, to attend their church and listen to homophobic teachings. He had attended the Jesus Christ Church, led by his father, Pastor Eni Folau. Israel Folau invoked the New Testament, raising the question whether his right to express his fundamentalist religious views should take precedence over the right of members of the LGBTI community to live free from vilification. And to complicate things further, there was Folau's right to work and have a life outside work.

Were Folau's exhortations harmful—particularly to closeted younger members of the queer community? Did they incite discrimination, bigotry, and violence? Or would the risk of those impacts be nullified by the widespread condemnation of his views? Australia's federal laws do not prohibit homophobic commentary or vilification. Was Folau's expression a form of hate speech, and should the parliament move to address it by legislative change? The Fair Work Act prohibits an employer from sacking an employee by reason of religion. Did that prohibition extend to religious proselytising, or should it be read more narrowly?

Simon Longstaff, the executive director of The Ethics Centre, entered the public fray, arguing that it was reasonable for companies to 'be free to take steps to protect themselves from the strategic risk caused by well-intentioned, loose cannons ...' In other words, Longstaff argued that companies should be able to fire staff with controversial views in order to protect their brands. On the other hand, he explained that 'it falls to the employee to accept (or not) the relevant conditions of employment', counselling that Folau had a 'choice': to play professional rugby or to find work with another organisation 'better suited to his values'. Next, Longstaff argued that 'if the conscience of an employee should be respected, then so should that of the employer'.[4]

The Ethics Centre is a not-for-profit organisation based in Sydney, offering programs 'designed to bring ethics to the centre of personal and professional life'. A year before the Folau controversy broke, a representative of the centre approached me and asked me to join a group known as 'The Ethics Alliance' to 'discuss ethics in a relaxed Chatham House environment' with a focus on the 'ethical issues our business community faces'. The alliance is made up of big corporations that pay the centre for membership. Among these companies were major banks, a major mining company, and one of the Big Four accounting firms: in the main, oligopolies. I declined the offer to join the alliance, explaining that I could not participate in an ethics discussion group with representatives of 'companies that routinely engage in illegal, improper and unethical conduct'. I was sceptical about chatting about ethics in a relaxed environment with a group of oligopolists, including companies I had sued or conceivably would sue in the future.

I was also conscious that professional ethicists are often wheeled out after a scandal involving professional athletes. A familiar script plays out: the athlete takes a period of leave, undergoes re-education, and duly appears at a press conference to pronounce, 'I take full responsibility for my actions. I have been on a journey of discovery, and I now appreciate that urinating on my teammate's head while he was asleep and posting it on YouTube was deeply wrong. I'm grateful for these learnings and humbled by the support that I have received ...' Each such performance has always struck me as an excruciating exercise in brand management.

Longstaff's interventions in the debate were both fascinating and deeply problematic. Here was a professional ethicist elevating the corporation's right to manage its brand above the right of an individual to quote the Bible. Then there was Longstaff's notion of 'choice' offered to Folau—to find another job or career. Longstaff was apparently unaware of the virtually identical company policies and codes of conduct that exist throughout the labour market. Consequently, Folau would have been hard-pressed to find another employer. The choice to cease playing professional sport? This characterisation was pure sophistry—a severe penalty dressed up as a 'choice'.

Longstaff's failure to acknowledge the existence of laws that prohibit an employer from sacking an employee because of their religion was more than passing strange. For Longstaff, Rugby Australia's contractual right to manage its brand took priority over Australia's anti-discrimination laws. According to such logic, if a company is able to use its employment contract and associated policies to override a legislated human right, presumably it could contract with an employee not to express their homosexuality, pursue a political affiliation, or get pregnant.

Folau sued Rugby Australia in the Federal Circuit Court, asserting that he had been unlawfully sacked because of his religion. Predictably, the case resolved before trial. Although the settlement sum was confidential, it was widely reported that Folau had been paid approximately $3 million, representing the balance he had been owed for the term of his contract. Nevertheless, Folau suffered a severe punishment. He lost his job and was forced to leave Australia to obtain work as a professional rugby player.

On 1 June 2019, I entered the fray by posting on Twitter:

> If you are a progressive arguing that Folau has caused harm to gay people that's fine but going to the barricades on contract law is an excruciatingly bad take. Ask Scott McIntyre, Yassmin Abdel-Mageid, Angela Williamson …

I was referring to notorious cases, such as those mentioned earlier, in which employees had lost their jobs after posting controversial, progressive views because their employers had decided that their political expression contravened their employment contracts.

I also criticised Folau's sacking in a television interview for *The Project*, arguing that determining complex moral and philosophical issues, including the bounds of acceptable speech, should not be the remit of corporations, but rather was the role of democratically elected politicians. I found myself in uncomfortable company: arguing alongside right-wing politicians and hard-right religious groups. I was aware that their invocation of human rights and free-speech discourse was disingenuous, and I tried to distinguish my position from theirs. Nevertheless, I was widely criticised and pilloried by parts of the left.

Of course, the strongest argument in favour of constraining Folau's religious expression was that his bigoted, homophobic views caused harm to the queer community, particularly its young and religious members. Comedian and podcaster Tom Ballard, who interviewed me about the controversy, instanced a young man from a Pacific Island background struggling to come to terms with his sexuality who could be harmed by Folau's rhetoric. And yet many progressives and liberals ignored the question of harm — as did

Longstaff, Jesuit priest Frank Brennan, and my friend and former race discrimination commissioner Tim Soutphommasane. Instead, they emphasised his obligations under the employment contract, and argued that Folau could choose to continue working or pursue his religious proselytising.

And then there was Longstaff's notion that a corporation had a conscience. How did that work? Are we to believe anthropomorphically that corporations such as Coca Cola, Amazon, ExxonMobil, and Qantas have a conscience?

The nature of a corporation

Unlike people, publicly traded corporations are entities created by law. And unlike people, capitalist corporations have one legal purpose: to make a profit. Directors and management must act in the best interests of shareholders to maximise their return.

Perhaps the most compelling critique of major corporations is provided by Canadian law professor Joel Bakan, who wrote that, 'The corporation's legally defined mandate is to pursue, relentlessly and without exception, its own self-interest, regardless of the often harmful consequences it might cause to others.'[5]

Bakan famously challenged the anthropomorphic lens applied to corporations by identifying their characteristics, which included self-interested but asocial self-aggrandising, and the inability to feel remorse or accept responsibility for their actions. As such, Bakan argued, if corporations were people, they would meet the diagnostic criteria for psychopaths.

For centuries prior to the rise of the capitalist corporations, incorporation was a privilege granted to further non-commercial objectives, including religious and charitable purposes.

The publicly traded profit-seeking corporation first emerged in the late-16th century in England, with the ascension of the East

India Company. Its constitution permitted it to 'wage war' to further its business of international trade. Led by Robert Clive, a 'violent, ruthless and psychologically unstable corporate predator', it relied on a private army of 260,000 men—twice the size of the British army—by which means it conquered great parts of the Indian subcontinent before colonising parts of South-East Asia and Hong Kong. As it rapidly expanded, it became 'not just the world's first great multinational corporation, it was also the first to run amok and show how large companies can become more powerful, and sometimes more dangerous, than nations or even empires'.[6]

The early years of English capitalist corporations were mired in financial scandals as stockbrokers routinely sourced capital from 'ignorant men, drawn in by the reputation, falsely raised and artfully spread, concerning the thriving state of the stock'.[7] By the time of the collapse of the South Sea Company in 1720, which caused catastrophic losses and bankruptcies for many investors, and widespread economic damage, the capitalist corporation had been so thoroughly discredited that the English parliament introduced laws banning the further creation of trading corporations.

The ban on corporations in England was not lifted until 1825, but they had been thriving in the US. From the mid-19th century, incorporation became a right—not a privilege. Laws established that the purpose of commercial corporations was maximising profit. By the late-19th century, capitalist corporations were booming in both Britain and the US, enabling vast sums of capital to finance the construction of rail networks and other critical infrastructure. In the US, they quickly developed into rich and powerful monopolies. Among them was Standard Oil, which by 1904 controlled 94 per cent of US oil production. It attained its monopoly by what the US Supreme Court described as:

Rebates, preferences, and other discriminatory practices in favour of the combination of railroad companies; restraint and monopolization by control of pipe lines, and unfair practices against competing pipe lines; contracts with competitors in restraint of trade; unfair methods of competition, such as local price cutting at the points where necessary to suppress competition; espionage of the business of competitors, the operation of bogus independent companies, and payment of rebates in oil, with the like intent.[8]

By the early 1900s, the US 'seemed condemned to monopoly capitalism, financial crisis, deep inequality, a loss of trust in institutions, and political violence'.[9]

President Theodore Roosevelt was confronted by the dilemma of how to address rampaging monopolies that resisted paying tax, crushed competing businesses by any means necessary, sacked injured and maimed workers while denying them decent wages, and fiercely resisted government regulation. In his first annual message to Congress on 3 December 1901, he stated that, 'Great corporations exist only because they are created and safeguarded by our institutions and it is therefore our right and our duty to see that they work in harmony with these institutions'. He railed against 'unfair money-getting' that created a 'small class of enormously wealthy and economically powerful men, whose chief object is to hold and increase their power'.

Companies routinely bribed American politicians to ensure that their interests were safeguarded, and Roosevelt was only too aware that many of his colleagues would not support proper regulation because they had been bought off. He courageously argued that the Republican Party did not deserve electoral success if it 'took the attitude of saying that corporations should not, when they receive great benefits and make a great deal of money, pay their share of the public burden'.

He legislated to break up monopolies, enact protections for workers, and create publicly owned national parks, ushering in 'a transformative period of corporate, regulatory, and financial reform that permanently altered the relationship between the government and corporations'.[10]

In response to growing public hostility and legislative reform, major corporations instigated campaigns to show that, like people, they cared for others. In 1908, for example, AT&T promoted itself as 'a friend and neighbour', and promised 'a new democracy of public ownership'.[11] Companies such as AT&T, General Motors, Standard Oil, and General Electric were at the frontier of the 'new capitalism'. If, like people, they were capable of moral decision-making, corporations could decide to do the right thing, thus rendering regulation unnecessary and undesirable. The new capitalism was the first attempt by corporations to engage in what we now call ethics-washing: the process by which corporations promote themselves as ethical and caring in order to discourage proper regulation.

'New capitalism' lived a short life; it was left to dwindle and die in the wake of the Great Depression. Following the ravages of the Depression, President Franklin Roosevelt introduced the New Deal in 1933, shortly after taking office, pledging to use all the levers of democratically elected government 'against the misuse of private economic power'. In his State of the Union address in January 1944, he argued that:

> The power of a few to manage the economic life of the nation must be diffused among the many or be transferred to the public and its democratically responsible government. If prices are to be managed and administered, if the nation's business is to be allotted by plan and not by competition, that power should not be vested in any private group or cartel, however benevolent its professions profess to be.

The president built upon the legacy of his cousin, Teddy, by modernising laws that regulated corporate power. They included consumer-protection laws and the introduction of the right of employees to bargain collectively.

The neoliberal corporation

In 1962, Milton Friedman published his book *Capitalism and Freedom*, in which he argued that a company had no 'social responsibility' to the public or society — its only obligations were to shareholders. A CEO's primary responsibility, he argued, was solely to owners of the business. On 13 September 1970, Friedman published a highly influential article in *The New York Times Magazine* entitled 'The Social Responsibility of Business is to Increase its Profits', which anticipated the conservative attacks on 'woke capitalism' by more than 60 years. He condemned businesses for professing a social conscience and their ambition to combat workplace discrimination and environmental pollution. To Friedman, this was 'preaching pure and unadulterated socialism'.

He went on to posit that business had but one social responsibility: 'to use its resources and engage in activities designed to improve its profits so long as it stays within the rules of the game, which is to say, engages in open and free competition, without deception and fraud'. Friedman's views were subsequently adopted by the peak business lobby group in the US, the Business Roundtable. As we have seen, Friedman came to be recognised as the leading proponent of neoliberalism, an ideology that is associated with deregulation, tax cuts, financialisation, and the privatisation of many public goods and services. But at the heart of the neoliberal project was a massive redistribution of wealth away from workers in favour of shareholders. What I have called the Great Wealth Redistribution relied on drastic changes to the labour market and the degradation of the notion of companies having to pay reasonable levels of tax.[12]

In the 1970s and 1980s, business schools, economists, and institutional investors insisted that businesses pare back their operations to focus on their 'core strengths'. The new consensus corporations had become too big and over-complicated:

> Where once the primary concern of every corporation was the production of goods, now production itself—running one's own factories, being responsible for tens of thousands of full-time, permanent employees—began to seem like a clunky liability.[13]

Wave after wave of restructuring and cost-cutting ensued. For many major companies, that meant outsourcing functions to external service-providers. Companies relinquished factories and production processes, payroll, IT, and accounting, together with the employees within those divisions. US academic Professor Weil coined the term 'the fissured workplace' for this development, observing that, 'As major companies have consciously invested in building brands and devoted customers as the cornerstone of their business strategy, they have also shed their role as the direct employer of the people responsible for providing good and services.'[14]

The initial wave of outsourcing focused on sourcing cheap labour in the developing world—a process that continues to be advocated by business schools, which describe it as 'labour arbitrage'. As the fissuring process continued, it took different forms, including the use of labour-hire agencies, contracting and sub-contracting, franchising, and, more recently, the gig economy. While it no longer employed its labour, the corporation maintained control over it, both to ensure the quality of production and the suppression of labour costs. The role of the corporation shifted from that of an employer required to negotiate wages through collective bargaining with securely employed workers to that of a lead company with the power to unilaterally set the price of precariously employed labour-hire workers.

In order to so radically redistribute wealth upwards, corporations in many OECD countries worked relentlessly to eliminate the bargaining power of employees. Politicians were leant on to enact pro-employer laws, and union-busting schemes were successfully unleashed across industries and workplaces.

In the 30 years to 1988, 92 per cent of US stockmarket gains were derived from economic growth. But in the decades since then, the majority of stockmarket growth has been driven by an underlying transfer from wages to shareholders as a result of labour cost-cutting: a massive, regressive redistribution of wealth. Across the US, the UK, and Australia, the share of economic growth enjoyed by business owners has reached record highs. The share afforded to employees has plummeted to record lows. In the US, executive remuneration has increased by an average 940 per cent since 1978, while average workers' pay has increased by 12 per cent.[15]

Setting fire to civilisation

If taxes are what we pay for civilised society, as US Supreme Court justice Oliver Wendell Holmes observed in 1927, then the neoliberal corporation set fire to civilisation. When Ronald Reagan declared that 'government is not the solution to the problem; government is the problem', he set out to unwind the relationship between the state and corporations. Government was designated as bad. Corporations were good. The clear implication was that tax revenue was wasteful. Economic reform was defined as measures that resulted in smaller government and lower tax rates.

In the late 1980s, multinational corporations started a race to the bottom on company tax, signalling their willingness to invest in countries with low corporate tax rates. Nation-states competed against each other to attract investment and business activity. The race was promoted by global institutions, including the IMF and the OECD, together with big-business lobbying organisations and their allies in politics, propagating the myth that tax competition, like market competition, was a boon for consumers. At the same time, increasingly sophisticated and aggressive tax-avoidance schemes were deployed by major corporations with the help of the Big Four accounting firms: Deloitte, Ernst & Young, PricewaterhouseCoopers, and Klynveld Peat Marwick Goerdeler (KPMG).

To take one example, in 2008 Goldman Sachs, the gigantic investment bank and financial services company, had an effective tax rate of 3.8 per cent (down from 34 per cent the year before). In 2007, it paid $6 billion in tax; in 2008, it paid just $14 million. Goldman Sachs's effective tax rate was achieved by shifting its earnings to subsidiaries in low- or no-tax nations, such as the Cayman Islands. A 2016 report by Citizens for Tax Justice stated that 'Goldman Sachs reports having 987 subsidiaries in offshore tax havens, 537 of which are in the Cayman Islands despite not operating a single legitimate office in that country ... The group officially holds $28.6 billion offshore.'[16]

The Business Council of Australia (BCA) is Australia's answer to the US Business Roundtable. It represents the CEOs of Australia's top listed companies, many of whom operate in highly concentrated markets. For decades, it has maintained a campaign for company tax cuts. Its chief executives enjoy membership of the Business Tax Working Group, which makes recommendations to government on tax policy. In 2010, mining companies, including BHP and Rio Tinto, both prominent members of the BCA, mounted an aggressive campaign that ultimately succeeded in destroying a super-profits mining tax proposed by the-then Rudd government. The companies invested $22 million in the campaign, which presented the proposed new tax as endangering new mining projects, workers' jobs, and economic prosperity.

As the campaign unfolded, and away from the public spotlight, the Australian Tax Office (ATO) was investigating whether both companies had illegally shifted profits to Singapore to avoid paying company tax. (Rio Tinto had paid as little as 5 per cent tax on profits shifted to Singapore from 2007 onward.) In November 2018, BHP settled its dispute with the ATO by making a payment of $529 million and a commitment that, from July 2019, all profits made from its Singaporean marketing hub would be 'fully subject to Australian tax'. In July 2022, Rio Tinto settled its decade-long tax dispute with the ATO for approximately $1 billion.

In 2010, Nathan Tinkler, who at the time was an Australian mining billionaire, filed a tax return declaring that his taxable income for that financial year was $9,834. In 2013–14, one-third of BCA member companies, including News Corp, paid no company tax at all.

The BCA liberally sprinkles its endless rent-seeking with econobabble — political spin dressed up as economic jargon. At various times, it has claimed that cutting the company tax rate would boost investment, productivity, and wage growth, and would cut unemployment — nothing yet about curing dandruff. In August 2023, the BCA released its 'Seize the Moment' report (which mimicked a 2021 report of the same name by the Confederation of British Industry), arguing that Australia would be left behind by competitors, while living standards would be eroded, unless substantial changes were made to the economy, including cuts to company tax.

In his famous 1958 book, *The Affluent Society*, John Kenneth Galbraith had noted that 'trickle-down economics' had been tried before in the United States in the 1890s. He explained that it was referred to at that time as 'horse and sparrow theory' by 'an older and less elegant generation', because 'If you feed the horse enough oats, some will pass through to the road for the sparrows.' The neoliberals promised that business tax cuts would trickle down to the rest of the community. The promise was false.

When multinationals effectively boycott the payment of company tax, billions of dollars are withheld from investment in health, education, social security, defence, and infrastructure. At the same time, taxpayer bailouts of big corporations at times of crisis—including the 2008 global financial crisis (GFC) and the Covid-19 pandemic—are an enduring feature of economic management. The corporations never knock back the government handouts.

The rise and fall of CSR

In his 2015 book, *Trust Me, PR is Dead*, public relations executive Robert Phillips recounts an approach made to him for advice from a highly anxious CEO of a major multinational. One of the factories in a developing country, which was part of his firm's supply chain, had caught fire, and 100 impoverished women had burned to death. 'My chairman's been giving me grief,' said the CEO. 'He thinks we're failing to get our message across. We are not emphasising our CSR [Corporate Social Responsibility] credentials well enough.' Phillips responded, 'While 100 women's bodies are still smouldering?' The CEO simply responded, 'Please help.'[17]

Milton Friedman hated CSR programs. Notwithstanding his exalted status in the business community, his views on CSR were largely ignored. The business community reasoned that Friedman was too much of a purist to understand the need for business to find a plausible cover for its otherwise reputation-busting activities.

The CSR industry grew exponentially in the 1980s and 1990s as big business brandished programs and sponsorships to help the needy and to save the climate.

Another form of ethics-washing, CSR is, like an alluring set of company values, brandished to convey a caring, ethical, and benevolent image. CSR helps companies to recruit and retain staff by seeking to persuade employees that the company is a good employer, or that it's not just driven by profit. Indeed, like conventional philanthropy, CSR programs can make a useful contribution by assisting charities, the arts, and non-governmental organisations. But CSR will never support efforts to tackle corporate tax avoidance, better regulate the private sector, or help trade unions to re-unionise the labour market.

In 1997, John Browne, the head of British Petroleum (BP), and known as the Sun King during his reign from 1995 to 2007, became a CSR hero, attracting global acclaim when he announced that his company had to address global warming and 'the reality and the concerns of the world in which' the company operated. BP endorsed the Kyoto Protocol, and its petrol stations suddenly turned green. Within two years, Browne was awarded a UN award for 'environmental leadership'.

However, during and after Browne's term as CEO, BP was responsible for environmental calamities. On 23 March 2005, an explosion and fire at its Texas City refinery killed 15 workers and injured another 170. In 2006, it suffered two leaks in its pipelines in Prudhoe Bay, in Alaska, with the first one, in March, leaking about 267,000 gallons of crude oil. Then, on 20 April 2010, an explosion on its Deepwater Horizon oil-drilling rig in the Gulf of Mexico resulted in the deaths of 11 workers and a massive oil spill, totalling millions of barrels, which is regarded as one of the worst environmental disasters in US history. The company pleaded guilty to 11 counts of manslaughter and a raft of other criminal charges in November 2012. It paid more than $18 billion in fines.

While Browne was widely lauded at the time for his environmental posturing, he achieved financial success for the company by implementing the most aggressive cost-cutting program in the company's history. He promoted low-cost individual work-safety rules while the budget for safe industrial processes was slashed. The National Commission on the BP Deepwater Horizon Oil Spill reported that the company's focus on 'individual worker occupational safety but not on process safety' was a key cause of the tragedy.

As at 2020, some 23 years after BP attracted acclaim for its environmental commitments, 96 per cent of BP's capital expenditure was dedicated to oil and gas. BP continues to brand itself as 'working to make energy cleaner'. In February 2020, BP once again attracted world headlines by announcing plans to eliminate or offset all carbon emissions from its operations and the fuel it sells by 2050.

Professor Joel Bakan recounts the efforts of Enron, another well-known US multinational that won several CSR awards and donated millions to charity:

> Each year the company produced a Corporate Responsibility Annual Report; the most recent one, unfortunately its last, vowed to cut greenhouse gas emissions and support multilateral agreements to help stop climate change. The company pledged further to put human rights, the environment, health and safety issues, biodiversity, indigenous rights, and transparency at the core of its business operations, and it created a well-staffed corporate social responsibility task force … It described the generous support it had provided … funding arts organisations, museums, educational institutions, environmental groups, and various causes throughout the world.[18]

Then, in December 2001, Enron collapsed. Some of its senior executives had hidden billions in losses, and had lied about its accounts. They were charged with criminal and other offences, including bank fraud, making false statements, money laundering, conspiracy, and insider trading. Sixteen people pleaded guilty to crimes committed while at the company. Chief accounting officer Rick Causey, for example, was sentenced to seven years in prison.

In 2012, Volkswagen was a recipient of the 'Ethics in Business Award' issued by the World Forum for Ethics in Business, in recognition of its efforts in environmental management and corporate social responsibility. In 2014, Volkswagen announced that 'environmental considerations are factored into every decision we make', proclaiming its aim to become the 'world's most environmentally compatible automaker' by 2018.[19] In September 2015, the news broke that Volkswagen had been lying to regulators and its customers about the amount of pollution emitted by its cars. Over a six-year period, at least 11 million VW cars were fitted with a software program that was able to cheat tests that measured pollution generated by the cars, allowing the company's vehicles to emit up to 40 times the legal limit. The deception was exposed through rigorous tests conducted by the International Council on Clean Transportation. The ICCT took its test results to the US Environmental Protection Agency, and VW was exposed. Since that time, VW has paid out more than 30 billion euros in fines, compensation, and legal costs.

After leaving BP, John Browne's thinking evolved. He now says that 'while corporate social responsibility was a very well-meaning and worthy thing to have started, it no longer serves a useful purpose in that it is detached from the basics of a business ... it is something that boards of directors only examine at 4.30 on a Friday afternoon'. Browne now argues that business should 'radically engage' with society. 'The more you engage with society, the more you have a reservoir of goodwill that will limit the risks – and the more you make money', Browne told *The Guardian* in a 2015 interview to promote his new book, *Connect*.[20] In June 2024, he criticised corporations for doing 'a poor job of reconciling corporate actions with the interests of society and the planet', and called for an end to the issuing of new North Sea oil and gas-drilling licences.[21]

Company values

Citing a breach of company values is standard operating procedure in defending decisions to sack employees for their controversial political, religious, or other expressions. Rugby Australia cited Israel Folau's failure to conform to its values in announcing its decision to sack him, as we have seen.

The values that are routinely promulgated by our major corporations are impeccable. They are helpfully listed on company websites under headings such as 'What we stand for'. Values such as 'Integrity', 'Trust', 'Transparency', 'Excellence', 'Respect', and 'Accountability'—always referred to in capital letters—are a given. More recently, 'Inclusiveness' has emerged. They embody the best qualities that a human being could aspire to.

But is the notion of corporate values an oxymoron? Is it another cynical form of anthropomorphism? Can an artificially created entity designed to maximise profit really nurture and harbour values? A cursory scan of the corporate landscape suggests the possibility of something even more troubling: an inverse relationship between a company's stated exemplary values, on the one hand, and its conduct, on the other.

In recent decades, one of the more popular—if not compulsory—company values has been 'Integrity'. It is proudly brandished on many corporate websites, including those of

Volkswagen, Rio Tinto, Chevron, Goldman Sachs, and 7-Eleven.

The Commonwealth Bank of Australia (CBA), established in 1911, is Australia's largest retail bank while also operating across Asia, the US, and the UK. It was privatised in 1996. During the 2008 global financial crisis, the CBA's deposits, like those of other major banks, were guaranteed by the federal government. The CBA is also ostensibly committed to 'Integrity', which it helpfully explains as 'saying and doing what is right for our customers, our people, our community and our shareholders'.

Instead, the 2017 Royal Commission into Banking and Financial Services found that the CBA had for years been engaged in a range of egregious misconduct, including:

- Charging dead people fees for financial-planning advice. For example, a CBA adviser knowingly charged a dead client's estate fees for more than a decade after death.
- Through its insurance arm, CommInsure, routinely ripping off its customers by denying them insurance that they were entitled to, including by manipulating medical reports. It now faces 87 criminal charges for hawking life insurance.
- Charging thousands of bank customers for financial planning advice that was not given to them. For this, the bank has had to repay more than $100 million to compensate customers.
- Selling credit card and loan-protection insurance to hundreds and thousands of customers who were ineligible to buy it or make a claim on that insurance because they were unemployed at the time.
- Being one of four banks that illegally sought to rig an interest-rate benchmark, the bank-bill swap rate, to advantage the bank at the expense of customers.
- Breaching anti-money-laundering and counter-terrorism-

financing laws. In June 2018, the CBA reached an agreement to pay a $700 million penalty for having contravened those laws on 53,750 occasions.

Royal commissioner Ken Hayne described this litany of crime and misconduct as the result of 'greed — the pursuit of short-term profit at the expense of basic standards of honesty'. 'How else is charging continuing advice fees to the dead to be explained?' he wrote. The misconduct was rife both before and after the GFC.

In 2016, the bank was aware that there were continuing investigations into its life insurance business; that it had violated anti-money-laundering laws; that thousands of customers and dead former customers had been charged fees for no service; and that it had sold consumer-credit insurance to ineligible customers. In that same year, the bank's CEO, Ian Narev, recommended that all CBA executives receive at least 100 per cent of their short-term bonuses. The recommendation was accepted by the board, other than for one employee, who received 95 per cent. Similarly, Narev received 108 per cent of his target bonus, worth $2.86 million, on top of his fixed pay.[22]

For decades, thousands of bank employees engaged in, or at least, were aware of the illegal and unethical conduct. All of them were violating their employment contract by failing to adhere to company values because they were not acting with integrity. There were at least two notable exceptions. Dr Benjamin Koh was chief medical officer of the bank's insurance business. He witnessed bank employees denying insurance to customers, including those who had suffered heart attacks, by manipulating medical opinions and using outdated medical definitions. He became aware that medical files had a tendency to disappear. His attempts to stop this misconduct were rebuffed. Having lost trust in those around him, he did what many whistleblowers do: he sent files containing relevant information to his private email address to ensure that the files did not disappear.

Having represented many whistleblowers, I am familiar with the usual corporate response. The standard script involves the company suspending the employee, pending an investigation into whether they have engaged in misconduct. At the same time, management is tasked with scanning the employees' work history and conduct in search of any flaws or failings that could be added to a misconduct charge. Often, the misconduct alleged against an employee involves their emailing of company documents to a personal email address—a step that is usually taken to enable the whistleblower to preserve materials essential to the reporting of the company's wrongdoing. The company then hires PR professionals who are required to try to discredit the whistleblower in off-the-record briefings to journalists.

In August 2015, Dr Koh was summoned to a meeting with CommInsure's CEO, Helen Troup, at which he was sacked. Koh was accused of having breached the bank's workplace policies by forwarding work files to his personal email account. The bank denied victimisation, stating that, 'Dr Koh's employment was not terminated for raising concerns. It was terminated primarily for serious and repeated breaches of customers' privacy and trust involving highly sensitive personal, medical and financial information over a lengthy period of time.' Its spokesman added that the bank 'encourages all employees to speak up if they see activities or behaviours that are fraudulent, illegal or inconsistent with our values'.[23]

The other whistleblower who stood up to the CBA was Jeff Morris from the bank's wealth-management division, whose customers included retirees. Morris took on the bank after witnessing its financial planners gain lucrative bonuses by persuading customers to invest in risky products, resulting in many of them suffering significant financial losses—some customers even lost their life savings. The bank responded to Morris's whistleblowing by compiling a dirt file on him and retaining spin doctors to background journalists in order to try to discredit him. The bank 'called in favours, heavied media bosses, launched sophisticated and sustained smear campaigns and had powerful politicians and regulators on speed dial'.[24] Morris's life was never the same.

The thousands of other bank employees who stayed quiet or participated in wrongdoing were not disciplined or sacked for failing to uphold the bank's values. In many cases, they were rewarded with bonuses. Throughout this period, the bank maintained its support for the education of young people. In 2017, the bank's Corporate Responsibility Report stated that 'over the last year 574,000 students have completed one of our in-school financial education programs, Start Smart'.[25]

There was a time in the wake of the GFC when it looked like stricter regulation of banks would protect their customers—particularly in the US, from where the crisis emanated. It didn't last. In 2016, Wells Fargo, one of the largest banks in the world, boasted of its 37-page 'Vision and Values' booklet, which used the word 'trust' 24 times. In bold letters under the heading, 'Vision and Values', Wells Fargo CEO John Stumpf stated that, 'Everything we do is built on trust. It doesn't happen with one transaction, in one day on the job or in one quarter. It's earned relationship by relationship.'

In late 2016, it was revealed that thousands of the bank's employees had opened deposit and credit-card accounts for customers without their knowledge to meet sales targets and to earn bonuses. According to the US Consumer Financial Protection Bureau, employees opened more than two million fraudulent accounts, fleecing customers of almost $2.5 million in fees. As a result, the bank fired 5,300 workers tied to the scandal and paid a record $185 million fine. John Stumpf retired in the wake of the scandal.

In Australia, the convenience retailer 7-Eleven also boasts that it acts 'with fairness and integrity' and embraces 'the highest standards'. As it promulgated such impeccable commitments, 7-Eleven was amassing enormous profits operating a business that depended on thousands of illegally underpaid workers, many of whom were vulnerable migrants relying on visas to remain in the country. Some were paid as little as $5.00 an hour—less than half the minimum wage. Others were initially required to work as trainees for several months without pay. Wage and pay records were falsified, and those who complained were threatened with deportation by the franchisees.

In August 2015, a joint investigation by the ABC and Fairfax exposed the systematic underpayment and abuse of workers in 7-Eleven stores. The workers were employed by 7-Eleven franchisees, all of whom had been forced to sign contracts with the company that were so unfair that the only way that the franchisees could survive was to grossly underpay their workers. These arrangements were phenomenally profitable for 7-Eleven.

Attempts by consumer advocate, Michael Fraser, to engage with the 7-Eleven board of directors and senior management over a period of several years were met with desultory letters advising him to take up the issue with the regulator. The company maintained a position of wilful blindness until publicly exposed. Following the revelations, the billionaire founder and director of the company, Russ Withers, stepped down as chairman of 7-Eleven and of the Australian Institute of Company Directors, a leading organisation promoting and teaching corporate governance in Australia. Withers also resigned his membership of the prestigious Australian Olympic Committee.

After its misconduct was exposed, 7-Eleven was hit with regulatory and legal action. It paid over $170 million in compensation to thousands of employees for underpayment of wages, and also settled a class action brought by franchisees for $98 million.

Meanwhile, on its website, multinational mining giant Rio Tinto also wants us to be impressed by its values and behaviour:

> **Business integrity underpins everything we do**. It requires that no matter where we are from or where we work, we demonstrate consistent ethical behaviours, put integrity at the centre of our decisions and hold ourselves and each other accountable for our choices.
>
> **What is 'integrity'?** Integrity means being honest, holding to strong moral and ethical principles and values and most importantly, having the courage to stand out from the crowd and object to something that you feel is wrong. For all of us, this translates into doing what is right not what is fastest or easiest.
>
> We consistently:
> - act honestly and transparently
> - speak up and challenge the status quo when something feels wrong
> - seek diverse opinions and advice
> - accept responsibility for our actions and accountability for our decisions
> - conduct our business in compliance with the law.

On 24 May 2020, Rio Tinto detonated an area of the Juukan Gorge in the Pilbara in Western Australia as part of its iron-ore mining operations, damaging two ancient rock shelters that held profound cultural significance to the Puutu Kunti Kurrama and Pinikura (PKKP) people. The site contained a cave that held evidence of continuous human occupation for over 46,000 years. The cave, which was a sacred site for the traditional owners, was destroyed in the blast.

A bipartisan parliamentary committee found that 'Rio knew the value of what they were destroying but blew it up anyway', citing 'severe deficiencies in the company's relationship practices with the PKKP', which reflected 'a corporate culture which prioritised commercial gain over the kind of meaningful engagement with Traditional Owners that should form a critical part of their social licence to operate'.[26] In the wake of the destruction of the sacred site, it emerged that Rio Tinto had for years negotiated mining agreements with traditional owners that contained an NDA, effectively gagging them from publicly criticising the company.

The chameleon corporation

Standing before the US Congress to deliver his State of the Union address in 1996, president Bill Clinton declared that, 'The era of big government is over.' Almost a decade later, in 2005, and shortly before assuming the mantle of the UK's prime ministership, Gordon Brown rejected 'the old model of regulation' with a 'better approach [that] trust[s] in the responsible company'. Brown was committed to ensuring that the City of London housed a financial services juggernaut. Brown's statement didn't age well. In 2008, the global financial crisis spawned the worst global recession since the Great Depression. By 2011, Brown was apologising for his mistaken faith in the 'responsible company'.

Several years later, the Financial Crisis Inquiry Commission, constituted by the US Congress after the 2008 GFC, delivered its report, which stated:

> The Commission concluded that this crisis was avoidable. It found widespread failures in financial regulation; dramatic breakdowns in corporate governance; excessive borrowing and risk-taking by households and Wall Street; policy makers who were ill prepared

for the crisis; and systemic breaches in accountability and ethics at all levels.[27]

In the immediate aftermath of the GFC, the-then Australian prime minister, Kevin Rudd, wrote:

> The current crisis is the culmination of a 30-year domination of economic policy by a free-market ideology that has been variously called neoliberalism, economic liberalism, economic fundamentalism, Thatcherism or the Washington consensus. The central thrust of this ideology has been that government activity should be constrained, and ultimately replaced, by market forces.[28]

As Rudd suggested, the global financial crisis should have prompted a fundamental realignment of the relationship between the state and the private sector, but it did not. Many big businesses socialised their losses in accepting government bailouts, and resumed where they left off.

Nevertheless, in this second Gilded Age, corporations have continued to reinvent themselves, just as General Electric and Standard Oil did in the first Gilded Age; this time, with more sophistication. A range of recycled and new ethical identities have been deployed in the course of this century. In the US in August 2019, the Business Roundtable issued a statement that was intended to redefine 'the Purpose of a Corporation' and to distance itself from the Friedmanite ideology that it had previously embraced: that the corporation existed solely for the benefit of shareholders. The new stated purpose of the corporation addressed the interests of 'all stakeholders', including customers, employees, suppliers, and local communities. The redefined purpose of a corporation—described as 'stakeholder capitalism'—was widely hailed around the globe as a major step forward.

In 2018, when he was CEO of the JPMorgan Chase bank, and chair of the Business Roundtable, Jamie Dimon's annual remuneration was $31 million (and later rose to $36 million). In April 2019, during a hearing of the House Financial Services Committee, Democratic Representative Katie Porter challenged Dimon about his bank's remuneration of employees. Porter described the monthly budget of a hypothetical new employee at a Chase bank in Irvine, California — a single mother who was earning $16.50 per hour. After paying the rent for a one-bedroom apartment that she shared with her daughter, plus the costs of utilities, food, childcare, and a basic mobile phone, Porter explained that the woman would be left with a $567 monthly deficit. 'How should she manage this budget shortfall while she's working full time at your bank?' Porter asked. Dimon responded that he 'would have to think about it'. Porter then asked, 'Would you recommend that she take out a JPMorgan Chase credit card and run a deficit?' Dimon answered, 'I don't know. I'd have to think about it.'[29]

Two years before embracing stakeholder capitalism, Dimon and the Business Roundtable had successfully lobbied to repeal 'unduly burdensome' regulations, including laws that set ozone and coal-fired plant emission standards, clean-water regulations, and minimum labour standards for the payment of overtime. President Trump duly embarked on a deregulation frenzy. When Trump introduced corporate tax cuts in 2019, JPMorgan Chase and its shareholders reaped a $5 billion windfall.

Lobbying efforts such as these are buttressed by an industry of consultants, managers, analysts, ethicists, and business school academics, all apparently devoted to helping business operate for a purpose other than maximising profit. In fact, the key consideration for corporations seeking to brand themselves as purpose-driven is to find a purpose that enhances — not detracts from — the bottom line. Business academics, including Rodriquez-Vila and Sundar Bharadwaj, explain the challenge in this way:

> An effective social-purpose strategy creates value by strengthening a brand's key attributes or building new adjacencies. At the same time, it mitigates the risk of negative associations among consumers and threats to stakeholder acceptance.[30]

Corporations' performative engagement with a range of environmental and social issues, known as Environmental, Social and Governance (ESG) reporting, has nevertheless provoked a ferocious reaction from US Republicans. In 2023, Republican politicians in 37 US states proposed 165 pieces of anti-ESG legislation, although a majority of them failed to be enacted. A 2023 report argued that the legislation was the product of intense lobbying by fossil-fuel interests, including billionaire Charles Koch.[31] Black Rock's Larry Fink has since stopped advocating for ESG, and other major corporations are following suit.

After the era that has brought us purpose, stakeholder capitalism, ESG, impact investing, creative capitalism, caring capitalism, and myriad other forms of ethics-washing, the ills that these measures promise to address remain fundamentally unchanged. As Professor Carl Rhodes observes, 'No amount of feel-good moral conviction will allow a corporation to engage in a politics that will harm its own financial fortunes or that of its owners and managers. If we want real progressive change, it's time to get woke to woke capitalism.'[32]

But are we getting woke to 'the wolf in woke clothing'? For almost a decade, US billionaire Nick Hanauer has been warning that super-rich entrepreneurs like himself are under threat. Hanauer founded an internet advertising company before selling it to Microsoft in 2007 for $6.4 billion. He describes himself as a member of the '.01 per centers' and as 'a proud and unapologetic capitalist'. In 2014, Hanauer wrote:

> And so I have a message for my fellow filthy rich, for all of us who live in our gated bubble worlds: Wake up, people. It won't last ... If we don't do something to fix the glaring inequities in this economy, the pitchforks are going to come for us. No society can sustain this kind of rising inequality. In fact, there is no example in human history where wealth accumulated like this and the pitchforks didn't eventually come out.[33]

However, the pitchforks haven't come for the plutocrats, but for democracy. A deeply orange cartoonish grifter incited the pitchforks on 6 January 2021 in a desperate effort to steal an election. It nearly worked. Authoritarians and fascists are on the march in the US, Israel, India, and Europe. Why is it that those who are being screwed by wealth inequality, stagnating wages, housing crises, and an angry climate are seemingly ignoring the role of big business in their suffering?

CHAPTER FOUR

The Ethically Washed Brand

> An overriding tension in debates about ethical brands is that of the incompatibility of ethics and capitalist modes of production and consumption.
> –'The ethics of the brand'[1]

In their journal article, cited above, Caryn Egan-Wyer, Sara Louise Muhr, Anna Pfeiffer, and Peter Svensson argue that ethics are transformed when situated in the sphere of capitalist logic, 'from being principles of human existence and social life, into a strategic resource to be exploited by the corporation' to assist in the race for competitive advantage. As a result, where that competitive advantage is threatened, the focus invariably shifts from what is right and wrong to what is going to maximise profit. The authors argue that the concept of ethical brands is riddled with paradoxes and dilemmas, and that 'ethical brands may indeed repress — or at least obfuscate — the most urgent ethical questions' posed by profit-seeking corporations. Corporations develop brands to establish customer loyalty. Then they manage the brands as part of an arcane, all-encompassing industry of 'stakeholder' management designed to persuade stakeholders—government, employees, and consumers—that what is good for the corporation is good for them, too. Since the 1980s, corporations have constructed and deployed their brands to garner consumer recognition and loyalty while engaged in a frenetic period of sackings and outsourcing to cheap labour in countries such as China, India, and Bangladesh. At the same time, major corporations have restructured to establish entities in tax havens—often with the expert assistance of the Big Four accounting firms. Along the way, the brands have moved from otherworldly nirvana to social and political activism.

Sir Richard Branson is credited with pioneering a radical reconceptualisation of branding after establishing Virgin Records in London in 1973. He has been widely quoted as saying that, 'Branding demands commitment; commitment to continual reinvention; striking chords with people to stir their emotions; and commitment to imagination.' Virgin morphed into a brand that conveys a set of ideas and values to attract customers to an array of Virgin businesses. Branson has since brought 400 businesses under the Virgin master-brand: from hotels to healthcare, airlines, bridal gowns, and financial services. The Virgin brand is now considered a major asset that can be attached to virtually any product or service.

In her acclaimed book *No Logo*, Naomi Klein documented how branding moved beyond specific products such as fried chicken or jeans into more extravagant terrain. 'The brand builders conquered and a new consensus was born: the products that will flourish in the future will be the ones presented not as "commodities" but as concepts; the brand as experience, as lifestyle.' IBM rejected the limitations of a computer brand in favour of offering an array of 'business solutions'. Nike moved from selling running shoes to establishing its credentials as a sports company that promised 'to enhance people's lives through sports and fitness'. Anita Roddick, founder of The Body Shop, explained to Klein in an interview that her stores conveyed a political philosophy about women, the environment, and ethical business.[2]

At the same time as corporations benefited from the wave of privatisation that neoliberalism introduced from the 1980s, branding became increasingly intrusive and ubiquitous. Branding became part of our experiences of sport, recreation, art, film, music, and education.

The fine line

Constructing a business brand and managing it are creative endeavours: an art form with the lure of immense riches. Brands embellish, obscure, and mask reality; stir our imagination and emotions; and garner our loyalty. But there is a fine line between creativity and deception. The deception is often achieved by the creation of an alternative reality through the disingenuous use of vocabulary and imagery. A number of companies such as Facebook and Twitter that have emerged out of Silicon Valley since the 1980s have branded themselves as glamorous and otherworldly, operating in a parallel universe in which earthly legal and regulatory frameworks simply aren't relevant to them. Gig-economy companies position themselves as so radically different from that which has come before that existing regulatory laws don't apply to them — or, failing that, shouldn't apply to them. Their survival depends on avoiding existing forms of labour-market regulation that apply to their competitors.

Finance journalist Alan Kohler argues that, 'Companies that posture as tech businesses but just use the internet to do non-tech business, like online retailers, fintechs that are just online banks and video peddlers such as TikTok, YouTube and Facebook, remain largely unregulated and are given ... outsize valuations on the sharemarket.'[3] Facebook and Twitter, for example, have fashioned the myth that they are not publishers of the content that appears on their platforms, in order to avoid taking responsibility for the harm that it can cause. The companies can and do choose what is published on their platforms, but acknowledging this reality would entail complying with regulatory regimes that apply to their competitors, and would hit their market valuations and profits.

Uber is not so much a futuristic revolution as a regression to a piecework labour market that prevailed in the feudal era. The novelty, such as it is, lies in the method of allocation of the piecework: by the use of an app. Uber drivers are paid well below minimum labour standards for employees. A 2018 study by the Centre for Future Work demonstrated that UberX drivers in Australia earnt $14.62 per hour driving for the company.[4] The basic statutory minimum wage in Australia at that time was $18.29 per hour.

The risk with carefully branded narratives is that they often collide with the real world in which the legal system resides. As Uber's recent travails show, expensive branded fantasies have their limitations. The company that is fond of declaring that it has relationships with 'partner' drivers to pursue mutually beneficial 'business opportunities' has had to fight legal challenges in many countries seeking to prove that Uber employs its drivers and that existing labour laws regulate their terms and conditions.

In 2016, for example a test case about the status of Uber drivers was heard by the British Employment Tribunal. The company argued that its London business constituted a 'mosaic of 30,000 small businesses linked by a common platform under which drivers are free to negotiate a bargain with each client'.[5] The tribunal described this notion as 'faintly ridiculous', and was satisfied that the supposed driver/passenger contract was 'a pure fiction which bears no relation to the real dealings and relationships between the parties'. The tribunal stated, 'In each case, the "business" consists of a man with a car' who is offered and accepts trips strictly on Uber's terms.

Meanwhile the slow-moving process of regulatory catch-up with Big Tech continues. In February 2024, the Australian government introduced laws to establish better labour standards for gig workers. Several months later, a class action against Uber brought on behalf of 8,000 taxi drivers was settled for $272 million.

Brand deception involves much more than obscuring dodgy employment arrangements. It is often to be found in misrepresentations of the qualities of the product or service that are promised or of the benefits that are said to flow from its consumption. Does this fruit juice contain any fruit? Does that moisturiser actually remove wrinkles or retard the ageing process? Do I really help the environment by buying these jeans or upgrading my SUV? If I'm a retiree living in a caravan, is this 'aggressive' investor product really suitable for me?

In the second Gilded Age, major corporations have avoided effective regulation by ethics-washing their brands and through constant reinvention. Indeed, ethics-washing can be of existential importance — a key determinant of whether a brand or the corporation behind it will survive. A British academic study found a clear correlation between brand resilience and ethical branding, revealing that, 'irresponsible corporate conduct, on its own, did not lead to any damage to reputations'. The 2019 study, which relied on an extensive survey of corporate misconduct and associated reputational harm, found that, while an adverse court ruling could harm a brand, there was no significant adverse impact on a company being exposed as benefiting, for example, from exploiting child labour. Fashion brands, including Nike, Zara, Gap, and H&M, experienced little discernible brand damage from their use of child labour to produce their products. Apple's brand had remained immune from a series of scandals that have implicated the company.[6]

The study illustrates that brands that have a strong reputation for being 'socially responsible' withstand scandals because of a 'halo effect', whereby past efforts to establish credibility and ethical conduct provide a strong measure of brand protection.

The study might help explain the different fate of two pharmaceutical companies, Purdue Pharmaceuticals and Johnson & Johnson. In May 2007, Purdue and three of its current and former executives pleaded guilty to criminal charges of 'misbranding'. The executives, who included the company's president and top-ranking in-house lawyer, admitted that they had misled regulators, doctors, and patients about its highly successful pain-killing drug, OxyContin. The company's deception lay in lying about the drug's risk of addiction and its potential to be abused.

To resolve criminal and civil charges it was facing, the parent company of Purdue agreed to pay some $600 million in fines and other payments. In a carefully curated statement, the company said:

> Nearly six years and longer ago, some employees made, or told other employees to make, certain statements about OxyContin to some health care professionals that were inconsistent with the F.D.A.-approved prescribing information for OxyContin and the express warnings it contained about risks associated with the medicine. The statements also violated written company policies requiring adherence to the prescribing information.[7]

The brand managers, who painstakingly prepared that statement, omitted to say that the company had repeatedly lied about OxyContin, and that as a result a lot of people were dead.

A decade earlier, Purdue had launched its marketing campaign for OxyContin with a laser-like focus on persuading physicians to prescribe it to all patients experiencing pain. It wasn't long before reports of abuse and addiction were made known to the company. Nevertheless, an army of sales representatives were instructed to assure doctors that 'fewer than 1 per cent' of patients who took OxyContin became addicted. (In 1999, Purdue-funded research found an addiction rate of 13 per cent.)

Purdue went to extraordinary lengths to persuade, cajole, and coerce doctors to prescribe the drug. The company funded research, and paid doctors to counter arguments about opioid addiction and to promote Oxycontin as a safe treatment for a wide range of maladies. It also paid several thousand doctors to attend medical conferences and deliver presentations promoting the drug. Doctors were offered all-expenses-paid trips to pain-management seminars, and were plied with branded merchandise, including fishing hats. The company advertised in medical journals, sponsored websites, and funded chronic-pain medical-support groups. Prescriptions for OxyContin duly took off.

The company was generous with its political donations to both Republicans and Democrats while its owners, the Sackler family, became the 14th-wealthiest family in the US.

Shortly after Purdue pleaded guilty to misbranding OxyContin, the company doubled down. It hired the world's most prestigious consulting company, McKinsey, to advise it and to assist with a new brand campaign. McKinsey describes itself as 'a values-driven organisation' that is committed to 'doing well by doing good'. However, as Walt Bogdanich and Michael Forsythe of *The New York Times* have documented, the company is 'the greatest legitimiser of mass layoffs ... in modern history' and has partnered with a staggering number of the world's largest polluting businesses. It has mastered the art of ignoring conflicts of interest, being 'deft at "playing offence and defense" — getting on all sides of a market, advising multiple competitors and regulators, private capital and public interests, and relying on its reputation to sanitise what in other eyes would represent a palpable and unconscionable conflict'.[8] In other words, it is a typical large consulting business.

McKinsey duly delivered a plan to 'turbocharge' sales of OxyContin and to overcome restrictions meant to curb the opioid crisis. The plan targeted doctors to convince them that opioids provided 'freedom' and 'peace of mind' that would give patients 'the best possible chance to live a full and active life'. McKinsey also advised Purdue to maximise its OxyContin profits by focusing on higher, more lucrative doses and scheduling more visits by its sales representatives to high-volume opioid prescribers. McKinsey worked with the company on ways to 'counter the emotional messages from mothers with teenagers that overdosed on OxyContin'. The consultancy advised Purdue to offer distributors rebates worth $14,810 for each customer that overdosed on the opioids.

As the opioid addiction crisis deepened and the body count exploded, Purdue moved into the next lucrative phase. 'Project Tango' was launched to boost the marketing of the company's overdose-reversal drug, Naxolone, together with buprenorphine, used to treat opioid addiction. Project Tango aimed to ensure that Purdue became a high-profit 'end to end pain provider', targeting doctors who prescribed OxyContin excessively and patients who had become addicted to it.

During the course of the opioid epidemic, over 750,000 Americans died and the Sackler family pocketed $10 billion. All the while, further lawsuits were mounting. In March 2022, Purdue reached a settlement of $6 billion, with the Sackler family compelled to pay the overwhelming majority of that sum while being protected from further claims. In June 2024, the Supreme Court disallowed the settlement, exposing the Sackler family to massive claims. Whatever happens, Purdue Pharmaceuticals was finished. It was rebranded as Knoa Pharma, which promises to develop and distribute opioid addiction treatment and overdose-reversal medicines at no profit.

Johnson & Johnson is a multinational pharmaceutical and medical-technologies corporation, and one of the most successful corporations in US history. It enjoys an extraordinary level of brand awareness. In May 2016, *Forbes* valued the company's brand at $312.6 billion. In 2022, Johnson & Johnson was named as a Top 50 All-Star on *Fortune*'s World's Most Admired Companies list for the 20th consecutive year.

Over its 120-year history, the company has established a strong, family-friendly brand. In 1943, it established its own 'Credo', which states:

> We must help people be healthier by supporting better access and care in more places around the world. We must be good citizens — support good works and charities, better health and education, and bear our fair share of taxes. We must maintain in good order the property we are privileged to use, protecting the environment and natural resources.

Mckinsey had also advised Johnson & Johnson on its opioid-product business, recommending that the company focus its marketing on 'high abuse-risk patients (males under 40)' and influence doctors' prescription behaviour in pain-management clinics. Johnson & Johnson got off lightly from the opioid crisis.

A Reuters investigation published in 2018 revealed that, 'from at least 1971 to the early 2000s, the company's raw talc and finished powders sometimes tested positive for small amounts of asbestos, and that company executives, mine managers, scientists, doctors, and lawyers fretted over the problem and how to address it while failing to disclose it to regulators or the public'.[9] It emerged that the company had faced an avalanche of lawsuits from thousands of consumers of its talc powder — mainly women — who had developed cancers, including mesothelioma and ovarian cancer. Documents produced in the legal cases also revealed the company's dishonest efforts to impede US regulators' plans to restrict the use of asbestos in cosmetic talc products.

In October 2021, the company created a subsidiary, LTL Management, and offloaded all liabilities from the lawsuits to it. Days later, LTL Management was placed into bankruptcy, a manoeuvre known as the Texas two-step. It was intended that the manoeuvre would have the effect of preventing 38,000 lawsuits from proceeding. The contrived bankruptcy prompted a fresh legal challenge, risking years of further delay to gain redress. In September 2022, *The New Yorker* reported that, 'Johnson & Johnson's most recent quarterly report shows twenty-four billion dollars in sales, and in the eleven months since it filed for bankruptcy, an average of one woman a day has died waiting to find out if her case against the company would ever be heard.'[10]

In April 2023, Johnson & Johnson announced that it would pay $8.9 billion to settle tens of thousands of lawsuits alleging that talc in its iconic baby powder and other products had caused cancer. After decades of denial, deception, and death, Johnson & Johnson also announced that it was stopping the use of talc-based powder in its products, including in its baby powder.

Unlike Purdue Pharmaceuticals, Johnson & Johnson has survived and continued to thrive — in no small part due to its long-term investment in branding itself as ethical and decent. We may never know whether its ethical branding was well-intentioned but doomed to fail, or a calculated commercial strategy, or, even, a combination of both. But after paying out its talc baby powder liabilities, it bounced back strongly in 2024 off the back of strong sales in its medical-devices division.

Branding in an online world

In the 2000s, the advent of social media and digital streaming splintered audiences' attention and allowed consumers to avoid advertising, forcing corporations to explore other ways to maintain their brands. Brands began to experiment by engaging with the online community, and discovered that social media were being used for political campaigns, such as the Occupy Movement and the Arab Spring. In 2004, Dove, a personal-care brand owned by Unilever, launched a righteous, socially responsible Campaign for Real Beauty. 'Beauty comes in all shapes and sizes', it declared. 'There is no one perfect shape.' The campaign was hailed a commercial success, with the company's sales boosted by its celebration of a gamut of body sizes, shapes, and appearances, together with its promotion of self-esteem and anti-discrimination workshops.[11]

Brand activism quickly become an entrenched feature of 21st-century capitalism, with brands competing to be seen as ethical change-agents. In 2017, Nike maintained $12.2 billion in offshore tax shelters; the next year, in September 2018, it signed Colin Kaepernick to a multi-million-dollar brand ambassador deal in which Kaepernick became the face of a socially progressive campaign known as 'Just Do It'. Announcing the campaign, Gino Fisanotti, Nike's vice-president of brand, said: 'We believe Colin is one of the most inspirational athletes of this generation, who has leveraged the power of sport to help move the world forward. We wanted to energise its meaning and introduce 'Just Do It' to a new generation of athletes.' It was a remarkable turnaround. Kaepernick had lost his career as a professional NFL footballer as a result of taking the knee in protest at police violence directed at black Americans. He rebounded rapidly from becoming a high-profile victim of brand management to making a new career as a brand ambassador.

Shortly after Donald Trump signed an order to temporarily close American borders to refugees in 2018, Airbnb released a We Accept advertisement depicting people of different nationalities alongside the words 'We believe no matter who you are, where you're from, who you love or who you worship, we all belong …'

Following the murder of George Floyd by Minneapolis police officer Derek Chauvin, the streets of many cities in the US erupted with millions of angry Americans protesting police brutality and racism. Corporate America raced to 'create sensitive, aesthetically pleasing responses', seeking to align their brands to the protest movement. Amazon released a statement expressing its support for 'the fight against systemic racism and injustice.'[12] Jamie Dimon publicly took the knee.

Technology company Pinterest joined the fray, expressing solidarity by posting, 'With everything we do, we will make it clear that our Black employees matter.' *Time Magazine* subsequently reported that, 'Over the next months, Pinterest's warm, fuzzy veneer would unravel like one of the platform's chunky knitted sweaters.'[13] Former executives, including Ifeoma Ozoma, who had settled gender- and race-discrimination claims against the company, broke their NDAs to condemn the company for its opportunism and hypocrisy. Their whistleblowing prompted a staff walkout, followed by a culture review and a shareholder lawsuit alleging the company had mishandled claims of unlawful race- and gender-based discrimination. The company subsequently settled a gender-discrimination claim for a record $22.5 million.

In 2021, Walmart, the global retailing behemoth and one of the world's largest companies, generated $559 billion in revenue and employed 2.3 million people. By any measure of ethics-washing,

Walmart is a standout. It brandishes its commitment to mitigating climate change and addressing soil erosion, systemic racism, plastic bags, gun violence, financial literacy, vaccine distribution, and recidivism rates.[14] Its Project Gigaton pledges to remove 1 billion metric tons of greenhouse-gas emissions from its supply chain by 2030. It boasts an impressive range of alliances with prominent NGOs, including the World Wide Fund for Nature. All the while, Walmart's parasitic business model depends on taxpayers to keep its employees fed and housed. It has the largest number of employees in the US who qualify for food stamps. Like Amazon, the enormous wealth it has generated is the result of paying poverty-level wages to its employees and using its immense commercial muscle to source products cheaply from suppliers.

Greenwashing is one of the most popular sub-categories of ethics-washing in the corporate world, and a burgeoning industry. It is difficult to find a major corporation that hasn't gone green — including fossil-fuel companies. A joint study by British and Dutch regulators found that 40 per cent of green claims made by corporations on their websites could be misleading consumers. Coca-Cola, the worst plastic polluter in the world, has loudly and repeatedly committed itself to ambitious environmental targets to mitigate climate change. The company was one of the key corporate sponsors of the 2022 COP27 UN climate summit. In the three years prior to the summit, Coca Cola increased its use of newly manufactured plastic by 3.5 per cent. Coca Cola promises that, 'Through our actions as local citizens, we strive every day to refresh the marketplace, enrich the workplace, preserve the environment and strengthen our communities.' A senior executive put it differently, stating that the company's aim was to 'encourage as many people as possible to drink as much Coca Cola as possible at the highest possible price so that the company could make even more money.'[15]

Cooper Energy, an Australian company that has strong expansion plans beyond 2030, has proclaimed that it is the country's 'first carbon neutral gas producer'. Like many others, the company claims to offset its emissions. In fact, it offsets its emissions for activities such as business travel and office stationery, but excludes from its calculations the emissions that come from burning fossil fuel. This means that it only offsets 1 per cent of its emissions.[16]

Creative accounting and dodgy carbon-offset programs are one of the key drivers of the greenwashing industry. Australia is leading the way in performative carbon offsets. Its carbon-offset scheme has been fiercely criticised by prominent experts as making no discernible impact on reducing carbon. The results of a peer-reviewed study conducted by 11 Australian academics and published in March 2024 found that forest regeneration, the main technique relied on for claimed carbon reduction, was ineffective.[17] Ampol, which claims to sell 'carbon-neutral fuel', relying on its Australian carbon offsets, is one of many prominent companies accused of greenwashing. Australia's highest-polluting corporation, AGL, has been certified as a 'climate champion' by Climate Active, in 'an ongoing partnership between the Australian Government and Australian businesses to drive voluntary climate action'.[18]

While corporate claims to carbon neutrality and to meeting net-zero climate targets are now spreading like a global pandemic, emissions from burning fossil fuels continue to increase, and the frequency and severity of climate disasters is undeniable. Kirsty Ruddock, a managing lawyer at the Environmental Defenders Office, an Australian NGO, says, 'It is no accident that a fossil fuel company in Australia can claim to be a carbon neutral organisation at the same time as telling shareholders it will be ramping up oil and gas production. This is the result of policy design and an absence of environmental standards.'[19]

The fashion industry is environmentally sustainable—according to the fashion industry. More to the point, fashion companies, including clothing-rental brands such as Rent the Runway and recycling brand ThredUp, brand their businesses as environmentally sustainable. The branding celebrates the 'circular economy', in which clothes move around the economy for longer, thereby delaying the need to replace them. But a peer-reviewed study published in the journal *Environmental Research Letters* concluded that renting clothes has the highest harmful climate impact because of the impact of repeatedly transporting the clothes. The study found that less damage is caused by wearing a garment and throwing it away.[20]

Alan Joyce: social justice CEO

Aviation company Qantas operates a quasi-monopoly in the Australian domestic aviation market. It was owned by the federal government from 1947 until its privatisation in 1992, in what became a potent symbol of the neoliberal transformation of the economy.

Notwithstanding its privatisation, Qantas has remained deeply embedded in Australian culture as the national airline, the 'flying Kangaroo'. The aviation industry is notoriously volatile, but Qantas can't really lose. It enjoys enormous political clout, effectively ensuring that it is underwritten by the Australian taxpayer. When times are tough, it is bailed out. When times are good, it's a shareholder feeding frenzy. It also relies on government deals to block international competition on its valuable routes. Politicians, judges, and public servants overwhelmingly fly Qantas. A select few are given access to its exclusive Chairman's Lounge, which includes a corporate wellness and resilience centre.

Alan Joyce took the helm as CEO of Qantas in 2008, and set about ruthlessly cutting costs. Old aeroplanes weren't replaced; they just got older and dirtier. Joyce outsourced jobs as if his life depended on it. Secure, directly employed employees were replaced with precarious labour-hire and agency workers. Jobs in maintenance, IT, catering, cabin crew, and call centres were outsourced, a process that saw the company send 'thousands of Australian jobs and hundreds of millions of dollars to overseas companies, many based in tax havens—such as Zurich, Abu Dhabi, and Singapore—some of which have appalling human rights records, such as the United Arab Emirates (UAE), that breach Qantas's code of ethics and its supplier code of conduct'.[21] By 2023, Qantas had engaged 21 external companies for labour across 17 subsidiaries. Qantas cabin crew worked for 14 different companies with varied pay rates.

In 2014, the year that Qantas announced its plan to shed 5,000 full-time jobs, Joyce's total pay package doubled to $24.6 million.

Joyce consistently advocated for cuts to company tax during his tenure. In 2016, he wrote that Qantas was 'paying or collecting $2 billion a year in taxes of all kinds for the government … So if you're asking the question of "what's in it for me" when it comes to a company tax cut for big business, remember that we're all part of the same economy. And as the saying goes, a rising tide lifts all boats'.[22] The only boats that were lifted were Joyce's and those of other major shareholders.

Under Joyce's leadership, Qantas committed itself to campaigning for social justice. He relished the role of being a social justice CEO, arguing that such advocacy was good for business by attracting staff and customers. 'Where other brands have gone backwards', he proclaimed, 'we've seen our brand improve in the last few years, supporting marriage equality, supporting gender equality and indigenous rights'.[23] In 2017, Joyce supported the successful same-sex marriage campaign. He was named a Companion of the Order of Australia, Australia's highest civil honour, the same year, for 'eminent service to the aviation transport industry, to the development of the national and international tourism sectors, to gender equity, inclusion and diversity, and to the community, particularly as a supporter of Indigenous education'.

Among the many businesses hit by the coronavirus pandemic, the aviation industry fared particularly badly. From early 2020, the industry was virtually shut down by lengthy lockdowns in Australia, cutting a swathe through aviation companies' revenues. A slow vaccination rollout in Australia prolonged and deepened the crisis. Joyce acted swiftly to shore up the company's balance sheet, raising $1.75 billion of debt and $1.4 billion of equity, standing down the workforce, and closing its international arm. Despite enormous losses, Qantas's survival was assured by a federal government bailout of $2.9 billion. Of that sum, the federal government earmarked aid of $900 million to ensure that employees retained their employment. Qantas's main competitor, Virgin, was not so fortunate, and was forced into insolvency.

Joyce wasn't going to waste a crisis. He loathed the Transport Workers Union (TWU), which represented Qantas's baggage handlers and ground staff. The union and its members enjoyed stronger bargaining power than other Qantas employees, and had thwarted his efforts to outsource their jobs for years. They had publicly criticised him and challenged his social justice credentials. Now their members were furloughed, stuck at home, unable to bargain or take industrial action. Joyce viewed the pandemic as a once-in-a-lifetime opportunity to smash the TWU. Soon after the lockdowns commenced, management assessed that the lockdowns would be likely to ease by early 2021, at which time the union and its members could bargain and take legally protected strike action. The company hatched a plan to exploit the crisis by sacking 1,800 baggage handlers and ground staff and replace them with cheaper labour-hire workers.

Joyce needed to be insulated from the plan, because he knew that otherwise the litigious union might sue and cross-examine him. Lawyers were brought in to work with the company on the plan. Subsequently, Joyce executed an 'instrument of delegation' to one of his loyal executive team, Andrew David. Contrary to all orthodox risk-management principles and the conventions of corporate governance, the decision to sack 1,800 staff in the middle of the pandemic was delegated to a single manager inside Qantas.

In August 2020, Qantas announced its decision to outsource the jobs, citing the pandemic as having prompted it to take a commercial decision that would save it at least $100 million annually. I was hired by the union, and recommended suing Qantas for breaching freedom-of-association laws that protect workers who intend to bargain from being sacked. When we started the case, we had little evidence beyond knowing that Qantas detested the union. However, as the case progressed, that changed. Qantas was compelled to produce documents that illustrated the company's antagonism to the union and cited the need to act quickly while there was a 'window of opportunity' to sack the workers before they got back to work and tried to block the move. The case got even stronger at trial when Qantas's witnesses got into the witness box: their evidence fell apart in material respects. The Federal Court found for the union, declaring that the outsourcing exercise was illegal. Qantas immediately appealed, and continued to fight for three more years, appealing its way up to the High Court. In September 2023, the High Court emphatically dismissed its appeal — by which time Joyce had resigned.

While the legal process was being fought, the walls were closing in on the company. When flying resumed after the pandemic lockdowns, Qantas became a badly run budget airline charging top dollar. The company embarked on widespread price-gouging, safe in the knowledge that it was a quasi-monopoly and that, after years of lockdown, there was enormous pent-up demand for its services. Prices skyrocketed at a rate only comparable to the rate of the airline's customers losing their luggage when flying. Flights were repeatedly cancelled, and it became clear that the airline was selling tickets to a lot of flights and then cancelling some of them in order to maximise capacity on those remaining. Australian airports became even more chaotic, and their customers more angry. Social media complaints ignited like a bonfire. Damaging footage of replacement baggage handlers violently throwing customers' bags onto conveyor belts circulated on social media. In the lexicon of the internet, the bags, like the customers, were being #Joyced. The brand damage intensified, but it didn't really matter to the company. Qantas was making big money.

On 24 August, Joyce proudly announced that Qantas had posted a record $2.47 billion full-year underlying profit, backed by strong travel demand and high ticket prices. The result reversed a $1.86 billion loss the previous year. This was quickly followed by the announcement of a $500 million share buyback. When questioned about whether Qantas should return some or all of the $2.9 billion in Covid-related taxpayer assistance that had been granted to the company, Joyce refused on two grounds. First, he claimed that Qantas was providing a service to the public. Then he claimed that Qantas paid company tax and therefore should not have to return the subsidy.

Days later, the competition watchdog, the Australian Competition and Consumer Commission (ACCC), launched a prosecution against Qantas for having engaged in false, misleading, and deceptive conduct in 2022 by continuing to sell seats on thousands of flights that had already been cancelled. The airline admitted to 4,149 cancellations, but the ACCC discovered more than 15,000. Just eight weeks earlier, as the ACCC investigation proceeded, Joyce had sold 90 per cent of his Qantas shares at the top of the market, raising $17 million to purchase an apartment.

At the same time, Qantas was coming under increasing pressure for failing to refund hundreds of millions of dollars that customers had paid for tickets during the lockdowns but had been unable to use. Since that time, the company had deliberately delayed and stymied attempts by customers to get refunds. Then it announced that it would not refund or credit customers for their purchases after the end of 2023. Amid the public backlash and growing scrutiny, and after Joyce faced a fiery Senate hearing, Qantas was forced to dump plans to cancel $570 million worth of outstanding pandemic-era flight credits on 31 December.

A leading business journalist at *The Australian Financial Review*, Joe Aston, one of the few to cut through the airline's brand-managed fiction, wrote:

> Why hasn't Qantas automatically refunded the balance owing to any customer's credit card that is yet to expire? Or why can't Qantas post a bank cheque to every customer it has a mailing address for (given most are members of its Frequent Flyer program)? ... Why can't Qantas transfer the money into the lost super system administered by the Australian Taxation Office? The answer: because any of that might actually work.[24]

When Aston challenged the prevailing hagiographic orthodoxy, Joyce imposed a ban on Qantas purchasing *The Australian Financial Review*. The ban reflected Joyce's tendency to punish criticism and silence dissent. In the wake of criticism of Joyce's performance by Fairfax journalist Adele Ferguson back in 2014, Joyce had withdrawn millions in advertising spending with Fairfax, and had removed

Fairfax newspapers from Qantas aircraft and lounges. When workplace safety representative Theo Seremetidis advised colleagues to cease work on Qantas planes arriving from China in early 2020, due to the risk of Covid-19 exposure, he too was punished. He was suspended, pending a disciplinary investigation into allegations that he had breached the company code of conduct. Qantas was subsequently convicted of a criminal offence for its mistreatment of Seremetidis.

The growing scandals and brand damage prompted a humiliated Alan Joyce, its social justice CEO, to announce on 5 September 2023 that he was leaving his role two months earlier than planned. 'I leave knowing that the company is fundamentally strong and has a bright future,' Joyce deadpanned. In fact, by this time, he had trashed the brand. As the price of Qantas shares tanked, Joyce left the company as a very rich man, having been paid more than $150 million during his tenure. Six million dollars of that amount was a bonus for the years 2020–2022, during which Qantas posted total losses of $6.3 billion.

In 2008, when Joyce began as CEO, the Qantas group had 37,000 employees. In March 2023, there were 23,500. Most of those jobs have been replaced by cheaper, precarious labour engaged by third parties. During his tenure, Qantas received tax credits worth $2.93 billion, but only paid $2.65 million in tax. It barely made an overall profit in those 15 years. It only managed to do so because Joyce delayed huge capital expenditure on upgrading the ageing fleet, and it banked $2.7 billion in government handouts. For that legacy, he left with immense wealth and a string of awards.

Joyce is far from unique. He is emblematic of the performative posturing adopted by many contemporary activist CEOs. A recent study argues that CEO interventions on social issues contribute a modest increase to 'firm value, increased quarterly sales, and a reduced likelihood of shareholder activism on social issues'. The study noted that CEO social justice statements 'are not necessarily an expression of their political views'.[25]

Brand damage

A brand is an intangible asset, albeit one that can be worth billions. Forbes calculates the value of the Coca-Cola brand at $56.4 billion, while Brandirectory measures it at $34.2 billion. Why the enormous divergence in valuation? A brand is not like a house or publicly traded shares. There is no orthodox or reliable method to calculate the value of an intangible. One brand-valuation method combines 'the financial performance of the branded products or services the role brand plays in purchase decisions, and the brand's competitive strength'.[26] There is no scientific way to measure the latter two characteristics. Other factors considered relevant to brand valuation include the value that customers are willing to pay over and above the cost of a competitor's product or service, the ability to attract and retain staff, and the ability to attract greater market share and to rebound from a setback.

In lockstep with contractual obligations that push employees unwittingly into the role of brand ambassadors, employees are encouraged to embrace the corporate activism program. In the words of the self-described Canadian 'CEO, Keynote Speaker, Leadership Strategist and Poet', Dan Pontefract:

> If an organization exhibits a high degree of purpose in its mission and objectives—taking a stand to benefit society—there is a very good likelihood that employees will more easily demonstrate purpose in their roles at work, become engaged, while adding to their own personal sense of purpose in life as well.[27]

Employees are encouraged to engage with the corporation's social responsibility initiatives, to sit on 'for purpose' committees, and otherwise to embrace the notion that it is 'making a difference'. At its most extreme, including in Silicon Valley, the brand management of employees can resemble a cult in which all employees are empowered to make the world a better place.

Like codes of conduct and workplace policies, training programs are brandished as evidence of companies making a difference. In recent years, there has been an explosion in diversity-and-inclusion training. According to Iris Bohnet, a public policy professor at Harvard's Kennedy School, diversity training in the US is an $8 billion per year industry. Bohnet has studied the impact of such training, concluding, 'sadly enough, I did not find a single study that found diversity training in fact leads to more diversity'. This echoes a growing body of research that questions whether unconscious bias training makes any positive difference in eliminating discrimination — either at or outside the workplace.

In May 2021, Apple fired a product engineer, Antonio Garcia Martinez, just four weeks into his employment with the company. The company explained that, 'At Apple, we have always strived to create an inclusive, welcoming workplace where everyone is respected and accepted. Behaviour that demeans or discriminates against people for who they are has no place here.'[28]

Garcia Martinez's sin occurred well before starting work at Apple. He had written *Chaos Monkeys*, described by *The New Yorker* as 'an acerbic Silicon Valley memoir'. The book, written in a gonzo style, depicted his work at Facebook some five years earlier. On its publication in 2016, the book received favourable reviews in *The New York Times*, *The Financial Times*, and *The Australian Financial Review*, and became a bestseller. It likened Facebook's culture to that of a fascist state, with the company's 'ministry of propaganda' preparing posters for staff featuring Mark Zuckerberg proclaiming 'PROCEED AND BE BOLD'. In the book, Martinez wrote of his admiration for a woman employee at the company, whom he compared favourably to 'most women in the Bay Area', whom he described as 'soft and weak, cosseted, and naïve, despite their claims of worldliness and generally full of shit'.

A petition from 2,000 Apple staff expressing dismay at the hiring of Martinez sealed his fate. The petition stated:

> We are deeply concerned about the recent hiring of Antonio García Martínez. His misogynistic statements in his autobiography … directly oppose Apple's commitment to Inclusion & Diversity. We are profoundly distraught by what this hire means for Apple's commitment to its inclusion goals, as well as its real and immediate impact on those working near Mr. García Martínez. It calls into question parts of our system of inclusion at Apple, including hiring panels, background checks, and our process to ensure our existing culture of inclusion is strong enough to withstand individuals who don't share our inclusive values.
>
> It is concerning that the views Mr. García Martínez expresses in his 2016 book 'Chaos Monkeys' were overlooked—or worse, excused—during his background check or hiring panel. We demand an investigation into how his published views on women and people of color were missed or ignored, along with a clear plan of action to prevent this from happening again.
>
> …. Given Mr. García Martínez's history of publishing overtly racist and sexist remarks about his former colleagues, we are concerned that his presence at Apple will contribute to an unsafe working environment for our colleagues who are at risk of public harassment and private bullying. We are entitled to insight into how the People team intends to mitigate this risk.[29]

Faced with a demand by 2,000 staff, Apple probably had no choice. Nevertheless, the actions of the 2,000 staff deserve serious scrutiny. Did Martinez's mere presence in the company threaten the culture of the workplace? Was he unsafe to work with? Should the company have denied him a job based on his satirical book containing sexist and or racist stereotypes? Is an inclusive workplace one in which each employee is vetted for any past sexist, racist, or otherwise unacceptable thoughts or expressions?

Workplace safety laws can be violated by employees engaging in racist and sexist mistreatment of other staff. There was no suggestion that Martinez had engaged in any unsafe conduct in his short career at Apple. On this occasion, the notion of safety was redefined as one in which a workplace is free of those who may have expressed objectionable words in the past — the campus debates about safe spaces revisited.

And then there is the issue of proportionality. Assuming that all major employers have diversity-and-inclusion policies in similar form to Apple, is Garcia Marquez, like Israel Folau, unemployable?

If a scandal exposes a corrupt or improper business model, implicating key executives, board members, and employees, the usual choice is to tough it out or make a key individual a sacrificial lamb. Corporate misconduct, including the misconduct of corporate executives, is a staple of commercial activity. Financial services companies are routinely exposed for predatory and illegal activities that fleece unsuspecting consumers. Mining and energy companies damage the environment, and, when operating in developing countries, routinely pay bribes (known as 'facilitation payments'). Gambling companies facilitate money laundering. In many instances where companies are exposed for their wrongdoing and the brand is harmed, there are little or no consequences for key personnel. The company and brand tend to rebound quickly, and the cycle resumes.

If measuring the value of a brand is a pseudoscience, quantifying claims of brand damage is even more elusive. Alan Joyce trashed the Qantas brand, was feted and fawned over, and became very rich. But when a lowly employee attracts controversy, it's often a different story. Brand managers can be professional catastrophists, prone to violently reacting to any sign of a negative social media post by shrieking 'brand damage'. The emergence of adverse media commentary or social media barbs often lead to what is effectively a Code Red alert, in which ruthless decisions are taken to protect the bottom line. Invariably, hyperbolic claims of corporate brand damage are asserted at high levels internally to justify the sacking of an employee who has engaged in controversial speech. Those same assertions of catastrophic brand damage are rarely interrogated, either in courts or tribunals, or in the court of public opinion.

The consequences for employees caught up in a Code Red is the subject of much of this book. Code Reds are an exercise in asset protection, with the brand as the asset. Even churches play this game: for centuries, the Catholic Church, among others, prioritised the protection of its enormous wealth at the expense of the health of children who were raped and sexually assaulted by its priests. Asset and brand protection is not about morality.

If an internal consensus is reached that the corporation's commercial interests will be protected by an unjust sacking over a trivial tweet, that decision will be taken. The public rationale for the decision will be rooted in some form of ethical principle: a breach of 'company values' or its code of conduct, which mandates respect, or a failure to adhere to its diversity-and-inclusion policy. Indeed, according to brand-management logic, each such sacking buttresses the strength of the socially responsible brand, allowing the corporation to tough out significant ethical scandals. This logic also helps explain why the corporation will protect a highly valued employee who engages in serious misconduct or otherwise harms the brand.

In July 2020, a Code Red befell Boeing executive Niel Golightly, who was forced to resign from the company. Some 33 years earlier, Golightly, a young navy pilot at the time, had written an article arguing that women should be excluded from the armed forces. In the December 1987 article, titled 'No Right to Fight', he wrote, 'At issue is not whether women can fire M-60s, dogfight MiGs, or drive tanks. Introducing women into combat would destroy the exclusively male intangibles of war, fighting and the feminine images of what men fight for—peace, home, family.'[30]

Months after Golightly joined Boeing in December 2019, a fellow employee submitted an anonymous complaint about the article, sealing Golightly's fate. As he left the company, Golightly stated:

> My article was a 29 year old Cold War navy pilot's misguided contribution to a debate that was live at the time … My article was embarrassingly wrong and offensive … The article is not a reflection of who I am; but nonetheless I have decided that in the interest of the company I will step down.

Golightly told staff that the exclusion of women from military service at the time was 'government policy and broadly supported in society. It was also wrong.' American women had won the right to serve in all combat roles in 2016, some 29 years after his article was published.

Golightly had no choice. If he had not 'stepped down', he would have been pushed. It was a sacking for the times. On this occasion, it was a fellow employee who was policing the company's workplace policies by lodging an internal, anonymous ethics complaint. One of the unfortunate dimensions of brand management is the overzealous enthusiasm of some employees to police the corporate brand.

Presumably, the complaint alleged a breach of diversity and inclusion or company values. And yet, on any reasonable view, an individual who expressed sexist views 33 years before joining a company could not breach that company's code of conduct. If we accept that many of us have grown up in sexist and racist societies, it follows that most of us will have had sexist or racist thoughts, and/or will have expressed those thoughts somewhere along the way.

Brand management moves to the beat of a perverse drum. Golightly's demise established a standard that few of us can meet: a requirement that we are not allowed to be wrong, make mistakes, or harbour wrong opinions—not now or ever—and that we will keep being punished for our mistakes long after we have learned from them. For all of that, Golightly didn't really lose his job because of his old sexist views. At the time of Golightly's departure, the company was under siege following two fatal crashes of its 737 MAX aircraft that killed 346 passengers and crew in late 2018 and March 2019. The crashes had been brought about by Boeing's faulty design and cost-cutting that tragically compromised the aircraft's safety. Thereafter it lied to a weak regulatory agency that was too close to the company. The 737 aircraft was grounded, and many billions of dollars in sales were cancelled while multiple investigations were instituted.

The company was charged with conspiracy to defraud the US federal aviation safety watchdog, and in January 2021 it pleaded guilty under a Deferred Prosecution Agreement (DPA). Boeing admitted to deceiving the US federal aviation regulator about an important component of the Maneuvering Characteristics Augmentation System (MCAS) flight-control system on its 737 MAX aircraft. Because of the deception, a key document published by the regulator lacked information about MCAS, and in turn, airplane manuals and pilot-training materials for US-based airlines lacked information about MCAS. The US Department of Justice stated that:

> The tragic crashes of Lion Air Flight 610 and Ethiopian Airlines Flight 302 exposed fraudulent and deceptive conduct by employees of one of the world's leading commercial airplane manufacturers ... Boeing's employees chose the path of profit over candour by concealing material information from the FAA concerning the operation of its 737 Max airplane and engaging in an effort to cover up their deception.[31]

Under the terms of the DPA, Boeing paid $2.5 billion in penalties and compensation, including to a fund, to compensate the heirs, relatives, and legal beneficiaries of the 346 passengers who died in the two crashes. The DPA has been strongly criticised as inadequate and too modest to deter such egregious conduct in the future.

Boeing cut Golightly loose in order to shore up its brand in the face of its horrific misconduct. Like Johnson & Johnson, the Boeing brand is resilient, not least because it operates in a virtual duopoly with Airbus. Just three years after the first of the fatal aircraft crashes, Boeing reported a boom in orders and a return to profitability. In 2023, the company recorded a 70 per cent increase in orders.

However, in January 2024, a door in a Boeing 737 Max-9 blew off shortly after take-off from Portland International Airport, prompting a further crisis for the company. Hundreds of Boeing aircraft were grounded across the globe, and the company faced renewed regulatory investigations and legal action. Many whistleblowers from the company have emerged with stories of cost-cutting affecting safety, and relaying their experiences of company retaliation for their telling the truth. The company's reputation continues to be tarnished. It is too early to assess the fate of the company, but notwithstanding the brand damage, its position in the market provides it with a measure of protection. Airbus simply can't fulfil all of the demand for aircraft.

CHAPTER FIVE

A Festival of Hypocrisy: free speech and cancel culture

> In the industrial age of traditional media, the state was the ultimate arbiter of speech whose limits it defined and enforced. However, in the digital age of social media, private platforms make more daily decisions about speech limits than most governments will ever face ... their content moderation has huge ramifications for the global spread of ideas and information.
>
> –Jacob Mchangama[1]

In 2015, there was an attempt to cancel me, an experience that was both traumatic and illuminating. The story began several years earlier in September 2011, when the Federal Court of Australia upheld a claim of racial vilification against Andrew Bolt, Australia's answer to Tucker Carlson. Bolt is a prominent tabloid journalist employed by the Murdoch media empire with close ties to the hard-right political establishment. He has a big audience and considerable political and cultural influence. In two articles titled 'It's so hip to be black' and 'White fellas in the black', Bolt targeted nine 'fair-skinned Aboriginals', describing them sarcastically as 'professional' or 'official' Aborigines, and claiming that they had made an opportunistic choice to live as Aboriginals in order to benefit from that choice.

In the articles, Bolt invoked common racist tropes deployed against Australia's Indigenous population, including that they are privileged and enjoy many advantages over the non-Indigenous population. The statistics on life expectancy, education, health, and rates of incarceration tell a very different story.

Bolt was successfully sued under section 18C of the Racial Discrimination Act, which prohibits an act that 'is reasonably likely, in all the circumstances, to offend, insult, humiliate or intimidate another person' where that act is done 'because of the race, colour or national or ethnic origin of the other person'. Section 18D provides defences for anything said or done 'reasonably and in good faith' in three circumstances: the 'performance, exhibition or distribution of an artistic work'; in the course of debate 'made or held for any genuine academic, artistic or scientific purpose; or any other genuine purpose in the public interest'. Bolt had no recourse to those defences because his articles had not been based on truth. Instead, they included misstatement of facts, distortion, and exaggeration. The court also found that the articles were riddled with errors and poor research, and, as a result, were not written 'reasonably and in good faith'.

As we have seen, a joke about American insularity and racism cost Justine Sacco her job in 2013. Bolt had no reason to worry about losing his job as his speech conformed with the brand of his employer, which, among other things, celebrates nihilism and punching down. In fact, after the adverse finding about Bolt's articles, the Murdoch press and the conservative political establishment locked in behind one of their favourite sons. Shortly after the court's decision was announced, the leader of the opposition, Tony Abbott, made a very public point of visiting Bolt's home to offer his support. Many other conservatives added their voices in support and clamoured for legislative reform. The law was stridently criticised on the grounds that there should not be a right to be protected from racist statements that merely offended their targets. In 2024, Murdoch media and its political allies discovered their anti-racist passion; or to be more precise, their passion for denouncing anti-Semitism, which was directed at those protesting against the war on Gaza.

The libertarian Institute of Public Affairs (IPA) weighed in, publishing advertisements in *The Australian* in 'support of free speech for Andrew Bolt and every Australian'. It argued that, 'If individuals have the right not to be offended then this right may circumscribe the right to freedom of speech. But there is no such right. An injunction against offensive speech necessarily fails because this purported right is incoherent and therefore inapplicable.'[2] The IPA and other critics appeared to ignore criminal laws against offensive speech and behaviour that had been on the statute books in Australia for decades. Under those laws, offensive or insulting conduct can lead to a prison sentence. Indeed, Indigenous Australians have been historically over-represented in being charged with such crimes.

Two years later, in 2013, the Tony Abbott-led Liberal Party swept to power in Australia. True to his word, one of Abbott's first priorities was weakening section 18C of the Racial Discrimination Act. In March 2014, attorney-general George Brandis foreshadowed the government's intention to amend the laws, declaring that people 'have a right to be bigots …' The declaration unleashed an at-times ugly and divisive debate. On the other side of the divide was the racial discrimination commissioner, Tim Soutphommasane, who worked with a coalition of leaders from the Asian, Muslim,

Aboriginal, African, and Jewish communities in leading the charge to keep the anti-racism laws intact.

Although strongly critical of the private sector's repressive regulation of employee speech and expression, I am no free-speech fundamentalist. My progressive parents educated me about racism and its links with violence from a young age. Although I didn't have a Jewish education, my name is undeniably Jewish. I had my first taste of anti-Semitism in primary school. In my high school years, I was periodically targeted by a neo-Nazi student who had carved a swastika tattoo into his forearm and repeatedly threatened to gas me.

As a law student at Melbourne University, I conducted research about racial-vilification laws, and penned a substantial essay that supported laws which regulated racist speech, arguing that there was an undeniable link between racist speech and violence. In my legal career, I had represented victims of racism in claims under the Racial Discrimination Act. Prior to the Bolt case, section 18C had worked well for many years without controversy. It had not had a dramatic or chilling effect.

Using my modest Twitter profile, I challenged the claim — propagated by the federal government and those supporting the campaign — that the existing law was extreme and repressive. I argued that it was relatively mild in comparison with anti-racism laws in Europe and Canada that criminalise hate speech. I explained that many claims under the Racial Discrimination Act were resolved before a trial, and that there was no evidence that suggested the legislation was having a detrimental effect. My intervention attracted the usual social media blowback: a mixture of condemnation, abuse, and racist threats. However, it also attracted the ire of someone on the other side of the globe who was monitoring the debate and was disgusted by my views. He did not respond, but methodically began to plan my punishment.

In the early hours of 10 April 2015, *The Times of Israel* published an article on its website under my name and with an accompanying photograph of me. I did not write the article, and had never read the newspaper or written anything for it. The article began with a parsing of the key ancient text of teachings for Jews, the Talmud, before deteriorating into a racist and violent diatribe against Palestinians. The article culminated in a call for the 'swift and merciless extermination' of Palestinians.

While I lay sleeping in another time zone, the real author of the article made sure that it was disseminated widely online across the globe. I am an atheist who has never studied the Talmud. I am a critic of Israel's human-rights abuses of Palestinians, and believe that Israel will never have security until there is dignity and justice for Palestinians. Those who know me would have been aware that the article was a dangerous and bizarre fake. But most people in the world don't know me.

I was shamed across the world. I awoke to an iPhone filled with messages of abuse and death threats. US author Naomi Wolf took to Facebook to label me 'deranged', 'genocidal', and 'psychotic'. (Subsequently, she apologised.) In shock, I struggled to understand what had happened. Instinctively, I responded to the online barrage, taking to Twitter with a post that stated, 'I am a secular atheist FFS. I didn't write this shit.' It was shortly followed by another post, stating that, 'I have not written anything for The Times of Israel. Ever. WTF???'

My tweets prompted the editorial team of *The Times of Israel* to contact me, confirm my identity and bona fides, and then apologise to me repeatedly for the clusterfuck. When they realised what had happened, they ripped the article from the site. They explained that someone impersonating me had applied to become a blogger with the newspaper weeks before. The application and approval process had been conducted online, and my impersonator had been granted blogger status. The impersonator had then proceeded to submit to the Israeli newspaper the text of earlier articles that I had written about politics, tax, and law, and that had previously been published by *The Guardian* in Australia. This continued for a month before the fake article appeared.

There were profuse apologies, and an article was immediately published correcting the record. But the damage had been done, as the fake article continued to circulate on the internet.

Initial clues suggested that the attack had been launched by white supremacists associated with the racist US website 4chan. In one of their posts, the group denigrated me as a 'subversive Jewish parasite', a 'human rights activist', an 'open borders advocate', and 'staunch supporter of hate speech laws'. The same photograph of me that had been published by *The Times of Israel* appeared on the 4chan website; this time, with a yellow Star of David emblazoned on my forehead. It later transpired that all of this was the work of my impersonator.

In response to the death threats, I contacted the Australian Federal Police (AFP). In an ominous sign, they referred me to the local police station. My initial dealings with local police were underwhelming. The situation deteriorated from there.

While the hoax article continued to circulate online, I decided that I should try to correct the record by explaining the situation as loudly and to as large an audience as possible. I gave some media interviews and penned an article about the experience for the US *Guardian*, in which I wrote:

> Social media shaming can escalate and spread all over the world at eye-watering speed. In the maelstrom that engulfed me for a time, I felt like I was standing in an amphitheatre surrounded by

a hostile and highly multicultural audience who were baying for my blood. And the crowd kept growing …

The threats and abuse died down within 36 hours.

After the initial shock, I treated the situation in much the same way I treated clients who came to see me about sexual harassment, bullying, and being disciplined or sacked: as a crisis-management exercise. I sought advice from a network of friends and political contacts, including several politicians and a former police commissioner. I called in all manner of favours. When the police advised me that their requests of Big Tech companies were routinely being ignored, I was able to obtain the assistance of a friend who was working in an executive role at Google. She was able to help to eradicate the fake article from all but the dark web.

But several weeks after the initial attack, a fake Twitter account was set up carrying my name and photograph. It published a sponsored tweet calling for the death of all Muslims. Another wave of death threats and online abuse descended on me as I walked through the city streets of Melbourne back to my office. Twitter had accepted payment for the sponsored tweet so that it reached more people. This also meant that Twitter had accepted payment to publish a genocidal threat. I contacted the special police task force that was assisting me and asked whether they had sought the payment details from Twitter to help track down the culprit. Once again, I received an underwhelming response. There was no point, they claimed: Twitter would ignore any such request. With help from highly supportive colleagues at work, I foiled an attempt to set up a fake account on Facebook under my name.

An even more frightening experience awaited me. A Twitter account, in the name of Australi Witness, a self-proclaimed IS jihadist, began to target me online. Australi Witness was followed by young aspiring jihadists, and was treated as a serious security threat by Australian intelligence agencies and security experts. The account tormented the police, who desperately tried to identify and arrest its owner.

In May 2015, Australi Witness condemned an art exhibition in Garland, Texas, that included images of the Prophet Muhammad. It posted a map of the exhibition centre, and called on 'brothers in Texas' to defend the prophet with 'weapons, bombs or knives' to attack the exhibition. Two young jihadists, Nadir Soofi and Elton Simpson, duly arrived at the exhibition wearing body armour and armed with assault rifles. They shot a security guard in the leg before being shot dead. Australi Witness hailed them as martyrs.

Australi Witness posted a detailed online guide on how to join ISIS, and a list of Australian synagogues. He boasted online of planning to 'shoot up local synagogues when the maximum amount of Jews are praying'. Bomb threats were made against synagogues in Melbourne and Perth.

There were many acts of kindness and generosity by friends and colleagues who rallied around me. Others were clearly worried about being in close proximity to me. I detected as much from the frightened eyes of a neighbour who asked me for an update. The union that represented employees in my workplace approached the CEO and expressed concern about their safety while working in proximity to me.

After several months under intense pressure, I started to dread looking at my iPhone. I continued to go to work, albeit in a heightened state. I flew to Canberra to lobby politicians on behalf of 10,000 workers with an intellectual disability whom I was representing in a class action against the federal government. The experience was surreal. I made representations to a range of politicians about the importance of the class action in improving wages for the most disadvantaged cohort in the labour market—some of whom were earning less than $1 an hour. As I lobbied, I was becoming hyper-vigilant, increasingly anxious about my safety and that of my family.

Then Australi Witness upped the ante, taking to Twitter to demand that jihadists find my address and punish me for the fake article and fake tweet. Police assured me that they were close to an arrest of the perpetrator, who they said was based in Perth. The arrest didn't happen. They then told me he was in Melbourne. Again, nothing. After complaining to the state attorney-general, Martin Pakula, I was put in touch with a more senior police officer. He drawled, 'Listen, mate. You sound pretty upset. You should look after yourself. Y'know, once upon a time these loonies used to leave an anonymous death threat in your letter box. These days, it's all online …'

When it became clear to me that the police had no idea what they were doing in trying to identify and arrest whoever was behind Australi Witness, I gave up on them. I became unwell, losing five kilos in two weeks. I couldn't sleep or concentrate. I couldn't look at my mobile phone. I realised that I needed help. I took a leaf out of the advice I usually give my clients, and visited a doctor. Her eyes bulged as I relayed the story. She wrote out multiple prescriptions, almost shouting at me that I had no choice but to take my medicine. I took the medicine. I was also referred to a psychologist.

As this was unfolding, two Australian journalists, Luke McMahon and Elise Potaka, were painstakingly trying to track down the individual behind the Australi Witness account by piecing together clues he had left on social media over a period of several months. McMahon had a particular interest in monitoring extreme right-wing online behaviour; Potaka's interest was piqued by an online interaction. They connected with each other, and began to share intelligence. They established that my tormentor had at least 10 Twitter personalities, including Australi Witness. The Twitter accounts communicated with one another, sometimes arguing with one another; at other times, egging each other on.

McMahon and Potaka established that this one individual had been single-handedly responsible for all of the attacks on me. He had stolen my identity to get access to *The Times of Israel*, he had penned the fake article, and he had ensured that the article was widely disseminated online. He had set up a fake Twitter account in my name. Using his Australi Witness account, he had incited jihadist attacks on me. He did all of this from the basement of his parents' home in Florida.

McMahon approached the Australian Federal Police and shared his research. Incredibly, he was initially rebuffed. A second attempt to engage them was more successful. The AFP then shared the information with the FBI. On 9 September 2015, Joshua Ryne Goldberg was arrested as he plotted the bombing of a ceremony in Kansas City, Missouri, to commemorate the victims of the 9/11 terrorist attacks. He had been instructing his accomplice on how to make a bomb similar to that used in the Boston Marathon attacks. He was subsequently charged, found guilty, and sentenced to 10 years' jail for attempted malicious damage and destruction of a building using an explosive. It emerged that, under the guise of Australi Witness, he had also incited a jihadist terrorist attack in Melbourne. Those who he incited were intercepted before the attacks occurred, and were subsequently jailed.

Why had Goldberg targeted me? He was a veteran of Gamergate (an online misogynistic harassment campaign) and was a free-speech absolutist who despised 'social justice warriors'. He had a particular obsession with Australia, which he described as the most 'anti-freedom of speech country in the English speaking world'. It appears that he was not familiar with the crime of hate speech in Canada, which carries a maximum prison term of two years. He had monitored the debate in Australia about the Racial Discrimination Act, and had decided to punish a number of its defenders, including me. When confronted by McMahon, he said, 'Personally, I find it nothing less than absolutely disgusting and depressing how people who claim to campaign for "human rights" are so opposed to the most basic human right of all: freedom of speech.'

Goldberg suffered from a range of psychiatric conditions, and was a dangerous fanatic. His online personas included feminists, peace activists, white supremacists, and jihadists. In 2014, he published an online essay titled 'Philosophy of Rape', advocating collective rape against 'whores and feminazis'. But he shared with other right-wing, self-proclaimed free-speech crusaders a profound ignorance of the many constraints on speech (including in the US), a highly selective outrage at laws regulating racist speech, and a frightening intolerance of different views. He was a free-speech terrorist who caused harm to many people, including me.

After three visits to a psychologist, my health bounced back quickly. Or so I thought. But years later, when *The Australian* newspaper unleashed a barrage of attacks on me in a series of articles, seeking to depict me as a misogynist, my mobile phone lit up much like it had in 2015. I had an unexpectedly strong reaction to my hyperactive iPhone. My mental health deteriorated rapidly. It was the first time I experienced PTSD. I realised that what Goldberg and the internet had done still impacted me and will probably never leave me.

My experience reinforced the paradox of the internet age. Social media, a product spawned by government research and development, and then private sector innovation, has both enhanced freedom of speech and imperilled democracy. The early days of the world wide web were fuelled by a strange brew of tech utopianism and libertarianism typified by John Perry Barlow's 1996 manifesto, 'A Declaration of the Independence of Cyberspace', delivered at the World Economic Forum in Davos, Switzerland. It stated, 'We are creating a world where anyone, anywhere may express his or her beliefs, no matter how singular, without fear of being coerced into silence or conformity.'

The companies promised universal, free access to information, enhancing knowledge and boosting democracy. Social media propelled movements for democracy in the Middle East and North Africa, and were hailed as heralding a golden age for free speech and progressive politics. Paul Mason, for example, argued that information technology was undercutting prices, and predicted that capitalism would be replaced by a socially just economy 'based on information, with its tendency to zero-cost products and weak property rights'.[3] This was way back in 2016.

But capitalism was going nowhere. Big Tech found new ways to kill off competition and to make vast sums of money involving covert surveillance and data-selling. Capitalism morphed into 'surveillance capitalism'. Social media still allow us to publish our thoughts, views, and dog pictures with the potential of reaching an international audience. There has never been more free speech.

Social media are variously linked with a rise in disinformation, misinformation, and conspiracy theories, including those disseminated by QAnon, a far-right political movement. They distort election campaigns and results, foment political extremism, terrorist attacks and other violence, and facilitate child sexual abuse and exploitation. The online revolution has unfolded at the same time as a 'democratic recession'. Terrorists and trolls can use the cloak of anonymity to create mayhem, and to harm, maim, and kill. In 2018, the Myanmar military used Facebook to incite genocide against its Muslim Rohingya minority. The United Nations described the ensuing carnage as 'a textbook example of ethnic cleansing'. In my case, a major multinational corporation took payment from a terrorist to publish a global death threat directed at all Muslims.

Twitter was out of control shortly after its inception. It is now called X, and is owned by an erratic degenerate who, like Joshua Goldberg, impersonates a free speech 'absolutist' while seeking to eliminate the speech of his enemies. Elon Musk has unplugged the sewer. Among the lowlights is a post of Musk's that targeted George Soros and stated, 'He wants to erode the fabric of civilisation.' It garnered 2.4 million views. Adam Serwer, an American journalist and author, has noted that, 'During his tenure at Twitter, Musk has suspended reporters and left-wing accounts that drew his ire, retaliated against media organisations perceived as liberal, ordered engineers to boost his tweets after he was humiliated when a tweet from President Joe Biden about the Super Bowl did better than his …'[4]

When the Center for Countering Digital Hate published research findings that hate speech on the platform had soared since Musk's takeover of the site, X sued it, claiming revenue loss due to 'false and misleading claims'. For years, Tesla required its employees to sign a confidentiality agreement that banned them from speaking with the media without its permission. After a lawsuit brought by the United Auto Workers' Union against it, the company was forced to water down the text. According to Yoel Roth, who quit his role as head of integrity and moderation at Twitter after Elon Musk assumed control, 'Elections, and especially elections that touch on divisive social and cultural issues, are prime targets for organised disinformation campaigns and abuse, both foreign and domestic.' Roth says that 'this playbook' has been deployed by Russia, Iran, and China, together with extremist groups around the world.[5]

Absolutism

There has never been a time when the bounds of permissible speech have been free of contention, but the rise of poorly regulated social media monopolies has driven the debate into overdrive. Much shouty conflict about free speech starts from a false premise: that in the good old days, speech was absolutely free. It degenerates from there. In fact, speech has never been completely free of restrictions. Laws restricting speech that harm others are as old as Methuselah. The Ten Commandments proscribed bearing 'false witness against your neighbour'.

Free-speech absolutists tend to invoke the legacy of John Stuart Mill and Voltaire. But Mill, one of the foremost British philosophers of the 19th century and a guru of classical liberalism, did not advocate unfettered free speech. In his book *On Liberty*, which was first published in 1859, Mill argued that the limitations to be placed on freedom of expression should be based on 'one very simple principle', usually referred to as the 'harm principle'. He wrote that, 'The only purpose for which power can be rightfully exercised over any member of a civilized community, against his will, is to prevent harm to others.'

The expression 'I disagree with what you say, but I will defend to the death your right to say it' is usually mistakenly attributed to Voltaire. (These were not his words, but those of his English biographer, Evelyn Beatrice Hall.) In fact, Voltaire supported laws that curtailed speech, including the crimes of libel, slander, incitement to violence, and treason.

While the First Amendment to the US Constitution enshrines the strongest protections for free speech in the Western world, it too is widely misunderstood. The amendment limits the US government's ability to restrict speech by prohibiting Congress from legislating to interfere with it, subject to critical exceptions. Laws protecting against the harm of libel, slander, perjury, fraud, false advertising, violations of intellectual property law, threats, speech integral to illegal conduct, and obscenity have since been upheld many times by the US Supreme Court. In 2022, the families of the Sandy Hook Elementary School massacre were successful in their defamation suits against Alex Jones. Jones had repeatedly broadcast a conspiracy theory, asserting that the massacre had been staged with actors as part of a plot by government to seize citizens' guns. Jones' broadcasts resulted in family members of children who died in the massacre being harassed, abused, and accused of lying about their grief. The families were awarded almost $1.5 billion in damages, prompting Jones and his company, Free Speech Systems, to file for bankruptcy.

The First Amendment doesn't apply to corporations, however. It doesn't prevent them from restricting the speech of their workers, including through the promiscuous use of NDAs. Ask Lynne Gobbell, who was sacked by her employer because her car sported a John Kerry bumper sticker in the lead-up to the 2004 presidential election. According to Jeanette Cox, in the US, 'Most workers have no protection from speech-related termination unless they can prove that their employer's motive for firing them violates a federal, state, or local law. The available statutory protections form an incomplete, and often indefinite patchwork that leaves large amounts of employee speech and political activity unprotected.'[6] (A similar situation exists for Australian employees.) In recent years, 32 US states have successfully passed laws banning or restricting boycotts in support of Palestinian rights.

In Australia, there is no constitutional right to free speech. In the words of Australia's High Court:

> Unlike the First Amendment to the United States Constitution, which has been interpreted to confer private rights, our

Constitution contains no express right of freedom of communication or expression. Within our legal system, communications are free only to the extent that they are left unburdened by laws that comply with the Constitution.[7]

In other words, speech is free provided that it doesn't violate a valid law.

Mill and Voltaire recognised that speech can cause immense harm. In recognition of this reality, many democracies provide some measure of protection against defamatory speech. For example, it's unlawful to falsely publish statements accusing another person of being a terrorist or a paedophile, as a false accusation of this kind can cause catastrophic consequences for the victim. Defamation laws are designed to regulate that risk of harm.

Media owners and journalists are in perpetual campaign mode against the laws, but are far less voluble about the myriad other incursions on free speech that apply to others. They are also silent about their immense power and the prevalence of NDAs in their industry. Self-interest is at play.

The laws that restrict freedom of speech in Australia are extensive, and include those operating in the areas of consumer protection against deceptive and misleading conduct, workplace bullying, electoral regulation, sexual harassment, anti-discrimination, copyright, confidential information, national security, privacy, obscenity, nuisance, grooming of children, treason, and contempt of court. Overwhelmingly, these curbs on speech don't excite outraged calls condemning cancel culture.

When Mark McInnes, the-then CEO of major retailer David Jones was sued for sexual harassment amid a blaze of publicity, no one argued that his freedom of speech had been cancelled. Among other things, the lawsuit alleged that he had encouraged an employee of the company, Kristy Fraser-Kirk, to try a dessert at a celebratory dinner by telling her, 'It's like a fuck in the mouth.' McInnes lost his job. His words and his actions were alleged to have been unwelcome sexual conduct.

In June 2017, the Supreme Court of Victoria was hearing an appeal against the leniency of the sentences imposed on three men convicted of terrorist offences. During the proceedings, three federal government ministers—Greg Hunt, Alan Tudge, and Michael Sukkar—combined with *The Australian* newspaper to launch an attack on the integrity of the three judges hearing the appeal. Sukkar, a lawyer, was quoted as condemning the 'appointment of hard-left activist judges' and suggesting that the approach of the judges 'has eroded any trust that remained in our legal system'. The ministers were summoned to court under the threat of contempt proceedings. They avoided punishment—which can be either imprisonment or a fine—by apologising 'unreservedly' for their comments.

Fraud, a criminal offence, also punishes those who deceive others with words. Laws against obscenity, blasphemy, and treason restrict speech. So, too, does the criminal offence of grooming a minor. All of these examples underline the inanity of free speech absolutism and the bankruptcy of much debate about free speech.

The question that debates about free speech invariably raise is whether the law should intervene to restrict speech to address a particular type of harm. Legislators are required to make difficult decisions about competing freedoms, including the freedom to act in a certain way and the freedom from being held responsible for the consequences of those actions.

Debates about legislation to restrict hate speech typically engage minority groups, churches, academics, the media, and politicians. Invariably, the problem confronting legislators is whether the right to free speech should take precedence over other freedoms, including the right to live free of racist or homophobic abuse and violence. History is replete with unimpeachable proof that racist speech is closely connected to racist violence. The attempt to water down racial-vilification laws in Australia failed because it galvanised strong opposition in the community. The issue has since receded, though racist incidents and attacks have not. Racism directed at Indigenous Australians remains a scourge. In 2020, Australia's intelligence chief warned of a 'real threat' to the country's security from neo-Nazis. He said 'small cells' of right-wing extremists were meeting regularly to salute Nazi flags and share their ideology. The response of the Morrison government was to ban security agencies from describing such groups as 'right wing'.

In June 2022, Victoria became the first Australian state to specifically ban the display of the Nazi swastika. Under a new law, people who intentionally exhibit the symbol face up to a year in jail or a $22,000 fine. The-then Victorian premier, Dan Andrews, said, 'Nobody has the right to spread racism, hate, or anti-Semitism.' No one took to the streets to protest against the law — not even neo-Nazis.

The contrast with the draconian restrictions imposed on the activities and speech of employees by their employment contract is stark. The restrictions on speech and expression are not the product of a democratic, deliberative process; they are unilaterally imposed. Unlike carefully drafted legislation, the restrictions are deliberately vague and imprecise. An employee cannot possibly know the parameters of the rules. The effect is chilling. Second, the major consideration driving the suppression of speech does not involve a careful balancing of freedoms and rights. Instead, the overwhelming imperative is corporate brand-management.

Democracies should encourage the exchange of different views and expressions of dissent. Corporate cancel culture, on the other hand, usually targets dissent and controversy in aid of furthering and protecting the corporation's interest in profit maximisation. Notwithstanding the widespread cancellation of employee speech, the phenomenon is routinely ignored in contemporary debates about free speech. The more that corporations cancel their employees' speech, the more they perpetuate the culture. Each cancellation feeds the beast — whether that beast is an online mob, a Murdoch media pile-on, or a combination of both.

It's not just the cancel — it's the culture

In many ways, the debate about cancel culture is a continuation of the conflict generated when the terms 'political correctness' moved from ironic mockery among American liberals in the 1960s to a term of right-wing abuse directed at the 'authoritarian left' in the 1980s and 1990s. In the 1980s and 1990s, the political right was directing its scorn at anti-discrimination laws and policies that had been introduced in preceding decades. It was also a useful political strategy to distract attention from the radically regressive redistribution of income underway as part of the neoliberal revolution: a 'deflection of social and class tensions into a different realm'.[8] Decades later, cancel culture and its close relative, wokeism, is the new political correctness that allows an increasingly reactionary right to distract the rest of the population from the smouldering wreckage of neoliberal excesses and its own far more systematic and brutal repression. And this time, the left has both fallen for the distraction and added its own form of cancel culture to the mix.

In July 2020, *Harper's Magazine* published an open letter with 153 signatories, including prominent writers and academics from across the political divide. The letter took aim at a burgeoning progressive sensibility that was driving 'an intolerance of opposing views, a vogue for public shaming and ostracism, and the tendency to dissolve complex policy issues in a blinding moral certainty.' The letter also referred to 'institutional leaders, in a spirit of panicked damage control', resorting to 'disproportionate punishments'—in an apparent reference to sackings of academics driven by university brand-management. Typical of the debate about cancel culture, private sector suppression of employee speech did not rate a mention in the letter.

Although the letter condemned the repressive censoriousness of 'the radical right' and Donald Trump, its real target was the left. The *Harper's* letter attracted fierce criticism from a raft of progressive voices, many of whom denied the existence of cancel culture. Typical of these was Hannah Giorgis, who wrote in *The Atlantic*:

> There's something darkly comical about the fretfulness of these elite petitioners. It's telling that the censoriousness they identify as a national plague isn't the racism that keeps Black journalists from reporting on political issues, or the transphobia that threatens their colleagues' lives.[9]

Michael Hobbes wrote in *The Huffington Post* that:

> The panic over 'cancel culture' is, at its core, a reactionary backlash. Conservative elites, threatened by changing social norms and an accelerating generational handover, are attempting to amplify their feelings of aggrievement into a national crisis. The Harper's statement, like nearly everything else written on this subject, could have been more efficiently summarised in four words: 'Get Off My Lawn.'[10]

The charge that cancel culture is a myth has been repeatedly argued from the pages of *Time Magazine* to those of *The New*

Statesman. It is prosecuted by many brilliant thinkers and writers that I admire. They argue that it is an attempt to discourage criticism of those who enjoy considerable cultural cache and who are accustomed to being venerated, such as JK Rowling. And further, that these influential figures have not had their speech cancelled. Or that it is the imposition of an overdue accountability on those who endanger others. Distinguished philosophers Kate Manne and Jason Stanley argue that when minorities assert their rights, they are subjected to 'tone policing':

> When oppressed people speak out—and up, toward those in power—their right to speak may be granted, yet their capacity to know of what they speak doubted as the result of ingrained prejudice … So it is not just that these people have to raise their voices in order to be audible; it's also that, when their tone becomes the issue, their speech is essentially being heard as mere noise, disruption, commotion. Their freedom of speech is radically undercut by what is aptly known as 'tone policing'.[11]

At one side of the divide are those who say their speech is being undercut by content policing that aims to humiliate and silence them. On the other side are those claiming their speech is being impeded by tone policing. The debate about cancel culture suffers from the same vice that afflicts arguments about free speech: the lack of a shared understanding of what we're arguing about. Corporate cancel culture involves shaming, sacking, and blacklisting employees. It's alive and thriving. It's one thing to be black-banned for a decade from a career in Hollywood because of your perceived communist affiliations. It's another altogether to be rendered unemployable and destined for years of compromised mental health because the internet didn't understand that you were cracking an edgy joke.

The act of cancelling can also be distinguished from the culture of cancelling. The unilateral imposition on millions of employees of obligations not to harm the brand serves to pre-emptively censor them in their lives outside work. That culture is reinforced when they observe the corporation shame and cancel a colleague. The chilling effect is reinforced each time we see the ritual play out.

The term 'cancel culture' is apt to describe the fate of those who are sacked for expressing a controversial view or even relaying a misconstrued joke. This is not a form of accountability, but rather a form of repressive abuse — a world in which brand-managed corporations can 'impose the equivalent of lifetime scarlet letters on people who have not been accused of anything remotely resembling a crime'.[12] No one should be sacked for relaying an ironic joke about racism that is misunderstood, or for sharing a peer-reviewed article about political strategy. Or for protesting against a war, taking the knee, or advocating a vote for John Kerry or better access to abortion. In fact, as a general rule, sacking an employee because of a controversial comment they make is not okay.

As journalist James Button reminds us, 'To cancel means to shame, silence, and cast out an individual to make a larger political point.' He observes that the cancel culture sceptics focus far too heavily on the word 'cancel' at the expense of 'culture'.[13] In other words, victims of cancel culture are not necessarily sacked, but are often silenced.

There is undoubtedly a cancel culture exercised by the left — centred in universities and the liberal arts, which is increasingly censorious and repressive. In November 2022, more than 700 'members of the writing, publishing, and broader literary community' published an open letter urging Penguin Random House US to cancel the publication of a book. The publisher had contracted with US Supreme Court judge Amy Coney Barrett to write a book about how judges should avoid personal feelings interfering with their judicial responsibilities. Coney Barrett is an avowed opponent of abortion. The letter stated that 'publishers should uphold their dedication to freedom of speech with a duty of care ... We recognize that harm is done to democracy not only in the form of censorship, but also in the form of assault on inalienable human rights.'[14]

That hundreds of people in the US publishing and literary community would try to block the publication of a yet-to-be-written book by a sitting Supreme Court judge was a breathtaking example of cancel culture. Do publishers have a duty of care not to publish views that many others disagree with? Or, say, not to publish books by anti-abortion advocates? American journalist Conor Friedersdorf describes 'the hijacking of liberalism's language toward an end that is fundamentally authoritarian', and observes that the logic of the open letter would wipe out *The Communist Manifesto* by Karl Marx because it rails against private property, itself a tenet of the Universal Declaration of Human Rights.[15] As it happens, Justice Barrett will not be cancelled. Penguin Random House is undeterred and will publish her book, but the attempt to can it speaks of a culture that tries to silence those that it disagrees with—a culture of progressive authoritarianism.

Progressives who condemn tone policing and insist that it's all about 'accountability' have not fully reckoned with the digital age. This is a failure of both imagination and empathy, as the amorality of social media frequently visits a wildly cruel and disproportionate punishment on a target. For those who are pursued by an online mob, it feels like living in *The Lord of The Flies*. If you can imagine being swarmed by 1,000 people in a prominent public space, you will get a sense of what it's like: many voices chorusing their condemnation and disapproval, interspersed with abuse and threats of violence. Even when an initial post is merely righteously indignant — not abusive — the responses not only amplify the criticism, but also generate abuse. Women and people of colour are subjected to the most extreme forms of online bullying. Even a member of the cultural elite such as JK Rowling can have her health compromised by such attacks. It's not a safe space for anyone. Those impacted by the mobbing, shaming, and sacking are liable to end up on medication and in a long-term professional relationship with a psychologist.

Corporations that sack their employees in response to the shaming mob serve to encourage and reinforce the brutality. They do not have to do so. They have a choice.

John Stuart Mill identified that repressive social mores can present just as much a threat to a healthy polity as the actions of a repressive government. Writing of the stifling culture of Victorian England, Mill condemned 'a social tyranny more formidable than many kinds of political oppression' that 'leaves fewer means of escape, penetrating much more deeply into the details of life, and enslaving the soul itself'.

Identity activists reject liberal orthodoxy, citing its failure to address enduring, entrenched racial and gender inequality. In response, both liberal and right-wing critics have a field day with the language of privilege-checking, safe spaces, and intersectionality, knowing that it's incomprehensible to the 98 per cent of the population who haven't undertaken a university course in cultural theory. At the same time, these activists' demands can also be viewed through a liberal lens because they are advocating for the right of people being targeted to be safe from words that harm them. In so doing, they are seeking to expand the categories of recognised harm — both for the targets of harm and to lower the bar on harms that should be protected against — to include microaggressions.

For example, progressives' rage directed at Trans Exclusionary

Radical Feminists (otherwise known as TERFs) is driven by the aim of protecting transgender people from harm. The transgender community is highly marginalised and susceptible to discrimination in the provision of healthcare and in the labour market. The community suffers higher rates of depression and suicide. Undoubtedly, it is deeply hurtful to have to debate your identity, to be told you aren't 'really' a woman or a man, and to face the risk of further vilification and abuse. But, rather than campaign for legislative reform, there is a tendency amongst the censorious left to vilify and abuse its opposition. And, in so doing, this produces a disturbing hypocrisy. Too often, the means of pursuing the objective of creating a safe space for the marginalised involves inflicting injury on others.

The hypocrisy doesn't end there. The onset of the Israel–Hamas war has again seen both conservatives and progressives perform 180-degree free speech turns. Pro-Israel conservatives have sought to stymie legitimate protest against Israel by urging the sackings of academics, journalists, and even doctors in retaliation for their anti-war and anti-Zionist advocacy. Universities have been pressured to crack down on student protests—by donors, politicians, lobby groups, and others. In so doing, they have repeatedly referred to the 'safety' of Jewish students and academics, thus aping the language of the left. While, undoubtedly, there have been some expressions of anti-Semitism in university protests, they have been overwhelming peaceful and attended by many Jewish activists who support them.

In performing their own spectacular U-turn, pro-Palestinian progressives have demanded the right to sing and chant slogans, even if they make Jewish students unsafe. And there is no doubt that many Jewish students are distressed and do feel unsafe when confronted with anti-Zionist rhetoric. It is too early to know whether the shift in position will produce a rethink about progressive cancel culture.

You call that cancel culture?

Dr Anthony Fauci has been an adviser to every US president since Ronald Reagan. A scientist and immunologist, he served as director of the National Institute of Allergy and Infectious Diseases (NAID) and as the chief medical adviser to the US president. His profile rose across the world during the coronavirus pandemic when, as a member of the White House Coronavirus Task Force, he shared the platform with President Trump.

While Trump ranged from spruiking disinformation about the pandemic and suggesting fake cures, including bleach and sunlight, Fauci steadfastly adhered to the science. As the pandemic took hold in the US, he advocated staying at home, social distancing, and mask wearing. Fauci's advocacy of strong mitigation measures increased in response to the country's rising death and illness toll, only for him to come under significant pressure from the administration and Republicans nationwide to downplay the seriousness of the situation. At the initial height of the pandemic in April 2020, Trump retweeted a call to #FireFauci from Republican congressional candidate DeAnna Lorraine.

As Trump ramped up the disinformation about Covid-19 during 2020 in the lead-up to the presidential election, Fauci continued to perform his crucial role, correcting falsehoods—such as about the availability of a vaccine, the measures required to minimise the death toll, and the seriousness of the disease. On 1 April 2020, the far-right Republican member of Congress Marjorie Taylor Greene introduced the Fire Fauci Act. In July 2020, Senator Rand Paul falsely accused Fauci of being responsible for millions of deaths. Florida Republican governor Ron DeSantis, a devotee of Hungarian President Orban, promoted 'Freedom over Faucism' at a concert in June 2021. On Fox News, Fauci was compared to Nazi doctor Josef Mengele.

In response, Fauci complained that, 'I have threats upon my life, harassment of my family and my children with obscene phone calls because people are lying about me.' In July 2021, a West Virginia man, Thomas Connally, who had threatened to beat Fauci and his family to death and set them on fire, was arrested. Connally's emails to Fauci included the lines, 'Hope you get a bullet in your compromised satanic skull today' and 'You and your entire family will be dragged into the street, beaten to death, and set on fire.' Fauci was one of a number of public health officials targeted by Connally. He subsequently pleaded guilty to the charges.

When interviewed in January 2022 by *The Washington Post*, Fauci and his family remained under the protection of security agents, with cameras around his house. He was clearly affected by what he described as the 'almost incomprehensible culture of lies'.[16] Security agents slept in a spare room in the family home. In August, Connally was sentenced to three years' jail for having threatened to kill Fauci. Fauci was not silenced by his appalling treatment. He persevered in spite of it. Undoubtedly, the attacks and threats had an impact on him, his life, and that of his family. It can't be any other way. All of us — even the most hardy and resilient — have a limit. In June 2024, as Fauci testified before a US house sub-committee, he and his family continued to receive death threats, stoked by attacks from Republican politicians. The family remains under around-the-clock protection.

Fauci's mistreatment makes the cancel culture of identity activists look like a tiptoe through the tulips. Even his retirement was met with unhinged conspiracy theories and calls by Elon Musk, among others, for his prosecution. 'My pronouns are Prosecute/Fauci', tweeted Musk.

The impact of his experience resonates well beyond Fauci and his immediate family, poisoning the culture. Fauci is one of many public health officials, scientists, and medical experts who received such treatment during the early years of the coronavirus pandemic. Many carried on stoically; others became unwell and retreated. We will never know how much their treatment silenced them or changed their public messaging. We do know about Lisa-Maria Kellermayr, an Austrian GP who was a vocal advocate of effective strategies to minimise the spread of Covid-19 and its progression. After months of enduring death threats from anti-vaxxers and conspiracy theorists, and failing to gain support from the police, she committed suicide in July 2022—the ultimate cancellation.

Contrary to suggestions otherwise, the greatest threat to free speech and liberal democracy is not the work of woke activists. The authoritarian right is by far the greatest exponent of cancel culture. In the 21st century, it is the right that has set fire to liberal democracy: to the Enlightenment; to science; to reason, to logic, to reasoned argument; and to democratic institutions and norms. As *The Economist* has observed, conservative parties are 'on fire and dangerous', having abandoned any pretensions to their liberal inheritance. Constitutionalism, the rule of law, the independence of the judiciary, a free press, and freedom of speech are all under threat.

The political onslaught of authoritarianism has swept Hungary, Poland, Turkey, the Netherlands, Israel, the US, the UK, and Australia. Hungary's Viktor Orban remains in the vanguard of the authoritarian right, proudly proclaiming his 'illiberalism' in standing up for his country's white, Christian culture against non-white, non-Christian migrants and their 'cosmopolitan' liberal protectors elsewhere in Europe. Far-right parties in France and Germany made major gains in the 2024 European elections, weakening their respective centrist governments in those countries.

Comparing the cancel culture of identity politics to that propelled by the right is like comparing an electric scooter with a Humvee. While identity activists campaign online and impact universities, parts of the media, publishing, and the arts, the authoritarian right uses the levers of government, media monopolies, social media, and violence to systematically silence their perceived enemies across industry and community sectors.

When Joshua Goldberg incited jihadists to attack me, he sought to silence my views by violence. As it happens, the death toll associated with right-wing cancel culture is extensive. It includes 22 people shot dead in a Walmart in El Paso, Texas, by Cesar Sayoc, a Trump acolyte who had published an online anti-immigrant manifesto before going on his killing spree. British MP Jo Cox was murdered by neo-Nazi Thomas Mair in 2016 as anti-immigration rhetoric escalated in the lead-up to the Brexit referendum. The earliest casualty of the Trump era was Heather Heyer, a young woman who counter-protested against the white nationalists in Charlottesville, Virginia, in 2017. The tally extends to victims of massacres carried out by right-wing radicals at the Charleston church in South Carolina in 2015, the Tree of Life synagogue in Pittsburgh in 2018, and two mosques in Christchurch, New Zealand, in 2019.

In September 2019, in the span of 24 hours, a Republican state lawmaker in Texas threatened to gun down Beto O'Rourke; a conservative political action committee released an inflammatory advertisement featuring a photo of Alexandria Ocasio-Cortez's face on fire; and a commentator on Fox Business promoted the need to shoot immigrants. When David DePape broke into Nancy Pelosi's home in November 2022, looking to break her kneecaps, he encountered Pelosi's husband. Before bashing Paul Pelosi with a hammer, he told him that, 'We've got to take them all out.'

The rise in right-wing political violence reflects the growth in speech that incites attacks—including from right-wing politicians in the US, the UK, and Australia. It includes the violent rhetoric routinely deployed by Murdoch media employees. In the US,

Republican politicians use social media to 'publicize the names and photographs of largely unknown local election officials, health officials, and school-board members who refuse to bow to political pressure, and who are then subjected to waves of vitriol, including threats of violence to themselves and their children, simply for doing their jobs'.[17] Such speech can involve a combination of rhetoric that dehumanises and presents an existential threat: an extreme form of othering. QAnon peddles a conspiracy theory about systemic child abuse and the Deep State to suggest that it can only be remedied by violent suppression.

What also distinguishes the authoritarian right is its addiction to lying. Masha Gessen argues that we live 'in a time of intentional, systematic, destabilizing lying … lying as a way to assert or capture political power has become the dominant factor in public life …'[18] The lying is compounded by disinformation propounded by the Murdoch media and online around the world. Unlike woke activists, the right disseminates lies to debase culture, destabilise institutions, and inculcate hatred and violence against their political enemies. Lies are weaponised to silence opponents. Like his counterparts Boris Johnson and Donald Trump, former prime minister Scott Morrison was variously described as a 'liar', a 'fraud', and a 'bully' who has 'no moral compass'—all by his conservative colleagues.

Right-wing cancel culture can destroy the career of an individual target ruthlessly and efficiently by using the levers of government, the Murdoch media, and social media. In the US, although Fauci survived, Colin Kaepernick's sporting career didn't. In Australia, journalists Scott McIntyre and Yassmin Abdel-Magied were eviscerated and forced out of the country by an authoritarian right spearheaded by the Murdoch empire and right-wing politicians.

The authoritarian right's cancel culture is far more ambitious, systematic, and effective than the progressive left's. It targets not only individuals, but institutions that protect democracy—including schools and universities, the public service, trade unions, the courts, non-government organisations, and public-interest media—with the aim of either controlling them, weakening them, or shutting them down.

Donald Trump attacked leftist cancel culture, stating:

> One of their political weapons is 'cancel culture'— driving people from their jobs, shaming dissenters, and demanding total submission from anyone who disagrees. This is the very definition of totalitarianism, and it is completely alien to our culture and our values, and it has absolutely no place in the United States of America.[19]

During his presidency, Trump called for the sacking of NFL players who took the knee, revoked the press passes of media outlets whose employees criticised him, called for a boycott of CNN and shared images that incited violence against the network, and banned Muslim immigration. He also demanded the sacking of economist and commentator Paul Krugman, television journalist and political analyst Chuck Todd, actress Debra Messing, Republican political consultant Karl Rove, and the editorial board of *The Wall Street Journal*. He urged the imprisoning of protesters who burned the flag, encouraged attacks on those who protested at his rallies, required staffers and interns to sign non-disclosure agreements, and threatened litigation against media outlets that criticised him. Finally, he incited a violent fascist riot. Since then, he has fanned the Great Lie that he won the presidential election: a purely fascist play.

Following Trump's defeat in the 2020 presidential election, the retreat from democracy has deepened in the US amid the 'the largest wave of state censorship since the second Red Scare'.[20] Republican

Party legislators in red states are enacting laws to prevent citizens from voting and engaging in protest action that interferes with economic activity; banning books, and teaching, about racism and sexism in schools and universities; and seeking to criminalise speech about abortion. As I write, there is a palpable fear in many parts of the globe that the US might elect its first convicted felon and fascist president in November 2024. Trump has made no secret of his agenda. A second Trump presidency would devastate free speech for his opponents.

In the months leading up to the 2024 presidential elections, American billionaires were rushing to donate to Donald Trump's campaign. Trump, like other authoritarians, performatively attacks 'elites' in seeking to maximise his constituency. Despite the 'grassroots' rhetoric, he is funded by big business, precisely because he will deliver business and billionaire tax cuts and wage suppression. In this way, authoritarianism and corporate cancel culture are distinct, but complementary, anti-democratic forces. The current wave of authoritarianism reinforces, rather than challenges, corporate power.

In Australia, authoritarian censorship is less overt, but nonetheless has had an enormous impact. Successive conservative governments sought to silence criticism and dissent by repressive laws and policies directed at trade unions, charities, NGOs, community legal centres, the independent public broadcaster, the public service, courts, and tribunals. Important institutions, including the chief state-funded scientific research body, the CSIRO, and the Bureau of Meteorology, were prevented from communicating about climate change. A web of Kafkaesque measures prevented journalists, public servants, doctors, and security guards from revealing the truth about the conditions visited upon refugees while in offshore mandatory detention. In 2023, a referendum that proposed constitutional recognition for Australia's

Indigenous community was soundly defeated at the hands of a Trumpian campaign of disinformation.

Like other institutions that are critical to a healthy democracy, universities are also threatened by the rising tide of authoritarian politics at a juncture in their history when corporate cancel culture has infiltrated their ranks.

CHAPTER SIX

Academic Freedom and the University Brand

In May 2016, Daniel Andrews, the-then premier of the State of Victoria, delivered a powerful address to the Victorian parliament, apologising for the historical mistreatment of the LGBTI community. Andrews said:

> We criminalised homosexual thoughts and deeds. We validated homophobic words and acts. And we set the tone for a society that ruthlessly punished the different – with a short sentence in prison, and a life sentence of shame. From now on, that shame is ours.
>
> This Parliament and this Government are to be formally held to account for designing a culture of darkness and shame.
>
> On behalf of the Parliament, the Government and the people of Victoria. For the laws we passed. And the lives we ruined. And the standards we set.
>
> We are so sorry. Humbly, deeply, sorry.

As Andrews spoke, the rainbow flag was hoisted above the Victorian parliament. Weeks later, Roz Ward, a left-wing academic and activist employed by La Trobe University, posted an image of a rainbow flag on her privately accessible Facebook account, accompanied by satirical text: 'Now we just need to get rid of the racist Australian flag on top of state parliament and get a red one up there and my work is done.'

Ward, a queer Marxist with a dry sense of humour, is perfect fodder for the culture wars. Ward had founded and led an anti-bullying program for schools established by the Safe Schools Coalition, which sought 'to help school staff create safer and more inclusive environments for same sex attracted, intersex and gender diverse students, school staff and families'.[1] The Safe Schools program had initially been adopted by schools in Victoria, and then expanded into other Australian states in 2013. At that time, the program received bipartisan support.

It was not to last. A right-wing backlash led by the Australian Christian Lobby, conservative politicians, and the Murdoch press saw the program become prime fodder for the culture wars. The program was variously condemned by this chorus for promoting 'gender fluidity', 'cultural Marxism', and 'radical sexual experimentation'. Senator George Christensen linked the Safe Schools program to paedophilia, while the Australian Christian Lobby's Lyle Shelton likened it to Nazi atrocities.

In February 2016, a review was ordered by the Turnbull government. *The Review of Appropriateness and Efficacy of the Safe Schools Coalition Australia Program Resources* was undertaken by Bill Louden, an emeritus professor of education at the University of Western Australia. It backed the program, finding that its opponents had grossly misrepresented it. Nevertheless, Ward remained a target of the hard right in Australia.

Ward's satirical Facebook post depicting her preferred Australian flag was leaked to the Murdoch newspaper *The Australian*, which had virulently railed against Safe Schools for years. It seized on the opportunity to campaign to remove Ward from her position with Safe Schools. Former Victorian premier Jeff Kennett—the chairman of mental-health awareness charity Beyondblue, which has been a major funder of La Trobe University—joined the attacks, telling journalists that if Ms Ward remained in her role with Safe Schools, he would personally argue against any further funding to the university. Acting premier James Merlino called Ward's Facebook comments 'appalling', 'offensive', and 'stupid', adding that he expected the university to investigate Ward's conduct.[2]

In response, on 1 June 2016, Ward was suspended by La Trobe University pending a full disciplinary investigation into her alleged 'serious misconduct' involving breaches of its code of conduct. Ward was handed a letter by the university alleging that her Facebook post:

> a. ... Undermined public confidence in the Safe Schools program by undermining public confidence in you as a researcher and as a person associated with the Safe Schools program.
> b. ... Damages the reputation of the Safe Schools program and aligns the Safe Schools program with views which have nothing to do with the program and its message and content.
> c. ... Has required members of the Victorian Government to take up their time in defending the Safe Schools program, rather than be positive advocates for the Safe Schools program.
> d. ... Has required senior staff at the University to take up their time in defending the Safe Schools program, rather than be positive advocates for the Safe Schools program or undertake other duties they have.
> e. ... Has drawn [your colleagues] into the negative publicity

around Safe Schools and this has impacted on their ability to continue with their research in a safe environment.[3]

A charge of 'serious misconduct' is usually a precursor to summary dismissal. Serious misconduct targets the most extremely bad workplace behaviour: sexual harassment, theft, workplace bullying, assault, misuse of confidential information, and fraud. But on this occasion the disciplinary charge had been triggered by a satirical Facebook post about the Australian flag. The content of the post was, in fact, a harmless joke. It had no rational connection to Ward's work at the university.

You can test this proposition by considering a counterfactual: Ward posts the flag and her satirical text; her Facebook friends respond; there is no leak to the Murdoch press; and La Trobe University does not allege serious misconduct. Once again, the counterfactual illustrates that it is not the conduct of the employee that leads to disciplinary action. It is the conduct of others: often, bad-faith actors seeking to silence and punish an ideological adversary by pressuring their employer to sack them.

At the time, Ward was a prominent left-wing activist. Had a video of her addressing a Marxist conference or attending a political protest been disseminated, she was likely to have faced the same sort of campaign. As seasoned culture warriors can attest, it is relatively easy to foment outrage and target a political opponent in this way. A press release, a few noxious newspaper articles, and social media posts all put pressure on the employer and other 'stakeholders'.

Roz Ward was actually one of the lucky few. She tore up the script that had been laid out for her by her adversaries and the university. She worked in a university with a strong trade union presence and a collective commitment to academic freedom. The union's collective agreement recognised her 'right to participate in public debate about political and social issues and to express unpopular or controversial views'. She was not left at the mercy of a non-negotiable employment contract. Within days of her suspension, a campaign in support of Ward erupted, garnering 10,000 signatures on a petition calling for her reinstatement. The obligatory 'We Stand with Roz Ward' Facebook page was launched.

I represented Ward and her union, the National Tertiary Education Union. When I gave Ward my obligatory lecture about the need to look after her mental health in the face of the public attacks on her, she looked at me with what could have passed for mild contempt. It was as if to say, 'You think that this is the worst that I've encountered?' We sprung into action, preparing to seek an urgent injunction to save Ward's job. On 3 June 2016, I despatched a letter to the university, threatening to apply for an urgent injunction compelling the university to withdraw the suspension and disciplinary proceedings. The letter alleged that it had breached the collective agreement and anti-discrimination laws protecting political expression. In part, the letter said:

> Constraining Ms Ward's right to express a political opinion because of the unreasonable and unfounded reaction of particular sections of the media, and the public to that opinion stifles public debate, gives in to fear and ignorance. It is the antithesis of … academic freedom that La Trobe professes to value.

As the deadline for a response approached a few days later, the university caved in, dropping the disciplinary investigation and allowing Ward back to work. On the day of her return to campus, Ward walked through a guard of honour of her supporters, adorned by rows of flags, holding up her clenched left fist. She addressed her supporters, telling them that, 'This is about more than me and my experience. Homophobia and transphobia are very much alive in young people's lives. We are trying to do something about it, but there are a lot of people trying to stop us from doing that work.'[4]

Ronald S Sullivan Jr, a law professor at Harvard Law School, was not so fortunate. He is among the most high-profile criminal-defence lawyers in the US. Sullivan represented American footballer Aaron Hernandez in his acquittal for a double homicide, and helped the family of Michael Brown reach a $1.5 million wrongful-death settlement with the city of Ferguson, Missouri. Sullivan also devoted much of his career to representing less-privileged defendants. In the wake of Hurricane Katrina, he helped free thousands of Louisianans who had been incarcerated for various offences without due process.

When Sullivan, the first African American faculty dean at Harvard, agreed to represent Harvey Weinstein in defending criminal charges in early 2019, students protested, including by circulating an online petition demanding that Sullivan resign as the faculty dean of Winthrop House. In response, Sullivan wrote an email to Winthrop residents, describing the importance of representing 'unpopular defendants'. Sullivan was verbally abused, and the residence where his family lived was vandalised with graffiti. A survivor of sexual assault whom Sullivan had helped in the past spoke to *The Boston Globe* in his defence, as did many of his colleagues at Harvard Law School.

A colleague of Sullivan's, professor Jeannie Suk Gersen, wrote:

> On the same day as the vandalism, Harvard announced that, in response to 'concerns about the impact of this decision on the support that students can expect to receive in the Winthrop community,' the College would undertake a 'climate review,' consisting of surveys and interviews of students, after which it would 'take actions, as appropriate'.[5]

A few days later, on 11 May, Rakesh Khurana, the dean of Harvard College, announced that Sullivan and his wife, Stephanie Robinson, would be leaving their roles as faculty deans:

> Over the last few weeks, students and staff have continued to communicate concerns about the climate in Winthrop House. The concerns expressed have been serious and numerous. The actions that have been taken to improve the climate have been ineffective, and the noticeable lack of faculty dean presence during critical moments has further deteriorated the climate in the House. I have concluded that the situation in the House is untenable.

Sullivan issued a dignified response, stating that:

> My decision to represent Mr. Weinstein sparked considerable discussion and activism around issues of sexual violence, the appropriate role and responsibilities of Harvard and its faculty in addressing those issues, and the tension between protecting the rights of those criminally accused and validating the experience of those who are survivors of sexual violence. My representation of those accused of sexual assault does not speak to my personal views on any of these matters.[6]

In fact, the experiences of Ward and Sullivan, in different universities on different continents, reflect the peculiar political and cultural maelstrom that is challenging the boundaries of speech both outside universities and within them. Ward's academic career was imperilled by right-wing politicians and the Murdoch media, which demanded that her employer punish her for her expression. Sullivan was brought down from within the institution by left-wing students contemptuous of the liberal shibboleth that those charged with crimes, no matter how unpopular, deserve legal representation. In both cases, the universities applied brand-management orthodoxy. Since both controversies, the situation has deteriorated for academics, particularly in the US.

The unique role of university academics

> Since the time of Martin Luther and Socrates, professors have been persecuted for their views — by state or religious authorities or by powerful interest groups who do not like dissenting views or uncomfortable truths.
>
> –Philip Altbach[7]

There are numerous categories of employees who, by reason of the circumstances of their work, enjoy less freedom of expression than does the general working population. The speech of Australian public servants, for example, is severely constrained by public sector legislation that, in effect, prevents them from communicating about politically sensitive matters. They do not enjoy freedom of speech even if they anonymise their social media commentary. Defence personnel, police officers, and intelligence agency employees are similarly restricted. In the US, public servants enjoy much stronger free speech protections, subsequent to Supreme Court rulings upholding their right to speak on matters of public interest.

On the other hand, academics are a rare breed in the labour market: employees who enjoy greater freedom of expression than just about any other category of employee. Their freedom is rooted in the history of universities and their unique place in liberal democracies.

Universities emerged in Europe from the 12th century as

autonomous institutions of higher learning. Hundreds of years before capitalist corporations were formed, universities were given corporate status to ensure their independence from church and state. The earliest universities pioneered the not-for-profit model with their own governance structures. Since the medieval era, the holy grail of universities has been to maintain their independence. Autonomy meant the ability to determine those who make up their academic ranks, to determine the content and manner of its teaching, and to choose who may study. The holy grail remains tantalisingly distant because, as universities repeatedly experience, funding—whether sourced from government, the private sector, or philanthropic organisations—is rarely granted unconditionally.

Founded in 1810, the University of Berlin is widely credited with having provided the model for many contemporary European and Western universities. The university was founded by Wilhelm von Humboldt, a diplomat, philosopher, linguist, and educational reformer who was committed to a humanist combination of research and study of the arts and sciences that would produce 'well-informed human beings and citizens'. Von Humboldt is also credited with creating the modern notion of academic freedom, arguing that teaching and research should be undertaken by scholars in universities that were free from political or religious influence.

The Humboldtian ideal focused on the freedom of professors to teach in their classrooms and to do research in their direct areas of expertise, but did not include the freedom to express views outside those areas. In the 19th century, German academics, including socialists and political dissidents, were disciplined and excluded.

Although the two notions are often conflated, academic freedom differs from freedom of speech because it extends to conduct in the form of research and teaching. Liberal democratic theory posits that academics should be free to rigorously conduct research and teaching in order to further knowledge and education. That freedom also extends to publicly communicating their research and to challenging intellectual orthodoxy. Academic freedom also encompasses the right to criticise the university and its governance in pursuit of these ideals. A further dimension, which is more contentious, is the right of academics to express opinions outside their sphere of expertise. The latter category aligns more with the conventional notion of freedom of speech. It is sometimes also described as 'free intellectual inquiry'.

The 1957 Murray Report, arguably the founding document for the modern university in Australia, commented:

> Here is one of the most valuable services which a university, as an independent community of scholars and inquirers, can perform for its country and for the world. The public, and even statesmen, are human enough to be restive or angry from time to time, when perhaps at inconvenient moments the scientist or scholar uses the licence which the academic freedom of universities allows him, and brings us all back to a consideration of the true evidence and what it may be taken to prove.
>
> … the best guarantee that mankind can have that somebody, whatever the circumstances, will continue to seek the truth and to make it known. Any free country welcomes this and expects this service of its universities.[8]

Academic freedom is legally recognised in different forms and to varying degrees in a number of countries, including the UK, Canada, New Zealand, and the US. In 1988, hundreds of universities worldwide signed onto the Magna Charta Universitatum. The charter declared that a university's 'research and teaching must be morally and intellectually independent of all political authority and economic power'. Similarly, the UK's *Education Reform Act 1988* conferred on academics the right to 'question and test received wisdom and to put forward new ideas and controversial or unpopular opinions without placing themselves in jeopardy of losing their jobs or the privileges that they have'.

In 1997, the General Conference of the United Nations Educational, Scientific and Cultural Organization adopted a recommendation concerning the status of higher-education teaching personnel, expressing 'concern regarding the vulnerability of the academic community to untoward political pressures which could undermine academic freedom', and asserting 'that the right to education, teaching and research can only be fully enjoyed in an atmosphere of academic freedom and autonomy for institutions of higher education and that the open communication of findings, hypotheses and opinions lies at the very heart of higher education and provides the strongest guarantee of the accuracy and objectivity of scholarship and research'.[9]

In February 2021, the Australian parliament legislated a definition of academic freedom for the first time. The term was defined broadly to encompass:

- the freedom to teach, discuss, and research;
- the freedom of academic staff and students to engage in intellectual inquiry, to express their opinions and beliefs, and to contribute to public debate about their study and research;
- the freedom of academic staff and students to express their opinions about the higher-education provider in which they work; and
- the freedom of academics and staff to participate in representative associations and bodies.

The National Tertiary Education Union has negotiated many collective agreements with Australian universities that confer rights on staff to protect academic freedom. One such agreement states that, 'The University promotes and protects Academic Freedom of Expression, as set out separately in University Policy.' The policy promises 'to preserve, defend and promote the traditional principles of academic freedom ... so that all scholars at the University are free to engage in critical enquiry, scholarly endeavour and public discourse without fear or favour.'

In effect, academics are paid to challenge the status quo, a vocation that will always threaten those with power, whether they are politicians, church leaders, or business leaders. Professor Jason Stanley writes that, 'The University educator is thus tasked with presenting their students with intellectually rigorous foundational challenges to tradition; that is the role of education in fostering autonomous thought. Fulfilling this mission will always threaten those in power, and that is why academic freedom is the University's core principle.'[10]

Controversies about the boundaries of academic speech have a lengthy history. US academic Irwin Polishook wrote that at the end of the 1890s, professors and presidents of American colleges were being dismissed 'for advocating free trade and greenbacks, participating in a Populist Convention, speaking against organised monopolies, favouring free silver, opposing imperialism and delivering a pro-labour speech'.[11] In 1900, Jane Stanford, the widow of Leland Stanford and Stanford University's sole trustee, directed its president to dismiss a prominent economist, Edward A. Ross, because he advocated abandoning the gold standard and restricting immigration in ways that were both racist and inconsistent with Leland Stanford's past railroad interests.

Academic freedom was championed by the American

Association of University Professors. Its 1915 'Declaration on Principles of Academic Freedom and Tenure' proclaimed the right of faculty to pursue and share knowledge without fear or favour, and was expanded in 1940, proclaiming that faculty are entitled to 'full freedom in research and the publication of the results'; 'freedom in the classroom in discussing their subject' (provided they avoid introducing unrelated 'controversial matter[s]'); and freedom from 'institutional censorship or discipline' when they 'speak or write as citizens', with the admonition that they should be accurate, restrained, and respectful of 'the opinions of others'.[12]

Nevertheless, in the first half of the 20th century, governments in both the US and Australia pressured universities that employed pacifist academics to sack them. In Russia during the 1930s, Stalin condemned the teaching of genetics as 'bourgeois pseudoscience'. Subsequently, thousands of Russian biologists were sacked, jailed, or killed. 'The reality that their knowledge may have helped prevent a tragic famine was not more important to Stalin than that their understanding of genetics contradicted government doctrine'.[13]

The McCarthyist witch hunts that swept through US universities in the 1950s also damaged the careers of left-leaning academics in Canada and Australia. McCarthyism also produced successful legal challenges. In 1954, New Hampshire economics professor Paul M Sweezy became the target of a state investigation into whether he had engaged in 'subversive behaviour'.[14] Sweezy, a Marxist, was suspected of membership of the Communist Party, and was interrogated by the New Hampshire attorney-general. During the interrogation, he refused to answer questions about his lectures and academic writing. He was sentenced to jail for 'contempt', a finding that was appealed to the US Supreme Court. The court overturned the conviction, prompting an eloquent defence of academic freedom, with Justice Felix Frankfurter stating:

> In a university knowledge is its own end, not merely a means to an end. A university ceases to be true to its own nature if it becomes the tool of Church or State or any sectional interest. A university is characterized by the spirit of free inquiry, its ideal being the ideal of Socrates—'to follow the argument where it leads'. This implies the right to examine, question, modify or reject traditional ideas and beliefs. Dogma and hypothesis are incompatible, and the concept of an immutable doctrine is repugnant to the spirit of a university. The concern of its scholars is not merely to add and revise facts in relation to an accepted framework, but to be ever examining and modifying the framework itself.[15]

In order to safeguard academic freedom, academics have enjoyed greater security of employment than most others in the labour market. The logic is simple and compelling: if academics are to pursue their profession rigorously, they must enjoy greater protections from dismissal. The forms of academic tenure vary significantly, but for those academics who enjoy it, it has operated to strongly limit the circumstances of dismissal for cause. However, as neoliberal politics have impacted universities, fewer academics are afforded tenure.

Protecting the right of employees to engage in controversial speech and secure employment are antithetical to the imperatives of brand-driven corporations. Brand management and academic freedom are mortal enemies.

The neoliberal academy

> To survive and prosper in rapidly changing world, universities must embrace the marketplace and become customer-focused, business enterprises.
>
> –Jan Currie[16]

The neoliberal project that swept developed economies in the 1980s heralded the end of an era of free university education in Australia. In 1987, federal government funding for tertiary education was halved and was replaced by the imposition of student fees and a student debt–repayment scheme. In 1990, the federal government introduced full fees for international students at Australian universities, and the sector was never the same again.

Australian universities were encouraged to fill the deficit in government funding by diversifying their revenue sources, including by maximising the enrolment of full fee–paying international students. Decades later, higher education is now a lucrative big business. It has also become Australia's third-largest export industry after coal and iron ore, attracting billions in revenue from international students. In 2019, the-then vice-chancellor of the University of Melbourne, Glyn Davis, likened the business of attracting international students to 'a mining boom'. Along the way, Australia's public universities have also moved into property development and financial services as they manage approximately $60 billion in assets.

The Enlightenment concept of the university as a public good has been replaced by the corporate university: an enterprise whose primary concern is with market share, global rankings, maximising economic return, suppressing labour costs, and gaining a competitive advantage in the 'Global Knowledge Economy'. Global competition between universities is fierce — for students, staff, grants, and the highest rankings. Academics James Guthrie and Adam Lucas argue that:

> Over the last three decades, however, university executives have been empowered by state and federal legislation to transform Australia's public educational institutions into for-profit property

development and investment vehicles. This has enabled the reshaping of universities into autocratic institutions that are unethical in their treatment of staff and students.[17]

The profile of the university labour market now closely apes that of a large corporation. At the top of the pyramid are highly remunerated vice-chancellors and CEOs, often earning sums in excess of $1 million annually. In 2022, the salaries of Australian vice-chancellors inched up past the $1.5 million mark, with Michael Spence at the University of Sydney pocketing $1.53 million, and the former University of Melbourne vice-chancellor Glyn Davis, $1.59 million. Australian vice-chancellors earn approximately double the salaries of their UK counterparts. The astronomical salary packages are rationalised in much the same way as is private sector CEO remuneration: the industry is said to operate in an internationally competitive market, and is increasingly complex. There is a hitch, of course. It's not-a-for profit corporation, and it still receives significant government funding.

Beneath the top tier are a raft of corporate managers covering operations, IT, marketing, human resources, and finance. The resulting managerialist culture involves 'incessant organisational restructuring, sharpening of incentives, and expansion in the number, power and remuneration of senior managers, with a corresponding downgrading of the role of skilled workers, and particularly of professionals'.[18]

Academics have been swept away from university governance. The few remaining academic staff representatives on university governing bodies are now a tiny minority, and are often treated with suspicion and disdain by management. These bodies, generally known as university councils, are supposed to exercise scrutiny over executive proposals and decisions. In practice, executives play a major role in selecting and appointing most members of council, who therefore have no incentive to disagree with executive decisions, and who are often not given sufficient information about major decisions by their executives to make informed judgements.

And then there are the brand managers. Since 2005, the numbers of marketing and public relations staff employed by British universities has increased nine times as fast as the number of academics.[19] The extraordinary devotion to brand management reflects the competition for lucrative international students and philanthropic donations. In the words of seasoned brand manager Ian Pearman even back in 1990, 'Wherever the target audience of an organisation faces a choice of alternative competitors, branding is incredibly important for justifying price, avoiding commoditisation, attracting and retaining talent and ultimately, resisting rivals. So a properly constructed brand is essential for any university competing in the modern global education market.'[20]

In 2014, Monash University ('are you monash-minded?') employed 130 staff for admissions, campaign management, channel management, marketing analytics, marketing communications and student recruitment, sales management, strategic communications, and brand services. A new brand identity ('make a bigger impact') was launched in 2017, and in the words of the university, 'The new brand identity, positioning and architecture are reinforcing its top-tier status in Australia.' University brand campaigns have even spawned 'University or Beer', a game in which participants guess whether marketing slogans comes from a beer manufacturer or a university brand campaign. The slogans include:

(a) Reach For Greatness
(b) Be Part of It
(c) Life beckons—choose wisely
(d) Change Your Life. Start here.

(e) Start your adventurous journey

(f) Dare to be different

The neoliberal transformation has produced a rapidly shrinking minority of tenured academics. A report published by the Australian Learning and Teaching Council in June 2008 found that all Australian universities depend heavily on sessional teaching staff, who were defined as 'any higher education instructors not in tenured or permanent positions, and employed on an hourly or honorary basis'.[21] Casualisation has accelerated since then. In late 2016, *The Guardian* reported that 53 per cent of academics performing teaching or research in British universities were retained on insecure work arrangements. In Australian universities, it's worse. A recent report has revealed that a record 69 per cent of staff are employed as casuals or on short-term contracts. The wealthiest university in the country, the University of Melbourne, employs a staggering 73 per cent of its staff on precarious forms of work.[22]

In 2013, I represented two long-serving academics working in Curtin University's Centre for Marine Science and Technology. The academics had worked under a total of 41 consecutive fixed-term contracts, despite having worked continuously for periods ranging from 15 to 20 years. Research engineer Frank Thomas worked at Curtin University under 17 consecutive fixed-term contracts. Research associate Amos Maggi was employed on 24 consecutive fixed-term contracts between 1993 and 2013. When the researchers were terminated in 2013, they missed out on a significant payout because the university argued that they had merely ended their period of fixed-term employment and therefore had not been made redundant.

At least Thomas and Maggi had a roof over their heads. University of London English lecturer and PhD student Aimee Le was unable to stay in her London flat when the rent was increased in 2016. She ended up living in a tent outdoors for two years while teaching and completing her PhD. It is difficult to exercise academic freedom while living in a tent. Le had been unable to obtain a secure academic job since completing her PhD in 2018.[23]

Mary-Faith Cerasoli has been reduced to 'sleeping in her car, showering at college athletic centers and applying for food stamps', *The New York Times* recently reported. Is she unemployed? No, in fact, she is a college professor—but an adjunct one, meaning she is hired on a short-term contract with no possibility of tenure. In 2020, half of American academics were adjunct professors on short-term contracts. According to the American Federation of Teachers, 25 per cent of adjuncts receive some form of public assistance, while 40 per cent can't meet basic expenses.

The precariat at universities are routinely underpaid for their hours of work, and many young, precariously employed academics are not paid at all for all of their hours of labour. In recent years, Australian universities have been repeatedly exposed for the illegal underpayment of casual staff. In June 2022, a Senate committee report revealed that at least 21 of Australia's 40 universities have been implicated in the underpayment of their staff. Less than a year later, in February 2023, a report released by the National Tertiary Education Union revealed that higher-education workers across Australia had been underpaid by $83.4 million over the three years from 2020 to 2023, with the University of Melbourne having underpaid $31.6 million during that period. The underpayment of precariously employed academics had clearly become an entrenched feature of the university business model and culture.

Managing the university brand

Months after his attempt to sack Roz Ward for her Facebook post about the Australian flag failed, La Trobe University's vice-chancellor,

John Dewar, courageously submitted to an interview with journalist and fellow academic Russell Marks. Dewar claimed to have acted against Ward as a means of protecting the Safe Schools program from further right-wing attacks. He had taken advice from in-house lawyers and other managers before charging her with serious misconduct and suspending her. He did not anticipate the ferocity of the counterattack.

As Marks wrote:

> The discursive world that the crisis inhabited, for Dewar, was the world of employment contracts, funding agreements and codes of employee conduct. The crisis may have begun on the pages of *The Australian*, but for the vice chancellor its resolution lay in managerialism.[24]

As managerialism has run rampant, so too has the reach of policies imposed on academic and other staff. As Carolyn Evans and Adrienne Stone observe, 'Many Australian universities have policies or guidelines that allow for action to be taken against staff who undermine the reputation of the university without regard to protecting academic freedom'.[25] In 2019, a federal government-commissioned report into academic freedom, the French report, observed that 'many ... higher education rules and policies use broad language capable of impinging on freedom of expression' by regulating conduct that shows a 'lack of respect' or is 'prejudicial to the good order of the University'.[26]

At the University of Melbourne, staff are required to 'not intentionally cause serious risk to the reputation or viability of the university consistent with their employment obligations'. At Flinders University, staff are required to consider the impact of social media commentary on the reputation of the university.

At the same time, universities promote their commitment to academic freedom. At James Cook University (JCU), the code of conduct blends both into a heady mix, conferring on staff the rights and duties to, among other things:

- behave with intellectual honesty;
- value academic freedom and freedom of speech, and enquire, examine, criticise, and challenge in the collegial and academic spirit of the search for knowledge, understanding and truth;
- have the right to make public comment in a professional, expert, or individual capacity;
- have the right to freedom of expression provided that their speech is lawful and respects the right of others;
- behave honestly, impartially with integrity in a way that upholds the values of the University; and
- treat fellow staff members, affiliates, students, and members of the public with respect and courtesy, and have regard for the rights and needs of others.

Once again, it is not possible for academics to observe all these duties at the same time. The obligation to 'behave with intellectual honesty' may involve a lack of courtesy or diminish the good reputation of the university. Views that are honestly held and expressed may offend others or become highly controversial, upsetting government, corporate, or philanthropic donors. In those circumstances, the policies authorise disciplinary action for failing to uphold the good reputation of the institution. An academic who publicly questions or criticises a university's treatment of its students or the quality of its teaching may be acting consistently with the highest ideals of academic freedom, and yet at the same time may face disciplinary action for damaging the brand.

The inevitable collision between academic-freedom rights enshrined in union collective agreements and university codes of conduct is at the heart of several recent legal challenges by academics who were sacked for espousing controversial views in Australia.

A series of disputes between dissident academic physicist Peter Ridd and JCU attracted considerable notoriety after the university sacked him for serious misconduct. In April 2016, JCU issued Dr Ridd with a formal censure after it found he had breached its code of conduct by sending an email to a journalist that accused other academics at the university of promoting 'bad science' and of circulating misleading statements that exaggerated the effects of climate change on the Great Barrier Reef.

In November 2017, JCU issued Dr Ridd with a second and final censure after determining that he had breached the code by making comments during a Sky News interview that JCU found had damaged its reputation and had denigrated and damaged the reputation of its 'stakeholders'. Dr Ridd was also censured for failing to maintain confidentiality regarding the disciplinary process. Ridd's status as an academic who criticised the scientific consensus on climate change and who was disciplined for comments made on Sky News guaranteed his martyr status among the Murdoch press and right-wing politicians.

In May 2018, JCU terminated Dr Ridd's employment for serious misconduct, including for breaching its code of conduct, by failing to treat others 'with respect and courtesy' in his public discussion of his research. Ridd's sacking became a cause célèbre among climate science conspiracists. Like Israel Folau, he was able to assemble an expensive legal challenge through crowdfunding.

In Ridd's case, the Federal Court observed that JCU's code-of-conduct standards 'are couched in vague and imprecise language. They do not readily provide clear guidance to staff as to whether particular conduct might breach the obligations outlined in the Code of Conduct ... Reasonable minds may differ about whether particular conduct in fact breaches the obligations on any given occasion.'[27]

The court's observations could equally be made of all codes of conduct and workplace policies that apply to millions of employees.

Ridd's case was ultimately appealed by the university to the High Court, which described academic freedom as 'a defining characteristic of universities and like institutions' and a foundational principle 'upon which the University is founded'. It explicitly asserted the right of academics to *not* act with respect or courtesy, finding that 'the purpose of intellectual freedom must permit of expression that departs from those civil norms'. The court found that the code of conduct should be subordinated so that 'intellectual freedom is not qualified by a requirement to afford respect and courtesy in the manner of its exercise'. While a prohibition upon disrespectful and discourteous conduct in intellectual expression might be a 'convenient plan for having peace in the intellectual world', the 'price paid for this sort of intellectual pacification is the sacrifice of the entire moral courage of the human mind'.[28] As a result, the court found that the censure given to Dr Ridd was not justified. However, Ridd's appeal against his dismissal was ultimately unsuccessful, as he had breached a range of other obligations, including a lawful direction to maintain confidentiality over the disciplinary investigation into his conduct.

In May 2019, Dr Gerd Schröder-Turk, a mathematics academic, appeared on the Australian Broadcasting Corporation's flagship current affairs program, *Four Corners*, to blow the whistle on Murdoch University's mistreatment of international students. Schröder-Turk was an elected staff representative on the university Senate, and had witnessed with growing unease the consequences of a dramatic increase in the enrolment of international students at his university: in 2017–18 there had been a 92 per cent increase in international students. Schröder-Turk was one of three academics at the university who were interviewed on the program and who expressed concerns about how international students with poor English skills were being enrolled, and about how pressure was being applied on academics to pass the students. Schröder-Turk told *Four Corners*:

> I've got very serious ethical concerns about the way the practices that we're applying in the international students' recruitment space. I'm concerned both about the welfare of the students and the wellbeing of the students, as well as about the academic integrity, or the problems related to academic integrity that result from this …
>
> Admitting students who don't have the right qualifications, or right prerequisites, or correct language capabilities is setting them up for failure …[29]

The retaliation was immediate. The university's chancellor, David Flanagan, circulated a resolution among Senate members seeking to remove Schröder-Turk from the university Senate. I was retained to represent Schröder-Turk, and sent an urgent letter, alleging that the retaliation was unlawful and demanding that the resolution be withdrawn. The university agreed to postpone its consideration of the resolution.

Within days, Schröder-Turk commenced legal proceedings against Murdoch University, seeking orders to stop the university from removing him from the Senate and upholding his right to academic freedom. This was only possible with the support of the National Tertiary Education Union (NTEU). Several weeks later, Murdoch University doubled down by adopting the same approach to whistleblowers as a multinational corporation would employ. It issued a multi-million-dollar counterclaim for damages against the academic, claiming that his public commentary had caused a substantial loss of international student revenue. This counterattack was designed to intimidate and distress the gently spoken maths professor. It worked. Schröder-Turk was traumatised by the fear that he might be bankrupted.

The move to personally sue a whistleblowing academic garnered headlines around the world, galvanising academics into action. The hashtag #IStandWithGerd was born. A petition in support of the academic quickly garnered 40,000 signatures, including from many distinguished academics. A visiting professor at the university, Robert Cribb, resigned in protest, calling the university's lawsuit a 'dangerous and uncollegial persecution of a principled academic colleague'.

A letter from 50 prominent academics sent to the university read in part, 'It is a long-established principle of academic freedom that academics must be able to criticise university governance. This right is especially important where aspects of university governance might compromise the integrity of teaching and research. The claim for damages is highly intimidatory to all Australian academics and therefore risks the capacity of Murdoch University and all Australian universities to pursue excellence in research and teaching.'[30]

The NTEU's national president, Dr Alison Barnes, said, 'The Associate Professor is the academic staff member elected by his peers to be a member of the university Senate. This continued attempt to silence the academic voice sends a chill through the entire higher education system, because academics must be involved in university governance at the highest levels.'[31]

As a result of the public pressure, the university eventually relented and dropped the retaliatory lawsuit. Months later, the university and Schröder-Turk resolved the whistleblower-protection case. The university permanently withdrew the motion to remove Schröder-Turk from his position as staff representative on the Senate, all litigation was resolved, and the university released the following statement: 'Associate Professor Schröder-Turk remains a valued member of both the Murdoch University academy and of the Murdoch University Senate.'

One of the reasons that US academics are more likely to be sacked for their expression is the lack of strong collective action. In September 2019, Jamie R Riley was forced out of his role as assistant vice-president and dean of students at the University of Alabama after the racist website *Breitbart* highlighted some of his old social media posts. Prior to joining the university, Riley had tweeted that the American flag 'represents a systemic history of racism for my people. Police are a part of that system. Is it that hard to see the correlation?' Within days of the hostile *Breitbart* coverage, the assistant director of the Division of Strategic Communications at Alabama University announced that Dr Jamie Riley had resigned his position at the university 'by mutual agreement'.

Shortly before another academic, Ilya Shapiro, was to take up an appointment with Georgetown University as executive director of its Center for the Constitution in February 2022, he tweeted in support of his preferred candidate for the vacant position on the US Supreme Court. His preferred candidate was Sri Srinivasan, a male judge of South Asian descent. Shapiro expressed his beliefs provocatively and offensively. He tweeted that, 'Objectively best pick for Biden is Sri Srinivasan, who is solid prog & v smart ... Even has identity politics benefit of being first Asian (Indian) American. But alas doesn't fit into the latest intersectionality hierarchy so we'll get lesser black woman.'

When Shapiro realised that some who read his tweet had interpreted it as suggesting that black women judges were racially inferior, he deleted it and apologised for his 'inartful phrasing'. He explained that he meant only that every other jurist, of any race, would be a lesser nominee than Srinivasan. Too late. Screenshots of the deleted tweet circulated on Twitter, tagging Georgetown University. Students protested and launched a petition. The law school 'suspended' Shapiro even before he started work, pending an investigation by its Office of Institutional Diversity, Equity and Affirmative Action into whether he had violated the university's policies on Equal Opportunity and Non-Discrimination in Employment and Education, and its Policy Statement on Harassment. The investigation took months before concluding that Shapiro was not guilty, as the policy did not apply to him prior to becoming an employee. Nevertheless, the report concluded that Shapiro's comments 'denigrated individuals based on race, gender, and sex,' that they 'had a significant negative impact on the Georgetown community', and that 'if he were to make another, similar or more serious remark as a Georgetown employee, a hostile environment based on race, gender, and sex likely would be created'. The investigation was a performance in brand management, theatrically playing to the crowd.

Following his reinstatement to the job that he had yet to commence, Shapiro resigned, explaining that the reality that a single ambiguously phrased comment followed by an apology and a deleted tweet could constitute the creation of an unsafe university climate made 'a laughing stock of the educational mission of the university to grapple with difficult ideas'. He added, 'I regretted the hurt that people felt. I never want to hurt people. And I certainly regretted the error in communication.'[32]

Concern for the 'wellbeing' of students informed the decision of Hamline University in Minnesota to sack adjunct professor Erika López Prater in January 2023. The art academic had included two images of a 14th-century painting depicting the Prophet Muhammad in a lesson on Islamic art, prompting a Muslim student in the class to complain. The course syllabus contained a warning about the images. López Prater also warned the class immediately before showing the depiction of the Prophet Muhammad. López Prater was to teach students about the 'rich diversity' of attitudes toward such imagery.

Hamline University responded to the student complaint by publicly condemning the class as 'disrespectful and Islamophobic' before terminating Prater, prompting a campaign to reinstate her by PEN America, the American Association of University Professors, and a former president of the university. University president Fayneese Miller staunchly defended the dismissal, stating that 'Prioritizing the well-being of our students does not in any way negate or minimize the rights and privileges assured by academic freedom.' Prater has issued legal proceedings, challenging her dismissal.

A free speech crisis on campus?

On 20 April 1968, British MP Enoch Powell gave his notorious 'Rivers of Blood' speech at a meeting of the Conservative Political Centre in Birmingham, warning against continued immigration to the United Kingdom. 'As I look ahead, I am filled with foreboding; like the Roman, I seem to see "the River Tiber foaming with much blood"', he declared. Powell had been prompted to make the speech in opposition to the Labour government's introduction of the *Race Relations Act 1968*, a new law that sought to outlaw racial discrimination in housing, employment, or the provision of public services. Powell's speech was widely condemned in the UK parliament and media for inciting racial hatred and violence.

British university students vented their fury at Powell in a series of angry demonstrations. In the years that followed, opposition to the Vietnam War and apartheid in South Africa grew on campus.

By 1974, the National Union of Students had embraced a policy of 'no platforming' of racists and fascists. Debate between the right and the left raged about universities, free speech, and no platforming, much as it continues to this day. In 1986, the Thatcher government legislated to require universities to take 'reasonable steps' to ensure freedom of speech on their campuses.

In the 21st century, academics around the world are finding their careers imperilled by authoritarian and fascist governments seeking not only to silence dissent, but also to dismantle entire fields of scholarship, all while brandishing their commitment to free speech. Education remains a source of power and influence, and therefore a threat to autocratic or fascist political movements at any time. That time is now for countries such as Russia, Hungary, Turkey, and Poland. The shift to authoritarian and fascist tendencies is also evident in the US and, to a lesser degree, among the right in Australia and the UK. A professor of philosophy at Yale University, Jason Stanley, argues that 'fascist politicians target professors they deem too political', and that universities that teach marginalised perspectives are particular targets: 'Fascism is about the dominant perspective, and so, during the fascist moments, there is strong support for figures to denounce disciplines that teach perspectives other than the dominant ones—such as gender studies or, in the United States, African American studies or Middle Eastern studies.'[33]

US political scientist Jeffrey Sachs assessed all cases of academics fired or forced to resign, arising from their exercise of political speech, between 2015 and 2017 in US non-profit tertiary institutions. Of the 45 cases, a clear majority lost their jobs for expressing 'liberal' views. Twenty-six faculty members lost their jobs in 2017, 19 of whom had expressed liberal views, including those criticised for being 'anti-white' or 'anti-Christian'. Conservative academics were targeted for expressing hostility to minorities and diversity initiatives.

In early 2019, President Trump signed an executive order requiring colleges and universities that received government funding to extend free speech protections on campus. In that same year, Trump's education department ordered Duke University and the University of North Carolina at Chapel Hill to 'remake' their Middle East studies program to include more positive depictions of Christianity and Judaism. In 2020, he signed an executive order banning publicly funded universities from holding diversity training that included any mention of 'systemic racism', 'intersectionality', or 'racial humility'.

Since then, the situation in the US has markedly deteriorated. Legislation banning the teaching of 'critical race theory' has been passed by Republican-dominated state legislatures, including Florida, Idaho, Oklahoma, Texas, New Hampshire, and Arizona. More Republican states are getting on board. The new laws ban any messaging to the effect that the US is inherently racist, and prohibit discussion of conscious and unconscious bias, privilege, discrimination, and oppression. The legislation also extends the ban to schools. The dangerous authoritarianism that is sweeping red states in the US is even fanning attacks on public libraries and librarians. In August 2022, reports emerged that a public library in Michigan was facing closure after a right-wing group launched a campaign to defund it. The campaign was generated by the presence of 90 books dealing with LGBTI matters — representing .015 per cent of its collection.

Since 2013, successive conservative governments in Australia have used the levers of power to compromise university autonomy and to suppress research, teaching, and academic freedom. In 2018, the-then minister for education, Simon Birmingham, overrode a peer-review selection process for highly competitive Australian Research Council grants. All grants vetoed by the minister were for research in the humanities. Australian Academy of the Humanities president Joy Damousi condemned the 'political interference' that undermined 'confidence and trust' in Australia's world-leading peer-review system and the 'incalculable effect' of the veto on the academics concerned. In July 2020, as the coronavirus pandemic decimated university balance sheets, the federal government announced an increase in fees for students taking arts degrees of 113 per cent.

At the same time, students aggressively brandishing identity politics and citing their concern for student safety, seemingly without irony, are seeking the scalps of academics who they see as transgressing red lines. The National Tertiary Education Union, which has been instrumental in defending academic-freedom rights, including in successfully overturning disciplinary action against academics in the courts, finds itself caught in the middle of a toxic conflict between trans-inclusive and gender-critical feminists. The former have sought to shut down gender-critical studies, research, and speech, and have called for the sacking of gender-critical academics, arguing that they are peddling unacceptable hate speech and transphobia. Attempts by the NTEU to support the academic freedom of gender-critical feminists have been met with fierce condemnation.

Undoubtedly, this wave of political activism has an impact on the culture of universities, and has muted and silenced expression. Whether academics are cancelled is not to the point. A growing cohort are inhibited from engaging in discussion about transgender issues for fear of the consequences. That speaks of a repressive culture that can't be denied.

The Israel–Hamas conflict that erupted in October 2023 has wreaked havoc on university campuses worldwide, unleashing a wave of protests, sackings, blacklistings, and fear. One of the first to be sacked was Michael Eisen, a genetics professor at UC Berkeley and the editor of the scientific journal *eLife*. Eisen was forced out of his job after reposting an article from the satirical magazine *The Onion* challenging the view that people should not criticise Israeli actions unless they first condemn Hamas. *The Onion* headline read: 'Dying Gazans Criticized for Not Using Last Words to Condemn Hamas'. Eisen, who is Jewish and has Israeli relatives, posted that *The Onion* 'speaks with more courage, insight and moral clarity than the leaders of every academic institution put together'. His post attracted criticism and controversy, including from Israeli scientists who labelled him a 'self-hating Jew'. The critics targeted the journal's major funders in their campaign against Eisen. The journal then posted on X:

> **eLife - the journal**
> @eLife
>
> eLife condemns the atrocities committed by Hamas last week. We wish to highlight that, while the opinions of eLife staff and editorial board are their own, they are covered by our code of conduct. We take breaches of this seriously and investigate accordingly
>
> 7:40 AM · 10/14/23 from Earth · **27.6K** Views

The journal's board asked Eisen to retract his tweet. He was reluctant to do so, but instead deleted his Twitter account. Then Eisen was given the choice of resigning or being fired.

He announced that he was being fired. Deputy editors, senior editors, reviewing editors, and one board member resigned in protest at the board's action. An open letter to *eLife* from researchers protesting his firing gathered nearly 2,000 signatures.

Weeks later, Eisen said, 'I think that they panicked and were overwhelmed by a Twitter mob and didn't function properly, and made a stupid decision in their tweet, and they made a bad decision in deciding to replace me under those terms. I think they did more damage to *eLife* than my tweet possibly could have.'

Eisen is also a rarity: a progressive who subscribed to the fashionable view that cancel culture doesn't exist, but who has now changed his mind. He acknowledges that, 'What happened with me, and with lots of other people, is that organizations don't like being involved in controversies', and that by setting the bar so low, in which 'you're only one political expression away from being fired', great harm is inflicted on free speech.[34] Amen.

The removal of Eisen is part of a wave of sackings and blacklistings in the wake of Hamas's slaughter of Israeli civilians on 7 October 2023 and Israel's retaliatory slaughter, killing tens of thousands of Palestinian civilians.

In late November 2023, research by the US Foundation for Individual Rights and Expression found that pro-Palestinian speech was more likely to get an academic disciplined or fired, while campaigns targeting pro-Israel speech had been more likely to succeed in de-platforming speakers.[35]

In 2024, universities around the globe were under enormous pressure as the protest movement against Israel's actions in Gaza grew. The situation has been likened to the student movement against the Vietnam War, particularly after thousands of pro-Palestinian protestors were arrested in the US in early May. Universities were at the forefront of a ferocious debate about the distinction between political protest and hate speech, particularly anti-Semitism. The conflict and ensuing protest movement spawned a wave of sackings of academics and blacklistings of students. It also produced an inversion of free speech orthodoxy on both the left and the right. Left-wing progressive activists who have led the anti-war movement have dismissed calls to tone down their slogans and rhetoric just because it makes pro-Israel supporters unsafe. For many, this is a radical departure from their previous advocacy for restrictions on teaching or permitting speakers on campus that hold views that make others feel subjectively unsafe. And let there be no doubt: Jewish students on campus who strongly identify with Israel have experienced great distress. The reasons for that distress are complex, but the feeling of being unsafe is real.

Those supporting the Israeli assault on Gaza and opposing the pro-Palestinian protest movement, many of whom profess to be free speech absolutists, have also reversed gear. At the instigation of US Republicans, on 1 May 2024, the US Congress passed legislation that would incorporate the International Holocaust Remembrance Alliance's definition of anti-Semitism in the Civil Rights Act of 1964, a federal anti-discrimination law that bars discrimination based on shared ancestry, ethnic characteristics, or national origin. It is unclear whether the Senate will follow suit.

This definition of anti-Semitism is deployed to silence criticism of Israel and its human rights record. In June 2024, former Israeli prime minister Ehud Barak condemned the government's 'goal of establishing a racist, ultranationalist, messianic and benighted religious dictatorship'.[36] Like many other Jews who are critical of the slaughter in Gaza, Barak would stand condemned as anti-Semitic under the IHRA definition. The deception involved in applying that definition doesn't end there: if the IHRA definition were to be applied to the anti-Apartheid movement targeting South Africa in decades past, it would characterise that successful campaign as anti-white Boer racism.

And yet, for all of tumult engulfing universities, the greatest threat to academic freedom is ignored: the proverbial elephant in the room. The neoliberal transformation of universities has eliminated academic tenure for more than 50 per cent of academic staff in many universities. In their place—whether in Europe, the US, or Australia—are precariously employed staff. In 2021, a UNESCO and International Labour Organization joint report on the state of higher education highlighted the 'international trend' of the increasing number of staff on fixed-term and temporary contracts in academia. The report said that these contracts 'undermined tenure' and 'weaken the full exercise of academic freedom and therefore, one of the fundamental pillars of excellence in teaching and research'.[37]

An academic sleeping in a tent or working a succession of insecure employment contracts is effectively silenced. The debate about academic freedom and freedom of speech fails to acknowledge that a majority of academics have no freedom to lose—their voice has been pre-emptively cancelled by the precarious terms on which they are employed. In a recent underpayment prosecution by the Australian workplace regulator, the Fair Work Ombudsman, the University of Melbourne was accused of refusing to pay two casual academics for hours that were worked outside those stipulated in their contracts. One academic was reportedly told by a manager that if she claimed payment for additional hours, 'Don't expect work next year.' Precariously employed academics are too frightened to express dissent or to challenge the status quo for fear of jeopardising their quest for tenure and career. It is too easy for a university to simply not renew a casual, part-time, or fixed-term contract.

The fate of the thousands of insecurely employed university employees echoes that of their counterparts working in major corporations. They toil at the bottom of the workplace hierarchy, and their voices are censored. In that part of the labour market, the worst abuses occur. Their fate is also a reminder that when we debate free speech, the choice of whose speech we argue about is deeply political.

CHAPTER SEVEN

The Journalism Paradox

> Professional news reporting is not easy. Its place in the world is still young—it really cannot be said to have existed in a full-bodied way for much more than a century. That's not a long stretch. But at its best, it has proved itself a bulwark of accountable democratic government and a thorn in the side of autocrats around the world.
>
> –Michael Schudson[1]

In May 2021, the US's Associated Press (AP) sacked Emily Wilder just two weeks into her new role as a news associate. Shortly after her sacking, Wilder stated, 'There's no question I was just cancelled.'[2] The AP claimed that a series of Wilder's pro-Palestinian tweets had violated its social media policy, which prohibited journalists from expressing opinions on news topics. 'Emily Wilder was let go because she had a series of social media posts that showed a clear bias toward one side and against another in one of the most divisive and difficult stories we cover,' said Brian Carovillano, the AP's managing editor.[3]

Before joining the AP, Wilder who is Jewish, was an active member of Stanford Students for Justice in Palestine at Stanford University in California. She was a proponent of Palestinian human rights, and a critic of the Israeli government. During the height of the 2021 Israel–Hamas conflict, she tweeted: '"Objectivity" feels fickle when the basic terms we use to report news implicitly stake a claim. Using "israel" but never "palestine," or "war" but not "siege and occupation" are political choices—yet media make those exact choices all the time without being flagged as biased.'

Two days earlier, the Israeli military had blown up the AP's office in the Gaza Strip, claiming that the Palestinian militant group Hamas had been operating out of the same high-rise building.

Wilder's ruminations about journalistic objectivity prompted a group of Stanford College Republicans to take to Twitter, attacking Wilder's pro-Palestinian activism while she was a student there, and condemning her as an 'anti-Israel agitator' who was responsible for promoting a 'blood libel' against her fellow Jews. *The Washington Free Beacon* then published an article headlined, 'AP Hires Anti-Israel Activist as News Associate: AP's objectivity in question amid revelations it shared office space with Hamas'. It republished her old tweets. That story was picked up on other forums, including Fox News. The campaign against Wilder was then amplified by conservative politicians and media personalities, including Ben Shapiro. The online mob duly descended. Wilder's safety was imperiled as she received an avalanche of violent, misogynist, racist, and anti-Semitic threats and abuse.

In defending its sacking of Wilder, AP management explained in a blog post that, 'Journalists' safety is at stake and the AP's credibility is at stake. Our credibility is constantly under attack. Our social media guidelines exist to protect that credibility, because protecting our credibility is the same as protecting journalists.' Wilder's colleagues at AP didn't accept the company's professed concern for their safety. Instead, they rallied in support of her. Wilder's union at AP (and the broader News Guild) called for her to be re-employed. More than 100 AP reporters signed an open letter to management protesting at their failure to protect staff from online harassment.

In the wake of her sacking, Wilder released a statement (on Twitter). It read in part:

> Last Monday, the Stanford College Republicans launched a smear campaign against me, attempting to 'expose' my already-public history of activism for Palestinian human rights at Stanford University ... my editors ... reassured me that I would not face punishment for my previous activism. I was told my editors were only hoping to support me as I received an onslaught of sexist, antisemitic, racist and violent comments and messages.
>
> Less than 48 hours later, the AP fired me. The reason given was my supposed violations of AP's social media policy between my first day and Wednesday. In that interim, powerful conservatives like Tom Cotton, Ben Shapiro and Robert Spencer repeatedly lambasted me online ... I am one victim of the asymmetrical enforcement of rules around objectivity and social media that has censored so many journalists ... What does it mean for this industry that even sharing the painful experiences of Palestinians or interrogating the language we use to describe them can be seen as 'irredeemably biased'?

'Amazing how quickly a talented young reporter's career can be snuffed out by a Twitter mob that decided to feign outrage over some college tweets,' *The Washington Post*'s Glenn Kessler observed.

As Wilder implicitly identified, she was not sacked for breaching a policy. She was sacked to mute a ferocious, partisan political campaign to punish her for her political activism as a student at Stanford University. AP sacked her to manage the brand. Even if a breach of the AP social media policy occurred, her sacking was a grossly disproportionate response. She was 22 years old, and two weeks into a very junior new role and career. Little did Wilder know, but her experience was a hint of what was to come just two years later when war erupted between Hamas and Israel.

Seven months later, in Australia, *The Sydney Morning Herald* fired Elizabeth Farrelly, a 30-year veteran of the newspaper with a passion for urban development and the environment. Farrelly had registered as a candidate for the Labor Party in the Strathfield local government election, and had not disclosed her registration to her employer. She claimed that the omission was an oversight. The newspaper stated that, 'Elizabeth's registration as a Labor candidate should have been disclosed to us and our readers …', adding that, 'Her registration makes future contributions very difficult given the close connection between urban development and politics.'[4]

Like academics, journalists occupy an unusual position in the labour market—both are employed in industries whose role is considered essential for a healthy democracy. Both work in pursuit of facts and the truth in roles that require them to challenge powerful interests and the status quo. But while academics enjoy enhanced democratic freedoms, including the freedom to speak out on controversial issues, journalists are in a different position.

Paradoxically, many journalists are required as a condition of working for news outlets—both privately owned and state-owned—to forgo many fundamental rights of democratic participation. The ideals of fairness, objectivity, and impartiality are invoked in support of the rules that severely restrict the human rights of their journalists. The rules forbid journalists from expressing political opinions, stating their political affiliations, and even participating in demonstrations. In effect, journalists exchange their rights to fully participate in civic life in order to enhance democracy. Some journalists, including *Washington Post* executive editor Len Downie and ABC journalist Virginia Trioli, don't vote at elections in deference to journalistic objectivity and impartiality.

While much corporate regulation of employees' out-of-hours expression is brand-driven and weakens democracy, the situation for the media industry is far more complicated. A respectable argument can be mounted that for serious news outlets which conform to 'journal of record' principles, their mission is undermined by the actual or perceived bias and partisanship of their journalists. It may be a respectable argument, but it's far from a settled orthodoxy. It is apparent that many journalists are hostile to the attempts to curtail their speech. There is considerable confusion both among journalists and the corporations that employ them about who should be restricted and what the restrictions require. And, like other businesses, the rules are often selectively and capriciously enforced, in response to dubious online shaming campaigns.

It's also apparent that newspaper corporations can cancel their employees not so much in the service of democracy, but to manage the brand.

The objectivity question

Unlike academia, the profession of journalism is relatively young. Universities carved out their unique role centuries before journals of record came into being. While academic freedom is an established feature of liberal democracy, being recognised in legislation, collective-bargaining agreements, and university policies, the rules of engagement in journalism are much more brittle. The two professions are also distinguishable by the complete absence of barriers to entry for journalists and the significant differences in approach to journalism among media companies.

The phrase 'journal of record' was coined by Adolph Ochs, an early proprietor of *The New York Times*. Ochs is credited with establishing the principle of objective reporting, writing in 1896:

> It will be my earnest aim that The New-York Times give the news, all the news, in concise and attractive form, in language that is parliamentary in good society, and give it as early, if not earlier, than it can be learned through any other reliable medium; to give the news impartially, without fear or favor, regardless of party, sect, or interests involved; to make of the columns of The New-York Times a forum for the consideration of all questions of public importance, and to that end to invite intelligent discussion from all shades of opinion.[5]

Ochs sensed a gap in the media market; to distinguish *The New York Times* from the 'yellow journalism' that dominated 19th-century newspapers. The term originated in the 1890s to describe *The New York World* and *The New York Journal*, both seeking to outdo each other with sensationalised stories of crime, good versus evil, and titillating sexual content. In the 19th century, many American newspapers also had strong party-political affiliations. Ochs sensed that he could craft a credible newspaper that appealed to Democrats and Republicans alike.

In 1893, US publisher Sam McClure established *McClure's Magazine*, employing a crack team of journalists, including Ida Tarbell, Ray Stannard Baker, and Lincoln Steffens. *McClure's* became famous for its in-depth exposés of the dark underbelly of the US during the Gilded Age. In doing so, it pioneered investigative journalism. McClure sent his writers on long, well-funded assignments of up to six months at a time, and directed them not to return until they had produced material of sufficient quality to 'shake the foundations'. For the next decade, the journalists produced lengthy, brilliant essays that exposed widespread corruption—monopolies that destroyed their competitors through illicit means, and the politicians bought off by those same companies—the endemic mistreatment of workers, and violence within the labour movement.

These investigative journalists, who were labelled 'muckrakers', saw themselves as crusaders for reform in the Progressive Era. President Theodore Roosevelt relied heavily on their exposés to push through a range of progressive reforms. When corporate interests called in favours with the Republican politicians who did their bidding in an endeavour to block Roosevelt's legislation, he relied on the journalists to expose their misconduct and shame the corrupt politicians into retreat. While the earliest investigative journalists relied on detailed, factual reporting, they were politically engaged reformists with no interest in a detached objectivity. That tension between tenacious investigative journalism and objectivity remains today.

Journalism scholar Jay Rosen traces the rise of journalistic objectivity to the 1920s and 1930s, when corporations started acquiring media assets and made a pact with their journalists. Under the agreement, journalists were permitted to report the news independently, provided they didn't insert their personal politics into their work. In 1935, Eugene Meyer, publisher of *The Washington Post*, promulgated 'Seven Principles for the Conduct of a Newspaper', an internal guiding document that included such principles as, 'In the pursuit of truth, the newspaper shall be prepared to make sacrifices of its material fortunes, if such course be necessary for the public good.' And, 'The newspaper shall not be the ally of any special interest, but shall be fair and free and wholesome in its outlook on public affairs

...' Meyer also distinguished between the public good and private interests of newspaper owners.[6]

Journalistic objectivity was successfully exported to the rest of the world. Nevertheless, criticism of the 'myth' of objectivity commenced soon after its inception. In its earliest incarnation, *The New York Times* was pro-business and reflexively supported the status quo. What was once considered sober and objective coverage of lynching in the 1890s failed 'to recognize a truth, that African-Americans were being terrorized across the nation.'[7] *Washington Post* scribe Alan Barth gave an address in 1952 to his peers, telling them that the way in which McCarthyism was 'reported in most papers serves Senator McCarthy's partisan political purposes much more than it serves the purposes of the press, the interests of truth'.[8] More recently, objectivity has been the cover for an egregious false balance — also known as 'both-sidesing' that has damaged journalism and the polity.

Even acclaimed journals of record around the world operate from a particular political perspective. The political leaning of many newspapers is not exactly a trade secret. *The Financial Times*, *Le Monde*, and *The New York Times* occupy a centre-left position. *The Wall Street Journal* and *The Spectator* occupy a conservative position. *The Australian* occupies a reactionary stance. *The Australian Financial Review* has close links to the Liberal Party and the Business Council of Australia.

Very few news outlets can lay claim to being purely journals of record. There has been a longstanding transformation away from event-based journalism towards opinion, analysis and commentary. Factual reporting is frequently fused with opinion and analysis. Many political journalists are followed for their commentary and analysis, and their political leanings can often be discerned. Then there is the commercial imperative. Increasingly, media outlets prize online clicks, which are often generated by content that is not generally sober and detached.

The frequent rationale invoked by news outlets for restricting journalists' civic rights is that the reputation of the masthead is harmed by any social media activity that demonstrates bias or partisanship. Promulgating rules to control the lives of journalists that are ostensibly directed at the objective or fair reporting of facts is problematic, when, as veteran American journalist James Fallows argues:

> Of course, taking a side is fundamental to the act of journalism. Everything we write or broadcast is something we're saying deserves more attention than what we're not discussing. The layout of a front page, in print or online; the airtime given to TV or radio reports; the tone and emphasis of headlines; and everything else down to the list of communication tools reflect choices. When we investigate and present exposés, we are taking a side in favor of the importance of these subjects, and the fidelity of our account.[9]

In rejecting objectivity in favour of what he calls a commitment to 'fairness and truth', journalist Wesley Lowery argued that journalists must provide readers with 'an assurance that we will devote ourselves to accuracy, that we will diligently seek out the perspectives of those with whom we personally may be inclined to disagree and that we will be just as sure to ask hard questions of those with whom we're inclined to agree'.[10]

Others, such as Canadian journalism academic Ivor Shapiro, argue that, 'Skepticism, not objectivity, is why democracies need journalists.'[11]

In the post-truth era and the second Gilded Age, the need for reliable and accurate information about the world around us has never been greater. But the traditional media are under assault from two different and destructive sources, both fuelling an age of extraordinary disinformation.

In the US, the UK, and Australia, the disinformation propagated by the Murdoch empire is an anti-democratic cancer, bringing to mind the chilling prophecy from publisher Joseph Pulitzer in 1904: 'A cynical, mercenary, demagogic press will produce in time a people as base as itself.' The Murdoch empire is a partisan political project, inverting the noble ideals of journals of record. It doesn't so much hold truth to power as shore up power with propaganda, and heap derision on the powerless. As a former News Corp director and son of Rupert, James Murdoch, stated, 'A contest of ideas shouldn't be used to legitimise disinformation … at great news organisations, the mission really should be to introduce fact to disperse doubt—not to sow doubt, to obscure fact …'[12]

The other major source of misinformation is social media, where almost anything goes.

While media corporations muzzle their journalists' speech and political expression by the imposition of policies and rules, there is increasing dispute about the legitimacy of their efforts. *The Sydney Morning Herald* and *The Age*, owned by Nine Entertainment, require their editorial staff not to 'editorialise, express personal biases, personally campaign or advocate for (or against) policies or do anything to undermine our reputation and stated objective of being "Independent. Always".'

That objective was spectacularly jettisoned in May 2019 when Nine Entertainment used its historic TV studios in the Sydney to host a $10,000-a-head corporate fundraiser for the Liberal Party. The event was hosted by Nine's CEO, Hugh Marks, and was attended by the prime minister, Scott Morrison, and other key ministers. The event was condemned by Nine journalists, who voiced their objection to 'independent journalism being compromised by the hosting of party-political fundraisers'. Neither Marks nor anyone else at Nine was disciplined for compromising the independence of the corporation.

The New York Times, *The Washington Post*, and the UK *Guardian* all promulgate social media policies embedded in their codes of conduct. *The New York Times*'s social media policy warns that, 'If our journalists are perceived as biased or if they engage in editorialising on social media, that can undercut the credibility of the entire newsroom.' *The Washington Post* has similar guidelines. In its policy, the *Post* says that, while using social media networks, 'nothing we do must call into question the impartiality of our news judgment'.

As Gabriel Snyder of the *Columbia Journalism Review* observed:

> The social media guidelines the *Times* demands its employees follow are vague, focused less on the content of a post and more on how it is read by others; the guidelines bar 'anything else that undercuts the *Times's* journalistic reputation' or that 'appear[s] to take sides on issues.' That means *Times* staffers do not have a clear way of knowing if they're committing a fireable offense before they press 'post'.[13]

As is apparent in other parts of the labour market, the rules are impossibly and deliberately vague. The *Times* staffers, like virtually every other employee, are left to try to intuit what they mean.

The uneasy state of play

Shortly after the election of Donald Trump as US president in 2016, Bérengère Viennot, a professional translator, published an essay in *Slate France* on the 'ethical' challenge that Trump posed for her translation of his comments to a French audience. Viennot observed:

> Trump is not easy to translate, first of all, because, most of the time, when he speaks he seems not to know quite where he's going ... He seems to hang onto a word in the question, or to a word that pops into his mind, repeating it over and over again. He shapes his thought around it and, sometimes, succeeds in giving part of an answer—often the same answer: namely, that he won the election. Trump seems to go from point A (the question) to point B (himself, most of the time) with no real logic. It's as if he had thematic clouds in his head that he would pick from with no need of a logical thread to link them.[14]

Viennot explained that translating Trump literally would befuddle French readers because French political leaders, regardless of their ideological leanings, were able to clearly articulate their thoughts. Such a proficiency was a base standard for French political life. And so Viennot was tempted to try to modify Trump's sentences to render them more coherent. Yet doing so involved deceit and an ethical betrayal.

Translating Trump to their audiences was ethically and professionally challenging for media companies and their journalists, too. The American people had elected an incompetent, incoherent, pathological liar with fascist tendencies to the most powerful office in the Western world. For several years, the truth was too confronting to convey. Many journalists refused to report Trump's lies; instead, they described them as 'untruths' because, they claimed, they couldn't see inside his head to determine if his lies were deliberate or not. It was only when the number of presidential lies exceeded 20,000 that the reporting began to change. All the while, Trump worked effectively to discredit and undermine trust in the media by his constant, strident attacks.

Journalists were also reluctant to report Trump's racism, as journalists Jon Allsop and Pete Vernon observed:

> In July 2019, after Trump tweeted that four Democratic Congresswomen of color (all bar one of whom were born in the US) should 'go back' to 'the totally broken and crime infested places they came from,' his remarks were described, variously, as 'racially infused,' 'racially charged,' and responsible for 'fanning the flames of a racial fire.' The language was so tortured that the *Daily Show* created a 'Trump Racist Euphemism Headline Generator' to parody it. ('Trump strolls along banks of eyebrow-raising racial misadventure.') [15]

As American democracy began to unravel, journalists employed by major news outlets rebelled against restrictions that the companies imposed on their speech. At the heart of the rebellion were questions of race and gender. In 2017, the #MeToo movement emerged. Several years later, Black Lives Matter protests erupted. Black journalists, among others, chafed at restrictions from news corporations that prohibited them from joining protest marches. Their activism and unrest prompted some extraordinary reactions.

The Washington Post took tried to restrict the online commentary of both its black and female journalists. An internal memo written about the newspaper's social media policy stated that, 'Expressing identity and personal experience can be particularly treacherous for certain reporters, as some aspects of personal identity are viewed as inherently political or controversial in our society, such as race and gender.' For 'race', the *Post* meant 'black'. The memo also described a 'two-tiered system', which meant that white male reporters were able to get away with more 'problematic' social media messages, 'while female and minority colleagues are not given the benefit of the doubt'.

The Washington Post was not up for challenging that expression of power. Instead, it banned its journalist Felicia Sonmez from reporting on sexual assault stories after she publicly disclosed a past experience of sexual abuse in 2018. The rationale for the ban was that her disclosure had created a perception of bias. The reality was different. Sonmez's disclosure had garnered right-wing attacks on her and her employer. The ban was a crude act of brand management.

Following the death of basketball star Kobe Bryant in early 2020, Sonmez tweeted a link to a newspaper article describing a rape allegation that had been made against Bryant in 2003. Sonmez made no comment about the newspaper article that she shared, but the response from Bryant's fans was swift and brutal. Sonmez received an enormous volume of online abuse, followed by death threats. Her home address was published online, and she went into hiding. In response, *The Washington Post* suspended Sonmez for breaching its social media policy. Marty Baron, the executive editor, wrote to Sonmez accusing her of a 'real lack of judgment' that had hurt the institution.

Her suspension outraged her colleagues, whose protests shamed the newspaper into reinstating her. A letter signed by *Washington Post* journalists to management accused the newspaper leadership of seeking to hide the unvarnished truth, stating, 'we believe it is our responsibility as a news organization to tell the public the whole truth as we know it—about figures and institutions both popular and unpopular, at moments timely and untimely.'[16] In this case, it was the journalists who exposed the newspaper for betraying its own professed standards by seeking to apply cynical brand-management strategies in response to criticisms, threats, and abuse directed at Sonmez.

Within a few months in 2020, the Black Lives Matter protests erupted on the streets of cities across the US, convulsing its newsrooms. Then, following the killing of George Floyd by police officer Derek Chauvin, *The New York Times* published an article by Tom Cotton, a Republican senator and ally of Donald Trump, titled 'Send in the Troops'. It called for the president to invoke the Insurrection Act of 1807 and to use US military forces to quell the protests.

In the days following its publication on 3 June 2020, numerous *New York Times* journalists protested at the decision to publish the article, arguing that it incited violence against people of colour and that it put 'black @nytimes staff in danger'. *The New York Times* responded by stating that the article 'fell short of our standards and should not have been published'. Its opinion editor, James Bennet, was compelled to resign. Following his resignation, *The New York Times*'s publisher, AG Sulzberger, said, 'We're not retreating from the principles of independence and objectivity. We don't pretend to be objective about things like human rights and racism.' Whatever view is taken of the removal of Bennet, Sulzberger was acknowledging the inevitable. Newspapers and their journalists make value judgements each day, with their judgements frequently having a political dimension.

More than 150 *Wall Street Journal* employees signed a letter in 2020 saying that they found 'the way we cover race to be problematic', while over 500 staff at *The Washington Post* endorsed demands for 'combating racism and discrimination' at the paper.[17]

Shortly after the attempted fascist insurrection on 6 January 2021 a tweet by *New York Times* journalist Lauren Wolfe brought her career to a halt. A news editor at the newspaper, Wolfe was watching the inauguration of Joe Biden on 20 January when she tweeted, 'Biden's plane landing at Joint Field Andrews. I have chills.' She also tweeted a criticism of Trump for having failed to provide a military plane for Biden, and then deleted it.

Her tweets elicited a strong online response, including accusations of liberal bias at *The New York Times*. Journalist Glenn Greenwald and Fox News commentator Brit Hume condemned her 'political bias'. Wolfe duly received the standard avalanche of revolting and violent threats. Wolfe claims that she then received a phone call from an editor advising that she was being fired over the 'chills' tweet. She argued that her tweet was being misread, as she was saying, 'I had chills, meaning after the attempted overthrow of our government, the nightmare we've all been through, I had chills watching the democratic process work.' For the record, the paper has since denied that Wolfe was fired for a single tweet, implying that there had been a history of policy contraventions by her. Either way, once again, firing an employee in this way was driven by the need to placate a mob acting in bad faith to suppress the voices of those they disagreed with. Wolfe's tweet caused no damage to *The New York Times*. Her firing did.

Wolfe has since had time to reflect on her sacking and her role as a journalist. In a post on her blog, *Chills*, she described the impossibility of not having a point of view; of not having biases. She argues that writing in a 'neutral voice' doesn't remove implicit bias, and that bias always guides the selection of stories that are published. As a journalist who had long written about war and human rights abuses, she acknowledged a quality shared with many of the best investigative journalists: she often wrote 'with an agenda—with an eye toward creating change'.

She added, 'I would describe the mission of my work the way ProPublica describes theirs: "To expose abuses of power and betrayals of the public trust by government, business and other institutions, using the moral force of investigative journalism to spur reform through the sustained spotlighting of wrongdoing."' Such a mission echoes that of the original muckrakers.

The media coverage of the Israel–Hamas conflict following the horrific slaughter of Israeli civilians inflicted by Hamas on 7 October 2023 has prompted a rebellion of journalists across multiple outlets across the globe, accusing their employers of bias. On 9 November, an open letter signed by over 1,000 past and present employees of US media outlets damned media coverage of the conflict, effectively accusing them of a longstanding pro-Israel bias. In some ways, the letter reflected the ruminations of Emily Wilder several years earlier.

Their letter urged 'an end to violence against journalists in Gaza', and called on 'Western newsroom leaders to be clear-eyed in coverage of Israel's repeated atrocities against Palestinians'. The letter attacked 'dehumanizing rhetoric that has served to justify ethnic cleansing of Palestinians', and stated that:

> Newsrooms have instead undermined Palestinian, Arab and Muslim perspectives, dismissing them as unreliable and have invoked inflammatory language that reinforces Islamophobic and racist tropes. They have printed misinformation spread by Israeli officials and failed to scrutinize indiscriminate killing of civilians in Gaza—committed with the support of the U.S. government.[18]

The *Los Angeles Times* responded by banning its staff from covering the Gaza war for at least three months.

A similar strongly worded letter signed by 53 journalists across major Australian media outlets criticised media coverage of the conflict. The letter damned the tendency to report Israeli government propaganda without sufficient scrutiny, suggested that civilian suffering in Gaza was being minimised by reporting and that media outlets were not covering the growing anti-war demonstrations in the country. The letter also demanded that journalists who had accepted all-expenses-paid trips to Israel should disclose these experiences when reporting on the conflict. A huge number of journalists, including those in senior editorial positions, have undertaken such trips. They were clearly embarrassed by the exposure.

In response, *The Sydney Morning Herald* put out a statement expressing pride in its coverage, 'which continues to abide by the highest standards of ethical journalism'. The statement added that 'newsroom staff who signed this latest industry letter will be unable to participate in any reporting or production relating to the war'.

Perhaps the most extraordinary response to the journalists' letter came from *The Guardian*. In early December 2023, its editors in the UK, the US, and Australia wrote to staff, stating:

> We know that a number of staff globally have signed open letters and petitions relating to the conflict. Although this may be well-intentioned, unfortunately it can be perceived as a potential conflict of interest that could hamper our ability to report the news in a fair and fact-based way. It has resulted in unwarranted scrutiny of *Guardian* journalism and accusations that our journalists and our journalism may be biased.

The Guardian's editors added that staff 'should not sign public petitions or open letters about matters that have, or could be perceived to have, a bearing on [the publication's] ability to report the news in a fair and fact-based way'. The statement accepted that journalists had a life outside work, provided that 'outside interests do not come into conflict with your role at the company'. Any staff defying the ban, which also extended to social media posts, would face 'appropriate action on a case by case basis'.[19]

The Guardian is an openly left-wing media outlet. Its political reporting and commentary largely and unapologetically support the British Labour Party, the Australian Labor Party and the

US Democrats. It is not a journal of record. Its most successful contribution to journalism is its brilliant opinion columns penned by journalists who rage against climate policy, Donald Trump, neoliberalism, racism, and sexism—both in their columns and on social media. Understood in this way, banning all staff from expressing an opinion on the Middle East, signing a petition, or engaging in other political activism when not at work was an extraordinary act of censorship. The staff directive did not distinguish between its opinion columnists, production staff, and other journalists. It applied across the board.

Public broadcasters and political pressure

Antoinette Lattouf's parents arrived in Australia in the 1970s as refugees, having fled Lebanon to avoid persecution by members of the Palestine Liberation Organisation. Many others lost their lives. Lattouf was born in 1983, and grew up in a working-class migrant family that experienced its fair share of hardship. She says that she survived and thrived because she was good at 'hustling'.

Her tenacity and charisma took her to university and then into the world of journalism with an activist bent, working across television, radio, print, and online. In 2017, she co-founded Media Diversity Australia to advocate for greater cultural diversity in the media. Two years later, she published her first book, *How to Lose Friends and Influence White People*, which she described as 'a guide through the balancing act of activist, advocate and ally'.

In December 2023, Lattouf was hired by ABC radio to fill in on a morning talkback show for one week while the usual presenter, Sarah Macdonald, was on leave. The brief was for her to be bubbly and light while the audience prepared for the Christmas holiday season. She was to talk about Christmas recipes and the looming holiday season.

After the third day of her five-day stint, Lattouf had a debrief with production staff, who were glowing in their feedback. A few minutes later, she was summoned to a further meeting with management, who told her that her stint was over because she had made a controversial post on social media about the war on Gaza. A shocked Lattouf was told to gather her belongings and go home. By the time that she got home, the news had broken that she had been sacked.

Prior to starting her stint at the ABC, Lattouf had expressed her opposition to the war on Gaza. She had also co-authored an article in *Crikey* casting doubt on reports that in the wake of 7 October, pro-Palestinian supporters in a Sydney protest had chanted 'Gas the Jews'. The *Crikey* article asserted that no such chant had occurred, although it reported that a small number of demonstrators had engaged in the anti-Semitic chant of 'Where are the Jews?'[20]

When Lattouf's upcoming role on ABC radio was first publicised, pro-Israel groups inundated the ABC with complaints alleging that she was anti-Semitic. Two WhatsApp groups, including one describing itself as 'Lawyers for Israel', orchestrated a campaign of complaints directed at the personal email addresses of the chair of the ABC board, Ita Buttrose, and its managing director, David Anderson. 'It is important ABC hears not just from individuals in the community but specifically lawyers so they feel there is an actual legal threat,' one of the lawyers wrote.

The complaints were referred to senior management. Lattouf was advised of the complaints before going on air. After a discussion about the issue, it was agreed that she could continue to post content from reputable sources, including human rights organisations such as Amnesty International.

On 18 December, Human Rights Watch published a report that asserted Israel was engaging in a war crime by using the starvation of civilians as a method of war in the Gaza Strip. It added that Israeli forces were deliberately blocking the delivery of water, food, and fuel while wilfully impeding humanitarian assistance that was essential to the survival of civilians. The ABC duly reported those claims.

Later, on 19 December, Lattouf shared a video from Human Rights Watch on her personal Instagram account, in which the organisation explained its report. Her post included the comment, 'HRW reporting starvation as tool of war'.

Subsequently, the ABC claimed that it took action against Lattouf for violating a direction 'not to post on social media about matters of controversy'.

The treatment of Lattouf aroused the ire of many of her colleagues at the ABC, culminating in a rare vote of no confidence in the ABC boss, David Anderson. The ABC board issued an emphatic statement in support of its management's actions. One of the broadcaster's most reputable journalists, global affairs editor John Lyons, reportedly told his colleagues that Lattouf's treatment marked 'one of [the ABC's] darkest days', adding that he 'was embarrassed that a group of 156 lawyers could laugh at how easy it was to manipulate the ABC'.

When I agreed to represent Antoinette Lattouf, I was labelled a 'traitor' by one of the Lawyers for Israel. Regrettably, she wasn't clumsily referring to my fondness for French cuisine.

As I write, the legal dispute continues. Strangely, the ABC has emphatically denied that it succumbed to public pressure. That denial continues even after the ABC unsuccessfully argued that it did not sack Lattouf, but instead merely 'varied her duties to nil'. At hearings before the Fair Work Commission, ABC management confirmed that Lattouf had not breached its social media policy and that a direction not to post controversial material had not, in fact, been given to her.

Through it all, Lattouf remains resolute, pledging to fight 'for as long as it takes'.

Contrary to the denials, the ABC had applied brand-management orthodoxy: it panicked and capitulated to a loud mob. It established a new, invidious benchmark for panicked brand managers: Lattouf was sacked for posting a fact.

Within months of these events, the ABC's political editor, Laura Tingle, attended the Sydney Writers' Festival and participated in a panel discussion about politics. In the course of a discussion about recent policy announcements by opposition leader Peter Dutton, Tingle stated that, 'We are a racist country, let's face it. We always have been, and it's very depressing.' The comments were leapt on by the Murdoch media, which ritually heaped scorn on the ABC over more supposed evidence of its left-wing bias. In response, the ABC put out a statement which detailed that she had been 'counselled' over her comments.

Tingle is also a staff-elected board member of the ABC and a member of the board that backed its sacking of Lattouf.

Following hot on the heels of the Tingle controversy, new ABC chair Kim Williams criticised the federal opposition's recently announced policy embracing nuclear energy. Williams, himself a panellist at Sydney's Vivid Festival, described the new nuclear policy as 'a sound bite, with no detail as to emissions targets', and lacking the 'normal fabric of policy formulation'. He stated that he was not speaking on behalf of the ABC, but in his capacity as an Australian citizen. Williams' defence of his right to free speech, to comment on matters of public policy and to fully participate in democracy in his capacity as a citizen, was powerful. However, it is a defence that is routinely denied to employees of the organisation that he chairs and to millions of other employees across the labour market, in the service of the corporate brand.

What are the governing principles for public broadcasters? The United Nations Educational, Scientific and Cultural Organization describes public service broadcasting as:

> broadcasting made, financed and controlled by the public, for the public. It is neither commercial nor state-owned, free from political interference and pressure from commercial forces. Through [public service broadcasting], citizens are informed, educated and also entertained. When guaranteed with pluralism, programming diversity, editorial independence, appropriate funding, accountability and transparency, public service broadcasting can serve as a cornerstone of democracy.

The British Broadcasting Corporation was created in 1922 promising to operate as the 'interrogator of democracy'. The Australian Broadcasting Corporation commenced broadcasting on 1 July 1932. Both organisations are required by law to operate in accordance with stringent standards, and have adopted guidelines and rules that regulate the lives of their staff.

The BBC principles emphasise 'due impartiality', rather than objectivity, stating that:

> 4.2.1 We must do all we can to ensure that 'controversial subjects' are treated with due impartiality in all our output.
> 4.2.2 News in whatever form must be treated with due impartiality, giving due weight to events, opinion and main strands of argument.
> 4.2.3 We seek to provide a broad range of subject matter and perspectives over an appropriate timeframe across our output as a whole.

The ABC Act requires its board to 'ensure that the gathering and presentation by the Corporation of news and information is accurate and impartial according to the recognized standards of objective journalism'.

It has a sophisticated set of editorial policies that includes a commitment to 'fundamental democratic principles including the rule of law, freedom of speech and religion, parliamentary democracy and equality of opportunity'. News and editorial staff are required to:

> 4.1 Gather and present news and information with due impartiality.
> 4.2 Present a diversity of perspectives so that, over time, no significant strand of thought or belief within the community is knowingly excluded or disproportionately represented.
> 4.5 Not unduly favour one perspective over another.

The policies implicitly acknowledge the impossibility of objectivity, noting that we all have 'different values and particular perspectives on disputed facts and issues. Objectivity in this context means testing information through disciplined, evidence-based, open-minded and fair journalism'.

The ABC's social media policy states that its employees' personal social media activity must not damage the ABC's reputation for impartiality and independence, mix the professional and the personal in ways likely to bring the ABC into disrepute, or imply ABC endorsement of their personal views:

> There is, of course, particular sensitivity for ABC staff working in news and current affairs, where the need to demonstrate impartiality and independence on all newsworthy and topical issues means it is almost always inappropriate to offer opinion on such matters.

In October 2020, the BBC issued a new set of social media guidelines that are some of the most repressive in the media industry. They apply to all BBC employees, including non-journalists, though they permit employees who work outside news and current affairs and factual journalism to attend marches, demonstrations, and protests as private individuals:

> Members of staff outside News and Current Affairs and some Factual output may attend marches, demonstrations and protests as private individuals.
>
> Staff are also able to participate in some parades, marches or gatherings, including events such as trade union rallies, under the banner of the BBC group to which they belong, but not representing the organisation as a whole.
>
> BBC News and Current Affairs staff and some Factual staff, as set out in the Guidelines, should not participate in public demonstrations or gatherings about controversial issues. As with social media, judgement is required as to what constitutes a controversial march or demonstration. If in doubt, advice should be sought before attending.

David Jordan, the BBC's director of editorial policy and standards, reportedly told a meeting of senior executives that the new rules included not attending 'political protests', such as Black Lives Matter events and LGBTI rights protests. Subsequently, he clarified that there was 'no ban on attending pride parades'. That too was qualified by this statement that, 'Attending Pride parades is possible within the guidelines, but due care needs to be given to the guidance and staff need to ensure that they are not seen to be taking a stand on politicised or contested issues.'[21]

The BBC's social media guidelines invoke a right-wing term of abuse in compelling all staff to 'avoid virtue signalling' and stating their personal views, 'no matter how apparently worthy the cause'. Such a directive would require staff to refrain even from expressing support for the Red Cross online.

The onslaught

Both the BBC and ABC are powerful institutions, wielding considerable cultural influence. They consistently rate highly as trusted sources of news and information, and stand as a bulwark against the neoliberal shibboleth that the market will always provide a superior product. Their investigative journalism has exposed scandalous misconduct by powerful individuals and organisations. They pose a commercial threat to commercial media organisations and to corrupt and authoritarian politicians.

In both the UK and Australia, conservative political parties and the Murdoch media have railed against the public broadcasters since the 1980s, deluging them with complaints of 'left-wing bias'. In Australia, conservative governments, which have been in office for 20 of the last 26 years, have engineered funding cuts, job cuts, program cuts, the stacking of the ABC board with right-wing apparatchiks, multiple inquiries and dubious reviews, boycotts of particular journalists or programs, the installation of a new breed of management, and a raft of recruits from the Murdoch ranks. The crusade has not let up. In June 2018, the Liberal Party Federal Council passed a resolution calling for the full privatisation of the ABC.

The BBC has suffered a similar fate. It has been starved of funds, and stacked with right-wingers, including former Conservative cabinet ministers and political advisers. Research carried out at Cardiff University in 2013 concluded that the BBC 'tends to reproduce a Conservative, Eurosceptic, pro-business version of the world, not a left-wing, anti-business agenda'.[22]

Prior to becoming a special adviser to prime minister Boris Johnson, Dominic Cummings was a conservative activist and think tank executive. Cummings was director of the New Frontiers Foundation in 2004 when it called the BBC the 'mortal enemy' of the Conservative Party and called for the establishment of a British equivalent to Fox News. During the 2019 election campaign, Johnson threatened to abolish the BBC's licence fee, arguing that it was a general tax that could no longer be justified.

Tim Davie, the BBC's director-general, is a former Conservative local council candidate. The previous BBC chair, Richard Sharp, is a former banker and one of the Tory Party's most generous benefactors. His appointment was recommended by a government-appointed panel. The panel included a Conservative Party donor and prospective Tory MP, as well as the wife of the former chair of *The Spectator* who worked with Boris Johnson. The government advised the selection panel that Sharp was the only candidate that it would support.

Sharp lasted just over two years in the job. In April 2023, he resigned after it was revealed that he had assisted in the process that led to Boris Johnson obtaining a secret, substantial loan. An investigation by the UK commissioner of public appointments found that Sharp had failed to declare his link to Johnson's loan, creating a 'potential perceived conflict of interest'.

The decades-long right-wing crusade against both public broadcasters has severely diminished both organisations, and has shifted their presentation of news and information to the right. As the cultural revolution within both broadcasters has unfolded, 'both-sidesing' (also known as 'false equivalence') has bled into hard-news reporting. Under the Morrison government, ABC journalists were pressured to 'balance' their reporting of government misconduct. Journalists faced disciplinary action if they breached impartiality requirements by factually reporting Coalition scandals. How do you report both sides of the corrupt misuse of taxpayer funds, gross negligence, or a blatant prime ministerial lie? There isn't a good answer, and nor should there be. Impartiality is not a quest for balance. It's a quest for truth.

At the same time, the regulation of employees' lives and the enforcement of its standards bear the same patterns observed in the private sector. Breaches of relevant standards are ignored or downplayed if they don't generate conservative political attacks and the flooding of the complaints process.

The public got a rare insight into internal ABC politics in September 2018 when it was revealed that the-then ABC board chair, Justin Milne, had fielded government complaints about two prominent journalists, including Emma Alberici. Milne texted the ABC's managing director, Michelle Guthrie, stating:

> They fricken hate her. She keeps sticking it to them with a clear bias against them. We clear her as ok. We r tarred with her brush. I just think it's simple. Get rid of her. My view is we need to save the corporation not Emma. There is no g'tee they will lose the next election [sic].

Alberici survived, but was made redundant several years later.

Not working in an editorial role is not enough to save a career. When an ABC in-house lawyer, Sebastien Maury, labelled Australian prime minister Scott Morrison a 'fascist' in a tweet, it was seized on by the Murdoch press and government politicians as evidence of ABC bias, and a disciplinary investigation ensued. Maury resigned before he was pushed.

On the other hand, Chris Uhlmann was appointed as the ABC's political editor in 2015, and during his tenure became a right-wing culture warrior—with impunity. Uhlmann penned a bizarre article for the Murdoch press invoking the anti-Semitic trope of cultural Marxism, in which he argued that neo-Marxist academics who fled Hitler's Germany had spread the 'intellectual virus' of critical theory in the US 'and set about systematically destroying the culture of the society that gave them sanctuary'.[23]

Uhlmann also repeatedly railed against the adoption of renewable energy. On 27 September 2016, a ferocious storm struck South Australia, delivering 80,000 lightning strikes and winds of up to 260 kilometres per hour, bringing down 22 power transmission towers. Much of the state experienced a blackout. Within hours of the storm hitting, Uhlmann went to air on the ABC nightly news bulletin, asserting that South Australia was too heavily reliant on intermittent wind power and that its wind turbines weren't working because the wind was 'blowing too fast'. In fact, the truth was far more complex and took months to determine. The investigation by the Australian Energy Market Operator found that the intermittency of wind was not a factor in the blackouts, but that overly sensitive turbine control-settings had contributed. Those flawed settings have since been changed.

While Uhlmann's right-wing culture-warrior antics attracted public criticism, the ABC took no apparent action to rein him in because his key messages echoed those of conservative politicians. Uhlmann has since left the ABC to become a political commentator for News Corp's Sky News Australia.

In April 2022, it was reported that ABC *Weekend Breakfast* presenter Fauziah Ibrahim maintained an online list of 'Labor Trolls/ Thugs' and 'Lobotomised sh**heads' that included prominent ALP politicians Tanya Plibersek and Doug Cameron. Ibrahim returned to air after a month-long 'break from on-camera duties'.

A number of highly talented ABC journalists, including Virginia

Trioli, Annabel Crabb, and Julia Baird, are involved in prosecuting feminist politics through books, commentary, and MCing gigs. Within weeks of Antoinette Lattouf's sacking, ABC journalists were posting about their participation in demonstrations against gendered violence. Arguably, such activity is inconsistent with the requirement to remain impartial, and yet none of these journalists have been disciplined. There is no suggestion that they are anything but professional in their ABC work, but, along with many others, they routinely breach the rules with impunity.

For good reason, the ABC has lost its reputation for the fearless pursuit of the truth. We only see a fraction of what goes on. Several years ago, one journalist described in detail to me how several news stories that were embarrassing to the-then Morrison government were left on the cutting-room floor after 'an intervention'. While it continues to produce outstanding content, staff are scared and intimidated. Consciously or otherwise, they censor their work and their lives outside work, especially involving subjects that might trigger the Murdoch media and conservative politicians into callout mode — subjects such as climate change mitigation or progressive social or economic policies. As another senior ABC journalist told me, 'We know one misplaced word, and it's lights out.'

Similar currents swirl around the BBC. In August 2022, former BBC journalist Emily Maitlis delivered the MacTaggart Memorial Lecture at the Edinburgh TV Festival. Her speech condemned the culture of fear within the institution created by repeated accusations of left-wing bias. She expressed regret that it had intimidated her from fearless truth-telling while being employed to anchor *Newswatch*. She revealed how she had been disciplined for an introduction she had delivered to a *Newswatch* programme in 2018, during which she had recounted that Boris Johnson's then key adviser, Dominic Cummings, had brazenly violated Covid-19 rules. This prompted a complaint from 10 Downing Street to the management of BBC News, which responded virtually instantaneously:

> What was not foreseen was the speed with which the BBC sought to pacify the complainant. Within hours, a very public apology was made, the programme was accused of a failure of impartiality, the recording disappeared from iPlayer, and there were paparazzi outside my front door.[24]

She went on to describe Sir Robbie Gibb, a BBC board member, as 'another active agent of the Conservative party—former Downing Street spin doctor, and former adviser to BBC rival GB News … as the arbiter of BBC impartiality.'

In April 2023, the BBC confronted an extraordinary backlash after its decision to suspend its popular football commentator Gary Lineker. The broadcaster had reacted to complaints made over a tweet posted by Lineker condemning a new hardline government policy on immigration that promised to turn back asylum seekers arriving by boat. The policy and rhetoric that accompanied its announcement by Prime Minister Rishi Sunak were replicas of Australia's controversial boat-turnback policy. Lineker condemned the policy, posting that, 'There is no huge influx. We take far fewer refugees than other major European countries. This is just an immeasurably cruel policy directed at the most vulnerable people in language that is not dissimilar to that used by Germany in the 30s …'

After complaints were made about Lineker's intervention by right-wing journalists and government MPs, he was required to 'step back' from his role on the popular *Match of the Day* program. The expression 'step back' is a brand-managed phrase meaning 'suspended'. The BBC asserted that Lineker's tweet had breached its social media rules.

Lineker's suspension prompted other BBC presenters, including Lineker's co-hosts, to withdraw their services, resulting in chaotic changes to television and radio programming. Many sports players also expressed their support for Lineker's free speech by boycotting BBC program interviews. Other BBC staff weighed in to support Lineker's democratic right to express views about political issues, and a petition to reinstate him garnered 200,000 signatures within days. The backlash became so fierce that the BBC's director-general, Tim Davie, faced calls for his resignation. Prime Minister Sunak sought to distance himself from the matter, apparently fearing a broader revolt against his new immigration policy.

Lineker survived and returned to air after several days of suspension. Crucially, he was not forced to withdraw his stated views. The BBC announced a review of its guidelines on social media and 'impartiality', but it is too soon to herald the dawn of a new era of workplace democracy. Lineker's views on human rights and immigration struck a chord at a time when the conservative British government was languishing in the polls. Had he expressed an unpopular opinion, the outcome may have been different.

Nevertheless, the uncertainty about what the staff of public broadcasters are allowed to say and do remains endemic. The ambiguity of their policies provides a potent recipe for confusion and the arbitrary regulation of journalists' lives. The notion of impartiality is discredited by the ritualistic overreaction to disingenuous right-wing campaigns that are designed to weaken and discredit the institution. In such an environment, producing journalism that is fearless and independent is dangerous. Instead, the culture gravitates to producing stories that will not upset right-wing crusaders. The moral of the story is that if you campaign systematically and flood the organisation with complaints, you shape the speech that the broadcaster produces.

CHAPTER EIGHT

Consensual Sex and Work

In 1921, Roscoe 'Fatty' Arbuckle was an American silent-film comedian with 'magical comic timing', a mentor to Charlie Chaplin and an actor at the height of his powers. His films were so successful that he was the first Hollywood star to earn $1 million per year. In 1918, Arbuckle signed a three-year contract with Paramount Pictures worth $3 million—the modern-day equivalent to about $160 million.

Arbuckle liked to party. On 5 September 2021, he and two friends, Lowell Sherman and Fred Fishback, checked into the St Francis Hotel in San Francisco, hiring several rooms, including one reserved for entertainment. That night, Arbuckle's career came crashing down after he was arrested and charged with the rape and murder of actress Virginia Rappe—a guest at a lavish party hosted by Arbuckle.

Throughout the saga, Arbuckle vigorously denied the charges. He claimed that he had found Rappe writhing in pain on the floor when he had gone to use his bathroom. He claimed to have carried her to the bed and later discovered that she had then fallen off it onto the floor. Her condition deteriorated, and she was taken to hospital. Three days later, Rappe died in hospital from peritonitis caused by a ruptured bladder. At the trial, it emerged that Rappe had long suffered from chronic cystitis.

Almost overnight, and in spite of his repeated protestations of innocence, Arbuckle was transformed from the darling of Hollywood into a widely reviled figure. Innuendo and rumour swamped him, amplifying the scandal. It was widely rumoured that Arbuckle, a large and heavy man, had pinned Rapke down and violently raped her, thereby rupturing her bladder. The sensational headlines and stories about Arbuckle, Rappe's death, and the moral depravity of Hollywood presented the US film industry with its first scandal 'with box office implications'.[1]

The drama continued in the courts. The charges against Arbuckle went to trial on three occasions. The first two trials ended in hung juries. At the third trial in 1922, he was acquitted, with the jury issuing an extraordinary statement, which read:

> Acquittal is not enough for Roscoe Arbuckle. We feel that a great injustice has been done to him ... There was not the slightest proof adduced to connect him in any way with the commission of a crime ... The happening at the hotel was an unfortunate affair for which Arbuckle, so the evidence shows, was in no way responsible. We wish him success and hope that the American people will take the judgment of fourteen men and women who have sat listening for thirty-one days to the evidence that Roscoe Arbuckle is entirely innocent and free from all blame.[2]

The jury's emphatic acquittal was to no avail. The episode dogged Arbuckle, and he was blacklisted by the film industry for over a decade. He tried to continue work as a scriptwriter under a pseudonym. In 1933, Warner Bros offered Arbuckle his first feature film role since the acquittal. Later that day, he died from a heart attack. He was 46 years of age.

In response to the loss of such a major commercial asset, the big Hollywood studios prepared new contractual obligations, described as 'morals clauses', which they insisted had to be included in their employment contracts with movie stars, producers, and writers. A sample morals clause read:

> The Actor shall conduct himself with due regard to the public conventions and morals. The Actor shall not, either while rendering such services to the producer or in his private life, commit an offense involving moral turpitude under Federal, state or local laws or ordinances. The Actor shall not do or commit any act or thing that will tend to degrade him in society or bring him into public hatred, public disrepute, contempt, scorn, or ridicule, or that will tend to shock, insult or offend the community or public morals or decency or prejudice the producer of the motion picture, theatrical or radio industry in general.[3]

Such provisions cast a wide net, giving the studios complete discretion to terminate a contract when their talent attracted public controversy. In effect, morals clauses banned employees from engaging in contentious behaviour—whether by word or deed. The employees were required to live their lives so as not to 'shock' or 'offend' the community, or cause prejudice to their employer or the entertainment industry in general. What might degrade an actor in society or bring them into disrepute, scorn, or ridicule was unclear, but was inevitably anchored in the politics and social mores of the day. Morals clauses enabled Hollywood studios to despatch movie stars who transgressed without the need to compensate the sacked employee. Lucrative contracts could be terminated by the studios with no recourse when it became convenient for the studio to do so.

The sexual morality of that era was also reflected in the Hays Code, a code of conduct developed by the Motion Picture Producers and Distributors of America, and introduced in 1934. The code provided that, 'No picture shall be produced which will lower the moral standards of those who see it', and forbade scenes depicting 'nudity', 'suggestive dances', 'lustful kisses', and 'scenes of passion'.

Morals clauses operated to suppress the sexuality of Hollywood actors and, in particular, homosexuality. The studios used private investigators to monitor the private lives of their talent and their compliance with morals clauses. Armed with incriminating evidence of nefarious activities, they could decide whether to try to safeguard the employee or cut them loose. If it made commercial sense for the studio to terminate a contract by invoking the morals clause: if the risk of public exposure was too great, it would be done. In other cases, an asset-protection strategy was adopted to ensure that the sexuality of the actor remained hidden.

Rock Hudson was a gay actor who shot to stardom in the 1950s. His films generated huge profits for Universal Studios—particularly when he was paired with Doris Day. Hudson enjoyed a lucrative contract with Universal that contained a morals clause. Away from the screen, Hudson had a busy sex life. His agent, Henry Wilson, reportedly paid off a blackmailer who threatened to expose Hudson's sexuality. Shortly afterwards, Wilson got word of a looming exposé to be published in *Confidential* magazine. With the support of Universal, which was keen to retain Hudson to safeguard the sizeable earnings he generated, a sham marriage was hastily organised with an employee of Wilson's, Phyllis Gates. The marriage was extensively reported. The ruse worked, so Hudson was able to continue his successful career.

In the McCarthyist era, morals clauses were directed at suppressing political expression and activity. They were invoked to sack left-wing activists, with devastating consequences. In 1947, the House Un-American Activities Committee (HUAC) established by the US House of Representatives, conducted public hearings to investigate the alleged infiltration of Hollywood by communist sympathisers. Approximately 40 actors and screenwriters were summoned to give evidence to the HUAC. At the hearings, they were required to name those they suspected of having links to the Communist Party. Many, such as celebrated director Elia Kazan, a member of the Communist Party between 1934 and 1936, succumbed to the pressure, and named colleagues and friends. A group known as the Hollywood Ten refused to comply. In a series of sensational hearings, the dissidents denounced the activities of the HUAC and refused to divulge any names, invoking the First Amendment.

The Hollywood Ten were cited for contempt by the HUAC and were then jailed for their defiance. A number were imprisoned for up to a year. Fearing adverse government or consumer boycotts, the major movie studios moved quickly to sack and then blacklist them. The board of Universal Studios resolved that any employee cited for contempt of Congress for failing to answer, whether or not they were a member of the Communist Party, would be sacked for breaching the morals clauses contained in their contracts.

Among them was Ring Lardner, an award-winning scriptwriter and political activist whose contract with Fox studios read:

[T]he artist shall perform the services herein contracted for in the manner that shall be conducive to the best interests of the producer, and of the business in which the producer is engaged, and if the artist shall conduct himself, either while rendering such services to the producer, or in his private life in such a manner as to commit an offense involving moral turpitude under Federal, state or local laws or ordinances, or shall conduct himself in a manner that shall offend against decency, morality or shall cause him to be held in public ridicule, scorn or contempt, or that shall cause public scandal, then, and upon the happening of any of the events herein described, the producer may, at its option and upon one week's notice to the artist, terminate this contract and the employment thereby created.[4]

Lardner was one of the Hollywood Ten who challenged the termination of his contract in the US Court of Appeals, on the grounds that it did not apply to political activity. His challenge failed, with the court finding that:

> [T]he natural result of the artist's refusal to answer the committee's questions was that the public would believe he was a Communist, and because a large segment of the public thought Communism was evil, the artist violated the express morals clause by failing to comport with public convention and morals.[5]

Morals clauses remain standard fare in contracts between corporations and their famous brand ambassadors. The exchange involves a lucrative financial package provided to the brand ambassador to be the public face of the brand and to promote it to consumers through various media channels and events. In exchange for the significant financial reward, the ambassador promises to conduct themselves in such a way as not to attract public opprobrium, based on the assumption that the individual's behaviour will be perceived as an extension of the beliefs and attitudes of the company. George Clooney, Rihanna, Leonardo di Caprio, Beyonce, Colin

Kaepernick, and David Beckham are all notable brand ambassadors. In 2003, Beckham signed up for a lifetime endorsement with Adidas for $160 million. Footballer Cristiano Ronaldo secured $1 billion in 2016 for such a deal with Nike.

In *What Money Can't Buy: the moral limits of markets*, prominent US philosopher Michael Sandel argues that, in recent decades, the West has been transformed from a market economy into a market society in which community values are increasingly subjugated to those of the market. In such a world, we are all human capital with a mission to build our personal brands. He questions the legitimacy of creating markets for almost everything. There are markets for goods or services that produce unjust outcomes or that can corrupt the good or service concerned. Markets for job-placement services, healthcare, water, or education spring to mind.

In the US, there is a commercial market for human kidneys. 'To determine whether kidneys should or shouldn't be up for sale,' Sandel writes, 'we have to engage in a moral inquiry.' Sandel also cites the market for places in queues: the phenomenon of time-poor, wealthy lobbyists hiring the time-rich, impoverished, and homeless to wait in queues for them outside the US Congress.[6] In a similar vein, we may question whether brand-ambassador contracts containing morals clauses are moral, desirable, or democratic. A healthy democracy requires the active participation and contribution of its citizenry. Should an individual be entitled to trade away their democratic right to full civic participation in exchange for a lucrative financial reward?

The labour market poses this dilemma beyond the realm of super-rich actors, sports stars, and musicians. Although the template employment contracts, codes of conduct, and other workplace policies that cross my desk each week don't explicitly contain morals clauses, the effect of their various provisions is much the same. As we have seen, the net effect of the standard obligations stipulated in the employment contract to conform to certain values, and the standard stipulation not to bring the company into disrepute, is to enable a corporation to sack an employee if their behaviour either at or outside work attracts public controversy. They also confer an enormous discretion upon corporations to dispense with employees who engage in controversial behaviour.

The effect is profound, rendering all employees brand ambassadors, but without the coin to show for it. Unlike the situation with highly remunerated brand ambassadors, these obligations are imposed on employees without any bargaining power. Most would be unaware that in entering into a wage-for-work bargain, the deal has a hidden anti-democratic sting. The chilling impact on public discourse and democratic participation is not confined to a small cohort, but extends to virtually all of the privately employed working population.

One hundred years after the demise of Roscoe Arbuckle, the arts—and specifically literature—is promoting a resurgence in morals clauses. In the wake of #MeToo, from 2017 onwards, allegations of sexual misconduct have been made against a number of US authors and other publishing-industry figures, prompting the industry to drop several authors and introduce morality clauses into their contracts with contemporary writers. Harper Collins' contracts, for example, permit it to terminate its contract with a writer in cases of 'conduct [that] evidences a lack of due regard for public conventions and morals', or in the case of a 'crime or any other act that will tend to bring the Author into serious contempt, and such behaviour would materially damage the Work's reputation or sales'.[7]

Consensual workplace relations

One hundred years after the Fatty Arbuckle scandal and the adoption of morals clauses, the private sector is no longer blacklisting communists and homosexuals; instead, it's targeting employees expressing controversial opinions, pursuing human rights issues, or engaging in consensual sexual relationships, particularly involving older men and younger women.

Take the case of my client Eugene (not his real name), an employee under investigation for engaging in 'inappropriate' consensual sex. The investigation is targeting his SMS messages.

'I can't wait to see you, babe. When I do, I'm going to run my lips across your neck, then your breasts and your pussy,' he enthuses in an email to his colleague and lover, Louise. It's February 2019, and I'm in my office neck-deep in emails about cunnilingus. It strikes me as mildly ludicrous that I'm being paid $700 per hour to trawl through emails and SMS messages about people going about the business of consensual sex.

Eugene is a serial philanderer and senior executive in the IT industry who is once again having an affair with a younger work colleague. His recidivism hasn't inspired any artfulness in his attempted erotica. Responding to his emailed cunnilingus commitment, Louise is an aspiring aphorist. 'Prrrrrr', she replies.

As the textbook of Human Resources requires, Eugene is confronted in his office late on a Friday afternoon by the CEO and a Human Resources manager. He is handed a letter advising him that he has been suspended from work on full pay pending a workplace investigation into allegations of misconduct. By having an affair with Louise and not declaring a potential conflict of interest, Eugene is said to have breached the company's values, workplace policies, and code of conduct. He is directed not to discuss the matter with anyone from work while suspended. He goes into shock, and his health declines as the investigation proceeds. Isolated and stuck at home, he ruminates and catastrophises.

To bolster the case against Eugene, it is also alleged that, eight months earlier, he threw a cocktail party at his apartment and invited a number of colleagues from work, including a recent recruit and attractive younger woman, Celia. She now says that a number of Eugene's guests at the party got drunk and spoke to her in a highly sexualised manner. One of the other guests — we will call her Sally — took Celia onto the balcony and showed her a short video on her iPhone depicting Sally having intercourse. Sally does not work for the IT company. She's a public servant.

What's that got to do with Eugene or his employer?

Under clause 6b of the company's code of conduct, all employees are required to treat other employees 'respectfully'. By having invited his colleague, Celia, to a cocktail party he was hosting at which she met other people who got drunk, talked about sex, and shared an iPhone video of consensual sex, Eugene is said to have failed in his obligation to afford respect to her. Eugene's health becomes so bad that he decides to stop fighting, and strikes a deal to resign quietly.

Within weeks of first sitting down with a distressed Eugene, I'm meeting with a senior academic accused of having failed to declare her affair with a younger male colleague. At least it makes for a change from the usual gender dynamic of these situations.

In the 1990s, US companies moved to ban or regulate consensual relationships between supervisors and employees. IBM's policy provided that, 'A manager may not date or have a romantic relationship with an employee who reports through his or her management chain, even when the relationship is voluntary and welcome.'[8] Some 'no fraternization' policies required one or both employees to be sacked for an infraction, while others required that one of the participants be reassigned. The policies were motivated by the advice of HR professionals and corporate lawyers that such relationships were high risk because they were disapproved of by other staff and might result in a sexual harassment claim upon dissolution of the relationship. To manage the litigation risk, some US companies required employees in such relationships to sign so-called love contracts, which typically read like this:

> I very much value our relationship and I certainly view it as voluntary, consensual, and welcome. And I have always felt that you feel the same. However, I know that sometimes an individual may feel compelled to engage in or continue a relationship against their will out of concern that it may affect the job or working relationships.
>
> It is very important to me that our relationship be on an equal footing and that you be fully comfortable that our relationship is at all times voluntary and welcome. I want to assure you that under no circumstances will I allow our relationship or, should it happen, the end of our relationship, to impact on your job or our working relationship.

In recent years, as consensual relationships have come under increasing scrutiny, love contracts are again 'becoming popular, requiring employees who are dating to report to HR to sign paperwork affirming that they are willingly taking part in a consensual relationship. ... This could be understood as HR mission creep.'[9] In fact, corporations do use employment contracts to achieve mission creep, as in this extract from a US waiver:

ACKNOWLEDGMENT AND WAIVER OF CLAIMS

_____, _____, and _____, _____, have notified the Company that they entered into a consensual relationship on or about [date] and said relationship continues until this date. In addition, they have notified the Company of their marriage plans. Both acknowledge that their relationship has been and is completely welcome and consensual. _____ and _____ further acknowledge that they believe this consensual relationship was not and is not harassment, sexual or otherwise, nor was it in violation of any federal, state or local law, regulation or ordinance.

_____ and _____ also acknowledge that:

Policies mandating disclosure of relationships between a supervisor/manager and an employee are now increasingly common in many corporate workplaces. Rules ranging from 'bonk bans' to mandating the disclosure of relationships with subordinates have been introduced. Meta, for example, requires that any staff who ask a colleague out on a date cannot ask a second time if the first request is declined.

Since #MeToo, several CEOs of US companies, including McDonald's, CNN, and Boeing, have been forced to resign for failing to disclose their consensual relationships with subordinates. Brian Krzanich resigned as chief executive of technology company Intel in 2018 after violating a 'non-fraternisation' code that applied to managers. In late 2021, German publishing multinational Axel Springer moved to require its 16,000 employees to disclose manager/subordinate sexual relationships. The move followed the removal of one of its editors, Julian Reichelt, after accusations of him having multiple affairs with interns and subordinates were investigated. (He was later reinstated.) While its new disclosure regime was introduced in the US, it was a different story in its German base. European workers are protected by the European convention on human rights, which provides a 'right to respect for privacy and family life'.

Investment giant Blackrock has gone further, promulgating a requirement of its 16,000 employees to disclose relationships with employees of 'external partners' — whether they are clients or suppliers. The policy says they should disclose any personal relationship they have at any 'service provider, vendor, or other third party (including a client), if the non-BlackRock employee is within a group that interacts with BlackRock'.[10]

The catalyst for the crackdown on consensual sex between employees was the #MeToo movement, which erupted in protest against sexual harassment and assault. In 2006, the American activist Tarana Burke founded the #MeToo campaign, seeking to ensure that the voices of survivors of sexual assault and harassment were heard. It was a slow burn until years later, when revelations about the industrial-scale sexual assault and harassment perpetrated by Harvey Weinstein and his enablers released the pent-up anger of generations of women at their mistreatment. In their wake, on 15 October 2017, the American actress Alyssa Milano tweeted a request to her followers to 'give people a sense of the magnitude of the problem': 'If you've been sexually harassed or assaulted write "me too" as a reply to this tweet.'

The effect was volcanic. Many other men who had harassed or assaulted women were named and shamed on social media. It started in Hollywood with reports of cases of abuse of women by men. Then Kevin Spacey was swamped with accusations of misconduct by younger men. His career went into freefall. (In July 2023, he was acquitted of all nine criminal charges that he faced.) The fallout spread from there, with sexual harassment allegations being aired in many industries — finance, technology, sport, and the law. All were engulfed. Google is reported to have sacked 48 employees for sexual harassment in response to #MeToo.

#MeToo unleashed a reckoning that reverberated across the globe. New policies, codes, and laws were introduced, industries rushed to embrace new gender-equality measures, and the silence-inducing shame and guilt that women experience in these cases was set aside as more and more women came forward to share their experiences. I felt both a sense of relief and exhilaration. Having represented many women who had been sexually harassed, I was only too aware of how widespread and entrenched their mistreatment was.

One of the first illustrations of the blurring of the non-consensual with the consensual occurred when more than 100 French women, including actress Catherine Deneuve, sought to discredit #MeToo. They signed an open letter condemning the movement for its 'hatred of men and of sexuality' and supporting men's 'liberté d'importuner' — men's freedom to make sexual advances toward women. Their letter characterised #MeToo as a 'vague purificatoire' — a puritanical wave unfairly targeting robust male sexuality. It described being 'fondled on a Metro' as a 'non-event' for some women.[11] The letter prompted a fierce counterattack by French feminists who branded its signatories as apologists for rape.

However, the protest was not enough to prevent the Macron government from enacting new laws designed to eliminate sexual harassment in France, including by introducing on-the-spot fines for men sexually harassing women in public places.

#MeToo had a dramatic impact on serving US politicians, forcing eight of them to resign after allegations of sexual harassment were aired. There was an outraged response to a US Congress report that revealed that, since 2003, taxpayer funds had been used by 13 US federal politicians to pay for settlements of sexual harassment allegations.

By February 2018, a bipartisan consensus reached among US legislators had resulted in new laws that radically altered the relationships between the politicians and their staff. The laws abolished policies that had allowed sexual harassers to resolve complaints confidentially, using taxpayer funds and with full access to taxpayer-funded lawyers and other support. The new laws required US politicians to personally fund any financial settlements for sexual harassment or cases of victimisation. In addition, the legislation explicitly banned sexual relationships between House members and 'any employee of the House that works under [their] supervision'.

The risks of rushing to judgement to condemn and deplore consensual relationships between older, more powerful men and younger women are neatly illustrated by the tale of Australian senator Barnaby Joyce. Joyce is a 'complex, intense, furious personality'[12] — a charismatic, yet generally unsympathetic character, except in his electorate of New England in New South Wales, which continues to re-elect him. At his worst, he is a rambling, incoherent reactionary, railing against climate science, public debt, and government. In February 2018, the Rupert Murdoch-owned tabloid *The Daily Telegraph* revealed that Joyce, the-then deputy prime minister, had left his wife and was having an affair with his former media adviser Vikki Campion. The front page featured a photograph of an obviously pregnant Campion walking across a street. The tabloids and other media justified this gross intrusion into their privacy by noting that Joyce had in recent years been a loud proponent of 'traditional family values', including being a vocal opponent of legislation to permit gay marriage.

After being outed, Joyce rejected any element of a power imbalance arising from his former position as Campion's boss, saying, 'there's nothing beyond the consensual'. In the ensuing media pile-on, Joyce was widely ridiculed and pilloried. In response to the political scandal, the-then prime minister, Malcolm Turnbull, announced a new code of conduct that would ban government ministers having consensual relationships with their staff. Turnbull claimed that he was following a well-trodden path already established in the private sector. I penned an article for *The Sydney Morning Herald*, criticising the move as overreach, and arguing that it was a 'misplaced attack on consensual sex'.

Turnbull did not pull his punches, condemning Joyce's 'shocking error of judgement in having an affair with a young woman working in his office' that had 'set off a world of woe'. He lamented the 'terrible hurt and humiliation that Barnaby, by his conduct, has visited on his wife Natalie and their daughters—and indeed his new partner'. Turnbull's condemnation occurred well after the relationship had begun and when Vikki Campion was about to give birth. The implication of Turnbull's posturing was that the relationship was illegitimate and that the soon-to-be-born baby was an 'error of judgement'. Several years later, the couple remain together and have two children.

Turnbull was performing his own version of brand management, but, in doing so, he fell into an all-too-common trap. Just after we eviscerate the philanderer, he leaves his wife, gets a divorce, and marries his younger female colleague. They have children, and live happily together evermore. We adjust. The disapproval subsides or disappears.

Journalist Julie Szego observed:

> [O]one dubious privilege of being a halfway rational adult entails understanding the boundless capacity of couples to inflict emotional damage on one another. As outsiders we cannot know what really went on in Joyce's marriage and who 'let down' who. Affairs happen. Sadly, marriages fail—and expecting Joyce or anyone else to manage their separation like a controlled landing, without emotional wreckage, is childish nonsense.[13]

Several years after these events, I spoke with Malcolm Turnbull about them. He was adamant that bonk bans were essential in ministerial offices. He explained that, in such a hothouse environment with a small number of staff, the minister is all-powerful, and that there is always resentment and fallout when an affair takes place. When the relationship ends, the woman always loses out, he said. Turnbull is right about that, but a ban on consensual relationships even in such environments is likely to have unintended consequences. Consensual relationships are likely to continue but be kept secret, or the woman is likely to be forced to leave her employment in order to pursue the relationship.

And then there's the law. I don't really want to encourage a new frontier of discrimination cases by powerful, older men, but if you ban a man from having a consensual relationship with a younger woman, there is a question as to whether you have contravened laws that prohibit age discrimination — impacting both parties.

Re-imagining consent

The law neatly delineates the divide between consensual affairs and sexual harassment and assault. It's a critical line in the sand, not least because unwelcome sexual attention, conduct, and assault often cause enormous trauma.

I have seen so much of this trauma that I have had to learn not to be overwhelmed by it. I have waded through unwelcome priapic pictures of partners in professional service firms and graphic 'Asian Anal' porn imagery sent by a real estate agent to his appalled female colleague. I have listened to accounts of workplace rape, of heads pushed towards assorted crotches, to stories of a judge manhandling his young employee on a hotel room bed as she tries to flee the room, and to myriad accounts of relentless stalking. Then — if you can forgive the technical legal expression — I have gone after the bastards.

While I cheered on #MeToo and the resulting progress in legal and policy reform, I don't have the same sentiment about consensual relationships.

Nevertheless, #MeToo also amplified a debate about the nature of consent that continues without a clear resolution. More than 20 years after Monica Lewinsky was reluctantly propelled into the international spotlight, #MeToo prompted her to revisit and reassess the nature of her sexual relationship with the-then 49-year-old US president, Bill Clinton. At that time, she was a 22-year-old White House intern. While Lewinsky had previously acknowledged that the relationship was consensual, her assessment has since changed. She now sees 'how problematic it was that the two of us even got to a place where there was a question of consent. Instead, the road that led there was littered with inappropriate abuse of authority, station, and privilege'.[14]

It is difficult to imagine a more extreme disparity in power and status than that between a serving US president and a young intern. Men at the top of a workplace hierarchy can seek to exploit their power by targeting much younger employees for sexual relationships. The relationships present a moral quandary. Do they involve an abuse of power, manipulation, or an explicit or implicit promise of career advancement? Will the woman be discarded and forced out of her job once he gets bored? Does such a relationship inherently negate, or somehow dilute, consent? At the same time, adult women should have autonomy and agency, including about their choice of sexual partner, even if that choice is questionable or, worse still, simply bad.

Such relationships also raise uncomfortable questions about what attracts women to older, more powerful men outside the workplace. There is a symmetry to the disapproval that we direct at such relationships. The male billionaire is damned for his adolescent sexual desire for a much younger woman, who most people believe could not possibly reciprocate or love him. His partner is assumed to be a golddigger: cynically relishing the wealth provided by her husband, all the while awaiting his death and an eye-watering inheritance.

The age differences and distribution of power between work colleagues having affairs remains a fraught and complex matter. There may be a power imbalance and a conflict of interest when one reports to or is subordinate to the other. If adultery is involved as well, some degree of disapproval or even hostility in the workplace is inevitable. That difficulty may be exacerbated for those others uncomfortably caught up in the deception. There may be questions of coercion, and real or perceived favouritism. The cliché of the serial male predator in management will not die any time soon, and certainly not before women share equally in senior roles. Yet, for all of that, the situation should not be conflated with sexual harassment. To do otherwise is to infantilise adult women and to suggest a moral equivalence with non-consensual, illegal, and harmful conduct—a false equivalence.

Shaming adulterers

Many major sporting codes are extremely lucrative big businesses, overwhelmingly driven by the bottom line. They attract astonishing sums of money from TV rights deals and membership enrolments, producing in the process ludicrously large pay packets for young athletes who are idolised for their sporting prowess. Not surprisingly, the codes frequently confront scandals involving corruption, match-fixing, racism, bribery, and other integrity challenges. The problem is that big sports clubs attract wealthy—and, often, colourfully wealthy—businessmen who buy them and wield them like a sparkling trophy, or who get a seat on the board to get up close to their sports-star heroes. That may render them and their employees ill equipped or reluctant to pass judgement on moral issues.

The adulation directed at and wealth gained by young, brilliant athletes often serves to give them licence to indulge in their instinct to regularly disgrace themselves. Think of simulated sex with animals. Or being photographed urinating into your own mouth — for kicks. Throw in the exponentially increasing sports-gambling market, and watch the moral turpitude unfold. In recent years, drug cheating has haunted cycling and swimming, FIFA has been exposed as a corruption racket, and cheating allegations have dogged professional cricket and tennis.

In Australia, the Australian Football League (AFL) is a corporation that operates the highly lucrative professional sport of Australian Rules football. It is both a commercial and cultural juggernaut, wielding influence in the halls of power, business, and the media. The rivers of gold that propel its growth flow from deals with commercial networks for the right to broadcast each season's games, and from an addiction to gambling company sponsorships. Despite spawning a steady stream of scandals — including epic bouts of racism, illicit drugs, misogyny, and violence — it is highly profitable and virtually untouchable. It employs an army of public relations and brand managers who work methodically to manage the journalists who write and talk about the AFL incessantly.

On Friday 14 July 2017, the-then CEO of the AFL, Gillon McLachlan, addressed a packed press conference at AFL headquarters, reading from a prepared statement. In an excruciating and highly choreographed performance that bore all the hallmarks of at least three dress rehearsals, a visibly pained McLachlan emphasised that he had 'no choice' but to accept the resignations of two managers, Simon Lethlean and Richard Simkiss. 'Two men had inappropriate relationships with two younger women who work in the AFL industry', he said. '… I expect my managers to be role models and set a standard for the rest of the organisation.' He confirmed that the affairs were consensual and that the women involved had not made any complaints against the men. (It was subsequently revealed that the women did not report to their lovers within the organisation, so there had been no conflict of interest involved.) He later explained that 'our organisation has a set of expectations around behaviours, and these guys understood they breached those', necessitating the making of 'very difficult decisions'. He continued:

> I can tell you there are relationships going on in my office. People know about them. There would be some between single people of the same age that people don't know about, and that is not an issue for me.
>
> The issue here is around ... the relationship status of the men. They go to the fact the women were younger women in the organisation; it talks to their positions on the executive.

Adultery had collided with the AFL's brand, and the brand won. Both senior managers were very publicly named and shamed. Both were married and had been having consensual affairs with younger, female employees who were also outed. One of the women involved was simultaneously in a relationship with a famous rugby player.

While the AFL's workplace policy on 'Responsibility and Respect' prohibited sexual harassment, it had nothing to say about consensual sex or adultery. There was no policy about or prohibition on workplace relationships. That absence was no impediment to the AFL, which moved to ruthlessly assert the moral high ground when the cameras started rolling. When pressed by a journalist, McLachlan said that the AFL might consider a formal code about consensual relationships, '[but] when you try to codify what we know what is right or wrong, and when there's all this nuance, you can potentially create a rod for your own back'.

Well before the press conference, the AFL had been made aware of the affairs. Four months before the senior managers' rushed exit, a journalist had sought answers to questions about the affairs from the AFL. He was brushed off. It was only when the AFL learned that a tabloid newspaper, Melbourne's *Herald Sun*, was investigating the affairs and was about to publish a tawdry exposé that it was prompted to act. Moving quickly, a decision was made to cut the managers loose. They were given a choice: resign or be sacked.

Out of the media limelight, a different approach was taken. McLachlan summoned AFL staff to a meeting at which he expressed his disgust that the story of the consensual affairs had been leaked to the press, and reportedly threatened to find and sack the culprit.[15]

There was no good reason for the men to lose their jobs, but if they were to do so, a press conference served to unleash pointless damage. A short, written statement acknowledging the departures would have sufficed. The press conference was a bloodbath in the service of the AFL's brand. By outing and shaming the married men having affairs, the AFL threw their wives, children, and other family members under a bus. The two women having affairs were given the same treatment. More trauma; more collateral damage. The brand was shored up while the human beings were humiliated.

In the manipulative lexicon of the modern spin doctor, there is no word more meaningless than 'inappropriate' — not so much a weasel word as a skunk word. It pollutes more than it illuminates, deployed to mask an absence of meaning. What was the problem here? That several adults were cheating on their partners? Adultery? Was it the age difference between the men and the women, and, if so, what is an acceptable age difference for a consensual relationship between an older man and a younger woman?

Journalist Gay Alcorn complained that the process was both regressive and sexist because the AFL assumed that 'somehow younger women need to be protected from older men, that they must inevitably be victims of an illicit affair, that they are not equal partners to a mistake'. Alcorn argued that women should not be consigned to stereotypical identities of '"innocent" wives', or "young" female temptresses, or victims of male desire. To treat them so isn't "respecting" women. It's infantilising them ...'[16]

Publicly shaming employees who engage in consensual sex provides a lamentable contrast with the standard operating procedure used by corporations when dealing with sexual harassment cases. A press conference to announce the sacking of a man for sexual harassment is a black swan event. Typically, such cases are cloaked in secrecy, with all relevant parties constrained by non-disclosure agreements. Even in the post-#MeToo era, that orthodoxy remains.

Not only did the AFL dive headlong into a murky and confused moral terrain, but its conduct was also illegal. Anti-discrimination legislation prevails over corporate codes of conduct or employment contracts where there is any inconsistency between them. The Victorian Equal Opportunity Act outlaws discrimination against employees because of 'lawful sexual relations'. As the Victorian Equal Opportunity and Human Rights Commission states on its website:

> Victoria's laws protect us all from discrimination because of lawful sexual activity. That means who you have sex with should have no bearing on whether you get a job, a promotion, accommodation, a loan or a place on a sporting team. Lawful sexual activity includes taking part in, or choosing not to take part in, any form of sexual activity that is legal in Victoria.

In late 2022, when the board of the University of Michigan unanimously decided to fire its president, Mark Schlissel, it engaged in an unprecedented act of cruelty. Following the receipt of an anonymous complaint that Schlissel may have been involved in an 'inappropriate relationship' with a university employee, an investigation began. The board subsequently released its letter of termination and 118 pages of emails between Schlissel and his lover 'in the interest of full public disclosure'.

The letter was littered with references to the need to free the university from sexual harassment and to make the campus community safe. Consensual sexual relationships were conflated with sexual harassment.

Schlissel's contract stipulated that his 'conduct and comportment shall at all times be consistent with promoting the dignity, reputation, and academic excellence of the University'. It was almost a morals clause. The university determined that Schlissel should be sacked for having breached the contract by communicating with a subordinate through the university's email system, 'using an inappropriate tone and inappropriate language', and for using university business to 'carry out a personal relationship with the subordinate'.

The university may have had good reason to sack Schlissel, but its stated reasons were odd. The emails between Schlissel and his subordinate lover were overwhelmingly cheery and banal. There was one email in which Schlissel linked to a *New Yorker* magazine story entitled 'Sexual fantasies of everyday New Yorkers'. I have read it. It's not very exciting. Did he spend university funds on flowers for his lover? Or book a hotel room on the university credit card? Or did the university board not appreciate Yiddish and misunderstand the word for a Jewish pastry stuffed with potato? In October 2019, when Schlissel emailed his lover about receiving a box of knishes, the woman replied that she liked them. Schlissel responded, 'Can I lure you to visit with the promise of a knish?' She responded, 'Laugh'.[17]

In fact, the university had endured a series of adverse events in earlier years relating to allegations of sexual harassment against a senior academic and its handling of the coronavirus pandemic. Schlissel was humiliated in order to shore up the university's damaged brand.

If there is anything to be redeemed from this story, it is that centuries after the medieval knysz emerged from Ukraine, the erotic potential of the humble knish may be about to be realised.

CHAPTER NINE

The Battle to Democratise Economic Power

> To strike at a man's food and shelter is to strike at his life, and in a society organized on a tooth-and-nail basis, such an act ... [is] menacing and terrible.
>
> It is for this reason that a laborer is so fiercely hostile to another laborer who offers to work for less pay or longer hours ... To sell his day's work for two dollars instead of two dollars and a half means that he, his wife, and his children will not have so good a roof over their heads, such warm clothes on their backs, such substantial food in their stomachs.
>
> –Jack London[1]

To understand how corporations have amassed such far-reaching powers over the lives of their employees, it's instructive to recount what happened to Henk Doevendans. A machine operator who had been employed by BHP Coal Pty Ltd for 24 years, Doevendans was a staunch union member and a valued delegate of the Mining and Energy Union. Union delegates perform a critical role for unions—they are the eyes and ears on the ground, the first port of call for workers with problems, and often a thorn in the side of hostile management. They require thick skins and an ability to argue. In his capacity as a union delegate, Doevendans had regular meetings with management to deal with problems at the mine site. After two years of attempts by the union to negotiate a new collective agreement, the negotiations stalled and the union took legally sanctioned industrial action in February 2012. The company reacted by bringing in scab labour. Doevendans was one of the workers protesting at the entrance to the Saraji Mine in central Queensland, and brandishing various signs, one of which read:

No principles
SCABS
No guts

Within days, he was presented with a letter from management, alleging that:

1. On Thursday 16 February 2012, between 4:25am and 6:55am, you were observed waving a sign that read 'No principles Scabs No guts' at cars that were entering and leaving Saraji Mine. The sign was white with black writing, with the word 'Scabs' written in capital letters in red.
2. On Friday 17 February 2012, between 4:30am and 7:05am, you were observed waving a sign that read 'No principles Scabs No guts' at cars that were entering and leaving Saraji Mine. The sign was white was with black writing, with the word 'Scabs' written in capital letters in red.
3. On Sunday 19 February 2012, at approximately 4:42pm, you

were observed waving a sign that read 'No principles Scabs No guts' at a white utility vehicle as it drove past.

4. On Sunday 19 February 2012, at approximately 6:03pm, you were observed waving a sign that read 'No principles Scabs No guts'.

Doevendans was accused of breaching the Workplace Conduct Policy, the company's Charter Values, and 'expected workplace behaviours' which required that employees 'always demonstrate courtesy and respect'.

At the conclusion of the company's investigation, BHP sacked Doevendans for misconduct. Notwithstanding his 24 years of service, management determined that termination of employment was the only appropriate outcome because he had 'demonstrated a lack of contrition, low potential to change or modify his behaviour', and was 'unwilling to learn any lesson from this incident'.

The mining union challenged the sacking, relying on laws that protect union members from adverse action taken because of their 'industrial activity'.[2] The legal case was fiercely contested and found its way up to the High Court. The court upheld a finding that Doevendans had been sacked for breaching company policies by failing to be respectful and courteous, and not because of his 'industrial activity'. BHP, a mining multinational with a rich history of undermining the tax system, was able to eliminate from its ranks a long-serving employee who was a staunch union delegate because he had failed to comport himself during a strike with courtesy and respect toward strike-breakers. This was a classic case of legally sanctioned union-busting.

Not for the first time, a legal ruling drove a Humvee through laws that are supposed to protect the rights of employees who join unions and speak with a collective voice. The court ruling effectively upheld a highly artificial distinction made by BHP; that in sacking Doevandans it was motivated by his breach of its behavioural policies and not by his union activity. Union delegates, like judges, do not afford courtesy and respect to others at all times.

Several years after the Henk Doevendans case, in 2020, and as set out in chapter 6, the High Court decided that academic freedom gave licence to academics, such as climate science dissident Peter Ridd, to not act with courtesy and respect so as 'not to sacrifice the moral courage of the human mind'.

Henk Doevendans' demise also helps explain why union membership has declined more severely in Australia than in virtually any other OECD country. The laws that notionally protect union speech and activity are ineffective, frequently ignored, or subverted. Conservative judicial interpretations exacerbate the problem. For some time, trade unionists have quipped that the High Court is the place where employee rights go to die. Approximately 50 per cent of workers were unionised in the early 1980s—the peak of union influence. Since then, union density has suffered a precipitous decline, hurtling towards US levels—a prospect that was once thought unimaginable. Currently, about 12.5 per cent of the workforce are union members, with density in the private sector at just 8.5 per cent. If the downward trajectory continues, Australia and the US will have the same union membership rates within a decade. As it is, 12 US states boast higher union density than Australia.

The uniquely repressive cocktail of anti-union laws that have de-unionised the labour market are a direct product of the outsized political power of corporations. The laws have progressively strangled union membership, collective bargaining, and employee voices. They discourage union membership by enabling free riders—those who choose not to join trade unions—to obtain the same employment conditions afforded to unionists, whose resources and work support improvements in pay and conditions for everyone. The laws, in effect, mean that unions are required to give away their services for free to the overwhelming majority of the labour market. A corporation required by law to offer its services or products for free to most consumers would dwindle and die. The only other comparable free-rider laws are to be found in some Republican Party-led states in the US.

The ability to enter workplaces and speak with workers is for unions akin to the right to breathe oxygen for the rest of us. Restrictive right-of-entry laws have been part of the smorgasbord of de-unionisation tools. One union has repeatedly ignored those laws: the construction union, also known as the CFMEU. In response to its defiance, even more draconian laws were enacted to try to de-unionise the construction industry, including by eliminating union speech and culture on construction sites. Publicly funded regulators were generously funded to enforce the laws.

On 6 November 2019, two inspectors from the Australian Building and Construction Commission (ABCC), the building industry workplace regulator, attended a construction site at Monash University in Melbourne's south-eastern suburbs. Upon entering the site, they found their way to the lunchroom, where they observed seven posters that had been placed on the walls promoting health and safety. One poster featured a chicken wearing a hard hat alongside the words, 'The chicken has a brain the size of a pea, and even it knows to get undercover when it starts raining. Don't let the boss make a chook out of you. When it's raining, come inside.' The inspectors' detailed notes, which were subsequently produced in court, said that the posters 'bore the logos, mottos or indicia' of construction industry unions.

Then things got even more confronting as the inspectors moved outside. There they discovered 'a flag bearing symbolism associated with the Eureka Rebellion' [more commonly and conveniently referred to as a 'Eureka flag'] that had been attached to the deck of one of the tower cranes. The Eureka flag is a favourite symbol of the CFMEU and adorns its merchandise. Subsequently, the regulator issued a notice alleging that Lendlease Corporation, the company managing the building project, had breached the Commonwealth Code for the Tendering and Performance of Building Work. The site had tested positive to trade unionism.

The Commonwealth code was a procurement policy used by the federal government to de-unionise the construction industry between 2016 and 2022. Under the code, government funding of building projects was made conditional on ensuring that no traces of union culture were permitted on building sites. In early March 2022, a comprehensive legal challenge to the ban on flags and posters was dismissed by the Federal Court.

In his zeal to prevent union officials from attending workplaces, Nigel Hadgkiss, the-then head of the ABCC, directed that incoming Labor government changes to union right-of-entry laws — which relaxed some restrictions — not be published by the agency. As a result, the regulator's website published misinformation encouraging employers to restrict unions from accessing workplaces in circumstances where this was illegal. After legal action was launched against him in 2017, Hadgkiss admitted that he had contravened the Fair Work Act, and resigned.

In 2018, a prosecution of union officials who visited a union delegate to catch up over a cup of tea on a worksite was condemned by a federal judge as a case where the regulator 'should be publicly exposed as having wasted public money without a proper basis for doing so'. The union organisers had visited their friend at a building site, and had discussed their shared passion for four-wheel-driving over a cup of tea. Federal Court judge Tony North said that the case was an 'abuse of power', where it seemed likely that 'reasonable members of the public would be offended by the use of community resources to prosecute a case such as this'.

In other cases, police raids have been orchestrated with media outlets in tow to maximise sensationalist headlines, suggesting sinister criminal conduct by trade unionists. In 2015, two union officials had their lives turned upside down when they were arrested and charged with blackmail over a meeting in a café with company executives to discuss an industrial dispute. The arrests were executed in a highly dramatic and public fashion, traumatising family members, and were coordinated with media outlets to achieve maximum public impact. The charges fell apart three years later, but the trauma endured.

The combination of anti-union laws, hostile, well-resourced regulators, and major union-busting operations conducted by large corporations has decimated union membership. Major corporations — including BHP, Telstra, Qantas, and the major banks — have all mounted and won aggressive union-elimination campaigns. I have spent the last four years in a legal battle against Qantas, challenging its union-busting. We won the case, but lost the war. Even if the company is forced to pay hundreds of millions of dollars in compensation and penalties, Qantas will have successfully eliminated the union and its members from its operations, and will also make a handsome profit.

The catastrophic decline of union membership in Australian workplaces is directly linked to an array of labour-market abuses. As we have seen, scandals exposing the widespread underpayment of wages have engulfed many major corporations and a majority of Australian universities.

A Senate committee inquiry into wage theft in March 2022 reported mounting evidence that 'wage theft practices have become widespread in the hospitality, retail, horticulture, franchise-heavy and higher education sectors ... The workers most vulnerable are migrants on temporary visas, young people, those in "low-skilled" jobs, non-unionised employees, and those in casual and insecure work ...'[3]

Corporate cancel culture is another form of abuse in the labour market that speaks of a radical redistribution of power away from employees. Once corporations eliminate the collective voice of employees, individuals don't stand a chance.

Union-busting in the United States

The political power enjoyed by major corporations guarantees that US trade unions continue to languish, notwithstanding 50 years of decline in the economic fortunes of employees and the resultant astonishing levels of income inequality in the country. On these measures, there has never been a better time to join a union. The percentage of Americans who say they support unions has spiked strongly, and in recent years there have been significant attempts to unionise major US corporates, including Amazon, Apple, Starbucks, Kellogg's, and Walmart. In 2023, workers organised about 400 strikes, including a successful 50-day strike by the United Auto Workers and the 148-day Hollywood writers' strike, conducted by the Writers Guild of America. Both in the UK and the US, there have been signs of growing membership and activism among women and younger workers.

Accordingly, David-and-Goliath successes in organising workplaces at multinationals, including Amazon, have generated many media headlines suggesting that trade unionism is on the precipice of a new era.

It's not.

Major corporations such as Amazon and Starbucks stop most attempts to unionise workplaces by breaking the law. Although the National Labor Relations Act makes it illegal for corporations to intimidate, coerce, or fire workers for participating in union-organising campaigns, corporations routinely flout the law because the penalty for non-compliance is minimal. Employers are charged with violations of federal law during 41.5 per cent of all union-organising campaigns.[4] According to Lynne Fox, the president of Workers United, the union that represents Starbucks workers, 'Violating workers' rights has simply become part of the cost of doing business', and is much cheaper than the cost of allowing companies to be unionised.[5] In recent years, the regulator has brought multiple complaints against Starbucks, alleging more than 1,000 illegal actions. Violations with minimal consequences include threatening employees, bribing employees, destroying union literature, firing union supporters, and lying to federal officials.

Strike-breaking has a rich and violent history in the US. In the first Gilded Age, major corporations were able to count on police, the military, and violent strike-breakers. Twenty-first-century union-busting has become far more sophisticated, with a recent surge in unionising campaigns galvanising a very American response: a burgeoning union-avoidance industry.

In April 2022, a two-day conference hosted by an organisation called CUE shared strategies for 'union avoidance'. CUE had been established in 1977 by the American National Association of Manufacturers, and was then known as the 'Council for a Union-Free Environment'. The organisation, which has since been rebranded as a 'Community for Positive Employee Relations', now provides research and training for the union-suppression industry. It is made up of lawyers and consultants who specialise in helping corporations defeat the threat of organised labour.

The dissonance of ethical brands engaged in illegal union-busting is stark. According to an exposé by *The Intercept*, one of the key union-suppression strategies promoted at the 2022 conference was the promulgation of diversity-and-inclusion activities at the workplace, guiding businesses 'to co-opt the language of social justice movements and embrace trends around self-growth and positive lifestyles to counter demands for unionization'.[6]

The roll call of speakers at the conference included 'human-capital managers' and 'diversity executives' offering 'to empower management with employee selection, retention, diversity training and skills, and union-avoidance tools and strategies'. Those strategies involve suppressing union speech while flooding the zone with anti-union speech. Employees are forced to attend lengthy meetings filled with anti-union propaganda, and are threatened with store (or factory) closures or the loss of their jobs if they vote to unionise. Starbucks stands accused of closing 23 of its stores to deter efforts to unionise. Walmart is one of the companies to favour the use of periodic union 'vulnerability' audits. The audits are increasingly sophisticated data-collection exercises used to flag the risk of union recruitment. Nissan and Volkswagen have used anti-union billboards, while Delta Airlines has preferred the humble poster.

A contract obtained by *The Intercept* shows that the Labor Pros consultancy provided a menu of options to Hilton Hotels in 2022 for persuading workers against joining a union. The firm offered up to four consultants to speak to 80 employees for four days at a cost of $43,120, plus per diems.

Inevitably, law firms are also a key plank of the union-avoidance industry. In 2016, IKEA used Ogletree Deakins to fend off unionisation in its Massachusetts stores. The law firm boasts of its pioneering work in 'developing strategies and practices that create positive employee relations. Through these legal, thoughtful approaches, enlightened employers work to develop a trust relationship with employees that minimize the risk of unionization'.

Government — by the corporation, for the corporation

Rutherford B Hayes, who served as American president from 1877 to 1891, identified the diabolical problem of the Gilded Age when he recorded in his diary that good government had been subordinated to 'government of the corporation, by the corporation, and for the corporation'. The evidence of a second Gilded Age is overwhelming: sprawling multinational monopolies; widening income inequality; the gaming of the political system; growing authoritarianism and fascism; a disastrous climate; a generation of billionaire plutocrats; and the regressive redistribution of wealth. The public service has been hollowed out and left dependent on the Big Four management consultants. For all of that, there are few signs of an imminent realignment of the relationship between the state and the corporation, raising the question whether corporations are too big and powerful to be tamed again.

The 21st-century corporation is remarkably resilient and adaptable: a chameleon that survives and thrives, no matter the harm it inflicts on others. An orgy of financialised corporate excess and inadequate regulation triggered the 2008 global financial crisis (GFC) and the greatest global recession since the 1930s. For major corporations, it was a mere flesh wound. Government bailouts ensured that the losses were socialised, and, after a brief flirtation with stricter regulation, business as usual resumed. The corporate tax system has continued to be subverted. Corporate regulators are still accepting staff on secondment from the companies they regulate, and are issuing jointly approved press releases. During the coronavirus pandemic, the state once again bailed out business to an eye-watering degree. The-then Australian treasurer, Josh Frydenberg, a loud and proud fan of Margaret Thatcher, famously wasted $27 billion of taxpayer funds in aid to businesses that remained profitable, notwithstanding the pandemic. In the US, workplace health-and-safety laws and enforcement were relaxed to allow corporations to continue their operations, including those operating abattoirs. Many workers at those abattoirs subsequently died of Covid-19.

While the death of neoliberalism has been repeatedly pronounced since the GFC, its spirit lives on. In October 2013, Australian prime minister Tony Abbott announced a commission of audit to review 'the role and scope of government', to examine the scope for privatisation, and to make recommendations about cuts to government expenditure. This was in 2013, not 1983. To head the commission, Abbott appointed Tony Shepherd, a former head of the corporate lobbying outfit the Business Council of Australia. There can be no more potent symbol of corporate capture than recruiting a veteran big-business lobbyist to make recommendations on the size of government, just five years after the GFC. To this day, conservative prominent businessmen are to be found in key roles within corporate regulators, public broadcasters, and central banks.

Monopolistic corporations have spawned a billionaire class that roams the earth in private jets assaulting democracy. One of their members is Anthony Pratt, chair of both Visy and Pratt Industries, two massive paper and packaging companies. Founded by Pratt's father, Visy has become Australia's second-biggest private company. According to the Bloomberg Billionaires Index, Pratt is worth $9.2 billion, making him the world's 213th-richest person. In October 2023, an investigation by *Sixty Minutes* and Nine revealed covert tape recordings of Pratt bragging of his strong links with Donald Trump. In those recordings, Pratt is recorded as saying, 'Being rich is my superpower.' He uses that superpower to support powerful and potentially helpful politicians. Pratt reportedly paid Trump lawyer Rudy Giuliani $1 million to attend Pratt's 60th birthday party.

When the roaming billionaires are not rent-seeking, there is much else to be done, including philanthropy and advancing public policy. Since stepping down from his role as CEO of Amazon, Jeff Bezos has established a $10 billion Earth Fund to contribute to the fight against climate change. While he does so, Amazon is emitting more carbon into the atmosphere than Portugal. According to a joint project of Oxfam and the Stockholm Environment Institute, the 'extravagant carbon footprints of the 0.1 per cent — from superyachts, private jets and mansions to space flights and doomsday bunkers — is 77 times higher than the upper level needed for global warming to peak at 1.5 per cent'.[7]

Corporate activism has moved beyond the brandishing of ethical values or loudly embracing social purposes into the realms of presenting corporations as an alternative to government, promising to change the world for the better. Indeed, corporations are promising to solve global warming in record numbers in a way that journalist Anand Ghiridaras observes 'not only fails to make things better, but also serves to keep things as they are'.[8]

In 2019, Larry Fink, a billionaire and head of investment behemoth BlackRock, wrote to the CEOs of companies in which BlackRock invests, saying that, 'Unnerved by fundamental economic challenges and the failure of government to provide lasting solutions, society is increasingly looking to companies ... to address pressing social and economic issues.'[9] Similar neoliberal posturing has become de rigueur at meetings of the World Economic Forum in Davos, where corporations and billionaires promise to end poverty, inequality, and climate change.

Paradoxically, one of the reasons for the disenchantment with political institutions is the gaming of the political system by big businesses and the neoliberal weakening of the state.

The corporate rent-seekers' handbook has become increasingly sophisticated and professionalised. Rent-seeking includes lobbying politicians; the provision of direct or indirect political donations and gifts; establishing or funding third-party entities, including think tanks; 'astroturfing' (setting up contrived grassroots protest groups); prosecuting political and media campaigns; political advertising; and 'partnering' with major media outlets and/or journalists.

Big business is not alone in lobbying politicians. It's just that it possesses the resources to out-lobby all the others. Those advocating on behalf of citizens, consumers, employees (including trade unions), the unemployed, and minorities tend to lose out more often. Politicians have long recognised the problem. Jimmy Carter once described political donations as 'legalised bribery'. In 2008, as Barack Obama campaigned for the US presidency, he promised that lobbyists 'will not run my White House ... and will not drown out the voices of the American people'.[10] Nothing changed.

In 2010, British prime minister David Cameron promised to shine 'the light of transparency on lobbying in our country and ... come clean about who is buying power and influence ... Commercial interests—not to mention government contracts—worth hundreds of billions of pounds are potentially at stake.'[11]

During Cameron's prime ministership, Greensill Capital enjoyed extraordinary access to his government. Later, in 2018, Cameron became an adviser to and lobbyist for Greensill, reportedly receiving millions of shares and remuneration of over $1 million for 25 days' work per year. In 2019, Cameron arranged for a private meeting with Lex Greensill and the secretary of state for health and social care, Matt Hancock. In 2020, several months before Greensill Capital collapsed, Cameron's lobbying on behalf of the company intensified, including through communications with the-then chancellor of the exchequer, Rishi Sunak.

In April 2024, as the campaign for the US presidential race intensified, Donald Trump cut to the chase when he offered oil and gas companies a 'deal': in exchange for a $1 billion donation, he would reverse President Biden's energy and environmental policies.[12]

It's the union, stupid

The battle for democracy at work is intimately connected with the broader democratic struggle. Workers acting collectively are one of the most critical forces that moderate the immense power wielded by corporations. By operating as a check on unbridled managerial force, unions reduce the wealth and associated power of corporations and their owners. They also participate in the political process to mitigate corporate influence. Strong democracies depend on robust trade unions. Weak democracies invariably contain weak and diminished unions. As journalist Eric Levitz has observed:

> [O]rganized labor does not merely democratize individual firms; it also democratizes economic power throughout the economy ... When workers organize, they secure a voice within the 'private governments' that rule their economic lives, and they (typically) use that voice to rationally advance their own material interests — which, most of the time, also advances the self-interest of most Americans (a.k.a. the public interest).[13]

When organised labour resists the suppression of employee speech on the altar of brand management, it moderates corporate excess. In January 2019, BP oil refinery worker and unionist Scott Tracey posted a video on Facebook deploying the much-parodied scene from the 2004 film *Downfall* about the last days of Hitler and Nazi Germany. Tracey's video satirically compared the position that the company had reached in collective-bargaining negotiations with the Australian Workers' Union to the last days of Hitler and Nazi Germany. The company sacked him for breaching company values.

BP's values included Respect. Satire doesn't comply with company values.

With the support of the union, Tracey challenged the decision, relying on unfair-dismissal laws. A two-year litigation battle ensued, with Tracey ultimately winning his job back and a substantial sum of compensation. After its loss, BP remained unrepentant, releasing a statement that emphasised the company's commitment to 'upholding our values and behaviours across our company'.[14]

The campaigns against academic sackings prosecuted by the National Tertiary Education Union (NTEU) against Australian universities, some of which are discussed in chapter 6, stand out as some of the most successful examples of resistance to corporate brand-management. The union has fiercely defended academic freedom, and has negotiated collective agreements that protect it. Those agreements have moderated the impact of employment contracts and workplace policies. In several notable attempts to counter the expunging of academics perceived to threaten a university's brand, the union not only went to court, but campaigned publicly and industrially in support of the targeted worker. Those efforts ultimately prevailed.

The NTEU, like other Australian unions, is waging these battles as a shadow of its former self. Membership density hovers at about 13 per cent. It lost the battle for security of employment so spectacularly that at least half of all university staff are now precariously employed. Many of the precariously employed have been ruthlessly exploited and underpaid. University employees are difficult to organise, and are prone to falling out with their colleagues and/or the union on matters of 'principle'. A significant number of progressive academics have resigned from the union on principle, but readily accept the gains made by their colleagues who have remained union members and continue to enable collective bargaining through membership fees and active participation. Some of the precariously employed resent those with tenure, and believe that the union hasn't always done enough to assist their cause. The union is also caught between its fierce attachment to academic freedom and the at-times furious debate among academics about identity politics. For all of the NTEU's travails, it stands out as a global beacon of hope in the democratic struggle against corporate cancel culture.

While it was not enough to save his football career, Colin Kaepernick successfully resolved a claim of unlawful collusion against the US's National Football League following his blacklisting for having taken the knee. He did so with the full support of the NFL Players Association. US labour laws have also been used successfully against corporations for sacking or disciplining workers whose speech outside work addressed wages or working conditions. The National Labor Relations Board has also ruled as unlawful provisions of company social media policies that inhibit discussions about work issues, even where they are highly critical of management.[15]

Restoring democracy requires, at a minimum, rebuilding the collective power of employees and their unions. That cannot be done without state support, and some moves in that direction are underway. Progressive parties have won government in the US, Australia, and Latin America. The United Kingdom elected a centrist Labour government in July 2024 with a massive majority, after years of Tory incompetence and dysfunction. And, although he failed to clearly articulate it, US President Joe Biden spearheaded a progressive shift from neoliberalism, notable for his administration's assertion of a greater role for the state, moves to reduce monopoly power, and support for increased union membership.

In 2023, Biden was the first president to join a union picket line and repeatedly proclaimed himself 'the most pro-union president in American history'. He supported a stronger, more dynamic role for trade unions, and committed himself to a range of measures that would strengthen collective-bargaining rights. That said, many of those measures have been frustrated by a hostile Congress. The federal minimum wage remains frozen at $US7.25 per hour. Nevertheless, real wage growth has spiked sharply as a result of strong government stimulus and a post-pandemic shortage of labour.

Vice President Kamala Harris oversaw the White House Task Force on Worker Organizing and Empowerment, which works with agencies on ways to use their existing statutory authority to support worker organising and bargaining. In August 2023, the US Treasury department released a comprehensive review of the role that labour unions play in the American economy. The report found that unions play an important role in addressing stagnant wages, high housing costs, and reduced intergenerational mobility. In doing so, unions contribute to a more robust and resilient economy, with the gains they make in bargaining flowing through to many others in the labour market.

Moderating corporate power must also involve reducing market concentration. Decades of neoliberalism have encouraged corporate consolidation to the extent that monopolies and oligopolies now dominate many industries. We are all paying a hefty price for this—as consumers, employees, taxpayers, and citizens.

In July 2021, President Biden issued an executive order which stated that 'excessive market concentration threatens basic economic liberties, democratic accountability and the welfare of workers, farmers, small businesses, start-ups and consumers'. Biden's order spurred multiple investigations of corporate power by the Federal Trade Commission, the Department of Justice, and the Consumer Financial Protection Bureau. Anti-trust cases are being pursued in the US in technology, aviation, and book-publishing industries. European competition regulators are zeroing in on Big Tech. The companies are so large and powerful that it may take decades to assess whether the regulators will succeed in breaking them up.

In July 2024, Biden was forced to withdraw from the presidential race, after a disastrous performance in the first debate with Trump, during which there was nowhere for him to hide his physical and cognitive decline. Kamala Harris's ascension gave the Democrats renewed hope, but nothing was guaranteed. Even if Harris were able to win the presidency, her position on corporate monopoly power was unclear.

A more cautious approach has been taken by Australia's Albanese government. Nevertheless, it has successfully legislated a commendable range of measures designed to improve employee bargaining power, promote collective bargaining, strengthen wage growth, and promote gender equality and job security. In doing so it has successfully stared down big-business campaigns. The Albanese government has made more modest steps to address market concentration, flagging increased penalties for anti-competitive behaviour and possible corporate-merger law reform. Australia has never had a divestment regime, although its opposition leader, Peter Dutton, has expressed support for breaking up its supermarket duopoloy. Curiously, Prime Minister Albanese has dismissed the idea of introducing a divestment regime on the basis that Australia 'is not the old Soviet Union'.

Can we escape the Second Gilded Age?

For decades, leading progressive intellectuals have called for renewed activism to counteract the influence of neoliberalism. In *Supercapitalism*, Robert Reich, a former secretary of labor in the Clinton administration, argued that genuine progressive reform can only occur 'if and when most citizens demand it'. He urged citizens and politicians to become better informed about corporate power and the brand-management techniques wielded to weaken government and avoid proper regulation. He added that, 'The most effective thing reformers can do is to reduce the effects of corporate money on politics, and enhance the voices of citizens.'[16] That was all the way back in 2007, before the GFC and the decision of the US Supreme Court to green-light the unlimited corporate funding of political campaigns. Since then, a tsunami of dark money has swamped American politics.

We have seen grass-roots activism and mass campaigns in the form of the Occupy Movement, #MeToo, and Black Lives Matter. Committed activists have also sought to shift the dial within the British Labour Party and the US Democrats, achieving far more success in the latter. All the while, many of the victims of neoliberalism have embraced authoritarian politicians.

French economist Tomas Piketty, ever the optimist, says that what he calls 'hypercapitalism' is destined to fail because that is always the fate of bankrupt ideologies. He takes the long view. In an interview in 2022, he said:

> We have become much more equal societies in terms of political equality, economic equality, social equality, as compared with 100 years ago, 200 years ago. This movement, which began with the French and U.S. revolutions, I think it is going to continue … Of course there are structural factors that make it difficult: the system of political finance, the structure of media finance, the basic democratic institutions are less democratic than they should be. This makes things complicated. But it's always been complicated.[17]

According to this analysis, the last 40 years across the West has been a bump in the road in the arc of progress that invariably moderates extremes in inequality. There is only one catch: what if Piketty is wrong?

The drift from neoliberalism to authoritarianism has prompted others, including Naomi Klein and playwright and journalist Van Badham, to urge progressives to learn from the playbook of authoritarian intellectuals such as Steve Bannon, an acolyte of the 'Breitbart Doctrine'. Andrew Breitbart, the founder of *Breitbart News* and co-founder of *Huffpost*, argued that 'politics flows downstream from culture'. Accordingly, if you want to change politics, you need to change culture; to change culture, you need to change how people think and react. Badham wants progressives to focus on the creative realm, including theatre, song, internet culture, and 'news entertainment'.[18] In some ways, Badham is responding to the thinking of Lewis Powell in 1971, who urged business groups to reshape culture in the interests of free enterprise. His targets were 'the perfectly respectable elements of society: from the college campus, the pulpit, the media, the intellectual and literary journals, the arts and the sciences ...' [19] As we have seen, his manifesto is considered instrumental in the triumph of neoliberalism.

Between the 20th and 21st centuries, there was a fundamental shift from a politics defined by the contest over economic inequality to the politics of identity. Increasingly, we no longer identify ourselves by our class, or position in the labour market, but rather by our ethnicity, gender, sexual identity, or disability status. How we define our identity is complex; we are all made up of multiple identities, multiple privileges, and multiple hurdles to overcome. The creative realm that Badham highlights is deeply immersed in an identity politics that rails against gender and racial inequality, but is far more subdued about class, economic inequality, and the critical power of collective-labour rights. We see the divergence play out each time that identity groups mobilise to urge the sacking of a transgressor (or micro-aggressor) at universities, or the black-banning of an artist. Progressive cancel culture can be extraordinarily puritanical and punitive, 'turning minor language infractions into major crimes', as Naomi Klein observes. For some of its most brutal exponents, the liberal progressive's 'casual racism' is more the enemy than the rabid racist.

Identity politics is inhibiting the progressive project in at least three ways. First, it is easily co-opted by corporations and their ethically washed brands because it poses no challenge to corporate power; company directors embrace identity politics as evidence of the corporation's 'purpose' and their credentials as 'change agents'. Second, and for precisely the same reasons, its most ardent exponents have little to offer to those who don't have a tertiary education, wealth, or secure housing, and who don't live in proximity to a major city; many are alienated by progressive identity politics, and have increasingly shifted their allegiance to authoritarians. Finally, it tends to produce a competition among progressives to claim multiple oppressed identities and to condemn the multiple privileges of others. In other words, identity politics undermines solidarity.

Conservative politics has embraced the post-truth era and relished the opportunity it has provided to shift the locus of political debate to identity, and to thereby avoid being held accountable for the detritus of neoliberal excesses. Stoking resentment against minorities and other tribes is proving a successful right-wing political formula. It has evolved into a violent and nihilistic project, deploying menacing rhetoric in a highly performative rendition of good versus evil, borrowing heavily from the culture of professional wrestling. That formula is now being exploited by a coalition of authoritarian states, including Russia, China, and Hungary, and allies in the Trumpish cult that describes itself as the US Republican Party. Those formidable forces are pumping social media, described by Klein as a 'filthy and crowded global toilet', with propaganda and misinformation designed to undermine democracy.

The relationship between corporations with ethically washed brands and authoritarian politicians is complex. On the one hand, corporations that publicly embrace progressive identity politics or that brandish environmental goals are condemned by right-wing populists for their 'wokeism'. In 2024, corporations are retreating from social and environmental progressive posturing. On the other hand, the right-wing anti-immigration agenda doesn't suit businesses that rely on importing specialist or cheap labour at will. Nevertheless, despite the tensions and the hostile rhetoric, their interests converge sharply on the fundamentals: business is good; corporate and billionaire taxes are bad; and trade unions are very, very bad. Both stakeholder corporations and authoritarian governments share an overwhelming interest in maintaining economic inequality and opposing redistributive government measures.

If Van Badham is right, and the creative realm is key to political transformation, there is another complication. Creatives are also muzzled by their employment contracts. Recently, for example, I took a call from a prominent comedian, who explained that she had just been offered a role in a new television series about families with young children. She was to be employed by a production company that had been commissioned by a television network to produce the series. Her contract with the company required her to comply with the social media policy of the network, including a prohibition on posting anything that was 'controversial'.

The comedian, who is an Arab Muslim, explained that she had been politically active in recent times, attending protests against the war on Gaza. She wanted to know what she was permitted to do if she signed the contract. I did not want to tell her to cease being politically active.

I responded, 'You can't do or say anything that is controversial.'

She asked, 'But what does that mean?'

I hesitated. 'You won't know until after the event. You will only know if something you say is controversial by the reaction of others.'

The comedian swore.

I added that, 'If an online lynch mob attacks you or the network, they may panic and you may be sacked. The sacking may be illegal, but they will still go ahead and do it. Just think of it this way: whoever chokes the system with complaints wins.'

Throughout this book, I have examined out-of-control corporations through the lens of their damaging impact on employee speech and expression. Of course, the harm caused when the state fails to properly regulate corporations is multifaceted. Neoliberalism has not only succeeded in transferring wealth and power from employees to the corporations that employ them, but has also diminished the state's capacity to regulate big business. The urgent need to address corporate censorship of speech and to rein in corporate power are democratic imperatives.

The decline in worker power mirrors the decline in the power of citizens, because they are inextricably linked. It follows that restoring the democratic rights of workers and citizens must be at the heart of the progressive project—a project that can only succeed if it involves a broad coalition that recognises the source of the harm and the shared interests of many people in addressing it. Such a coalition must include those harmed by economic inequality and other forms of inequality, including race and gender. Global multinationals are all-conquering and can buy influence in elections, but they can't vote. An organised combination of employees, members of minority groups, the unemployed and underemployed, environmental activists, students, and young people locked out of affordable rentals or home ownership have the capacity to see off the second Gilded Age and restore a functioning democracy.

We will know that we are making progress in repairing democracy when the next online pile-on pressuring a corporation to sack an outspoken employee is met with a standard-form statement that reads something like this:

> We sell goods and services for profit. We employ many people who harbour a range of values and views. We support our employees' fundamental right as citizens to participate in debate and other forms of civic life, including by expressing unpopular views. Their views are their own. They don't speak for the company. We will not censor, sack, or discipline them for exercising their rights.

Acknowledgements

The most important must come first. My love and gratitude to Tali, Esther, and Maya for your support, encouragement, and forbearance while I was swallowed up by the front room for an eternity to write and angst.

I am indebted to Sally Heath, who taught me how to pitch to a publisher.

Many thanks to Henry Rosenbloom of Scribe for taking a chance and supporting this book, and for his editing chops. I'm also grateful to the team at Scribe, including Christopher Black, Sarina Gale, and Tina Gumnior for their support and assistance.

I would like to thank Viktorija Melnikova, Patrick Coghlan, Madeleine O'Brien, Rachel Grove, and Jayne Hardy for their invaluable assistance in research.

I have benefited from suggestions, discussions, debate, and, yes, even disagreement, with a range of good folks, including Anthony Kitchener, Alison Penington, Giri Sivaraman, Emily Millane, Professor Jim Stanford, Kieran Pender, Catherine Deveny, Tim Soutphommasane, Nick Feik, Siobhan Kelly, Louise Adler, and Ian Mannix.

Many thanks to Professor Joel Bakan, who was generous in

reviewing an early draft of my chapter on corporations and who provided other helpful pointers. My thanks also to Ken McAlpine for his assistance in sourcing material about academic freedom.

Kudos to comedian Tom Ballard, who challenged my thinking and otherwise put me through my paces when interviewing me about corporate cancel culture for his podcast, 'Like I'm a Six-Year Old'.

Thank you also to Dr Costantino Grasso, Dr Dawn Carpenter, and Dr Luca d'Ambrosio, who invited me to present a seminar entitled 'Working for the Brand: how corporations are silencing employees', with support from the Centre for Financial and Corporate Integrity (CFCI) at Coventry University.

Some of the ideas in this book feature in articles and essays that I have penned over the last decade for media outlets including Nine/Fairfax, *The Guardian*, *The Monthly*, and the ABC. I am enormously grateful to the editors that I have worked with at those outlets.

Finally, I would like to pay tribute to the courage of the dissidents, contrarians, and inconvenient truth-tellers whose story I tell. All too often, they pay a terrible price for their convictions.

Notes

Chapter One: Rage and Revenge

1 'So you want to be a film critic?', *The Age*, 26 April 2006.
2 Bret Stephens, 'Free speech and the necessity of discomfort', *The New York Times*, 22 February 2018.
3 David Karpf, 'I called Bret Stephens a bedbug. Then he tried to squelch my freedom of speech. What a day', *Esquire*, 27 August 2019.
4 Luke O'Neill, 'NYT columnist quits Twitter after daring critic to "call me a bedbug to my face"', *The Guardian*, 28 August 2019.
5 Sacha Baron Cohen, 'Sacha Baron Cohen's keynote address at ADL's 2019 Never is Now summit on anti-Semitism and hate', *Anti Defamation League*, 21 November 2019. https://www.adl.org/resources/news/sacha-baron-cohens-keynote-address-adls-2019-never-now-summit-anti-semitism-and-hate.
6 Jon Ronson, *So You've Been Publicly Shamed*, Pan Macmillan, 3 September 2015.
7 Brian Stelter, '"Ashamed": Ex-PR exec Justine Sacco apologises for AIDS in Africa tweet', *CNN*, 22 December 2013.
8 Phillip Dwyer, 'Anzacs behaving badly: Scott McIntyre and contested history', *The Conversation*, 25 April 2017.
9 'How Anzac Day came to occupy a sacred place in Australians' hearts', *The Conversation*, 25 April 2017.
10 Wendy Bacon, 'Getting Scott McIntyre: lest we forget the role of pundits, politicians and a social media mob', *The New Matilda*,

5 May 2015.
11 Louise Hall, 'Scott McIntyre not sacked for controversial Anzac Day opinion: SBS', *Sydney Morning Herald*, 17 December 2015.
12 Sessions v. Dimaya, 138 S. Ct. 1204 (2018).
13 Australian Associated Press, 'SBS and sacked reporter Scott McIntyre resolve dispute over Anzac Day tweets', *The Guardian*, 11 April 2016.

Chapter Two: Flexible Control

1 Elizabeth S. Anderson, *Private Government: how employers rule our lives (and why we don't talk about it)*, Princeton University Press, 2019.
2 Rana Faroohar, '"Big Brother" managers should turn the lens on themselves', *Financial Times*, 23 October 2022.
3 Spencer Soper, 'Amazon warehouse workers complain of harsh conditions', *Los Angeles Times*, 1 October 2011.
4 Patrick Hatch, 'In Amazon's "hellscape", workers face insecurity and rushing targets', *Sydney Morning Herald*, 7 September 2018.
5 Emily Guendelsberger, 'I worked at an Amazon Fulfillment Center; they treat workers like robots', *Time Magazine*, 18 July 2019.
6 Philippa Collins, 'Automated dismissal decisions, data protection and the law of unfair dismissal', UK Labour Law blog, 19 October 2021.
7 Alexander JS Colvin, 'The growing use of mandatory arbitration', *Economic Policy Institute*, 27 September 2017, updated 6 April 2018.
8 Paul Karp, 'From dance instructors to boilermakers: Labor says non-compete clauses are holding back wages', *The Guardian*, 4 April 2024.
9 Paul Davies and Mark Freedland (eds.), *Kahn-Freund's Labour and the Law*, 3rd ed, 1983, Stevens & Sons, p. 198.
10 Suresh Naidu and Yoam Yuchtman, 'Coercive Contract Enforcement: law and the labor market in nineteenth century industrial Britain', *American Economic Review*, 2013, 103(1), 198.
11 Elizabeth Anderson, *Private Government*, p. 49.

12 Jacob S Hacker and Paul Pierson, *Winner-Take-All Politics: how Washington made the rich richer—and turned its back on the middle class*, Simon & Schuster, 2010, p. 117.
13 Jane Mayer, *Dark Money: how a secretive group of billionaires is trying to buy political control in the US*, Scribe, 2016, p. 75.
14 Miya Tokimitsu, 'The United States of Work', *The New Republic*, 18 April 2017.
15 'Text of Prime Minister's statement on workplace relations', *Sydney Morning Herald*, 26 May 2005.
16 Glen Dyer and Bernard Keane, 'Non-debate over productivity turns to attacking treasury', *Crikey*, 12 July 2012.
17 Ronald McCallum, *Employer Controls Over Private Life*, University of New South Wales Press, 2000.
18 Mark Irving, *The Contract of Employment*, LexisNexis Butterworths, 2nd ed, p. 26.
19 Graeme Orr and Alexandra Wells, 'Horizontal Censorship? Restriction of socio-political expression by employers', 2020, 32, *Australian Journal of Labour Law*, 290 at 316.
20 Orly Lobel, 'NDAs are out of control: here's what needs to change', *Harvard Business Review*, 30 January 2018.
21 Jenna Price, 'Harassment report a rate chance for workplace justice', *The Canberra Times*, 2 July 2021.
22 Australian Human Rights Commission, 'Respect@Work: Sexual Harassment National Inquiry Report, 2020.

Chapter Three: Do Corporations Have Feelings?

1 Quoted at the Iowa State Fair, when he was campaigning as the Republican presidential candidate. See, for example, *The Washington Post*, 11 August 2011.
2 'Israel Folau issued with Rugby Australia code of conduct breach notice, given 48 hours to respond', *ABC Online*, 15 April 2019.

3   Jamie Tarabay and Isabella Kwai, 'How a rugby star's homophobic posts got Australians arguing about religion', *The New York Times*, 1 July 2019.
4   Simon Longstaff, 'The Israel Folau crowdfunding saga is not about freedom of religion', *ABC Online*, 25 June 2019.
5   Joel Bakan, *The Corporation: the pathological pursuit of profit and power*, Simon & Schuster, 2004, p. 1.
6   William Dalrymple, 'Lessons for capitalism from the East India Company', *Financial Times*, 30 August 2010.
7   CF Smith, 'The early history of the London Stock Exchange', *The American Economic Review*, vol. 19, no. 2, June 1929, pp. 206–16.
8   Standard Oil Co. of New Jersey v. United States, 221 U.S. 1 (1911).
9   Anne Applebaum and Peter Pomerantsev, 'How to put out democracy's dumpster fire', *The Atlantic*, 8 March 2021.
10 Daniel Schulman, 'When Gilded Age lawmakers saved America from plutocracy', *Mother Jones*, January–February 2024.
11 Joel Bakan, 'Corporate capitalism's moral lack', *Business History Review*, vol. 98, no. 1, spring 2024.
12 Josh Bornstein, 'The great wealth redistribution', *The Monthly*, 31 March 2022.
13 Naomi Klein, *No Logo*, Flamingo, 2000, p. 4.
14 David Weil, *The Fissured Workplace: why work became so bad for so many and what can be done to improve it*, Harvard University Press, 2014, p. 570.
15 Daniel Moritz-Rabson, 'CEO compensation has risen 940 percent since 1978, but worker compensation has only increased 12 per cent', *Newsweek*, 14 August 2019.
16 Polly Hemming, 'How the government supports greenwashing', *The Saturday Paper*, 29 October 2022.
17 André Spicer, 'From Inboxing to Thought Showers: how business bullshit took over', *The Guardian*, 23 November 2017.

18 Joel Bakan, *The Corporation:* , pp. 57–8.
19 Joel Bakan, *The New Corporation: how 'good' corporations are bad for democracy*, Vintage, 2020.
20 David Hellier, 'Former BP boss on VW scandal: 'With these big crises, you have to overreact', *The Guardian*, 27 September 2015.
21 Kenza Bryan and Attracta Mooney, 'How companies are starting to back away from green targets', *Financial Times*, 21 June 2024.
22 Michael Janda, 'Banking royal commission: CBA chairman Livingstone answers for the bank's remuneration breakdown', *ABC News online*, 21 November 2018.
23 Rebecca Armitage, 'CommInsure whistleblower Dr Koh suing for wrongful, "farcical" dismissal', *ABC News online*, 10 March 2016.
24 Adele Ferguson with Mario Christodoulou, 'The inside account of how Commonwealth Bank tried to bury the scandal that sparked a royal commission', *Background Briefing / The Whistleblowers*, ABC Radio National, 11 November 2023.
25 'CBA Corporate Responsibility Report', Commonwealth Bank of Australia, 2017.
26 Peter Ker, 'The inside story of how Juukan Gorge was lost', *Australian Financial Review*, 12 December 2020.
27 Frank James, 'Financial crisis panel says disaster was avoidable', NPR, 27 January 2011.
28 Kevin Rudd, 'The global financial crisis', *The Monthly*, February 2009.
29 Caroline Kelly, 'Freshman Democrat presses JPMorgan CEO Jamie Dimon', *CNN*, 11 April 2019.
30 Omar Rodríguez-Vilá and Sundar Bharadwaj, 'Competing on Social Purpose', *Harvard Business Review*, September–October 2017.
31 Dharna Noor, 'Rightwing war on "woke capitalism" partly driven by fossil fuel interests and allies', *The Guardian*, 22 June 2023.
32 Carl Rhodes, 'Getting woke to woke capitalism', Transforming Society, 9 November 2021.

33 Nick Hanauer, 'The pitchforks are coming ... for us plutocrats', *Politico*, July/August 2014.

Chapter Four: The Ethically Washed Brand

1   Caris Egan-Wyer, Sarah Louise Muhr, Anna Pfeiffer, and Peter Svensson (eds), 'The ethics of the brand', *Ephemera*, vol. 14, no. 1, p. 2.
2   Naomi Klein, *No Logo*, Flamingo, 2000, p. 24.
3   Alan Kohler, 'The seductive, destructive technology illusion', *The New Daily*, 28 July 2021.
4   Amy McNeilage, 'Uber's underpayment of drivers keeping it afloat, report finds', *The Guardian*, 7 March 2018.
5   Hilary Osborne, 'Uber loses right to classify UK drivers as self-employed', *The Guardian*, 29 October 2016.
6   Giulio Nardella, Stephen Brammer, and Irina Surdu, 'Shame on who? The effects of corporate irresponsibility and social performance on organizational reputation', *British Journal of Management*, vol. 31, no. 1, May 2019.
7   Barry Meier, 'In Guilty Plea, OxyContin Maker to Pay $600 Million', *The New York Times*, 10 May 2007.
8   Gideon Haigh reviewing Walt Bogdanich and Michael Forsythe, *When McKinsey Comes to Town: the hidden influence of the world's most powerful consulting firm*, Bodley Head, 2022, in 'Amorality for hire', *Inside Story*, 13 October 2022.
9   Lisa Girion, 'Johnson & Johnson knew for decades that asbestos lurked in its baby powder', *Reuters*, 14 December 2018.
10 Casey Cep, 'Damages: Johnson & Johnson and a new war on consumer protection', *The New York Times*, 12 September 2022.
11 Amanda Mull, 'Brands have nothing real to say about racism', *The Atlantic*, 3 June 2020.
12 Ibid.
13 Janice Min, 'Pinterest and the subtle poison of sexism and racism in

Silicon Valley', *Time Magazine*, 22 March 2021.
14 Andrew Edgecliffe-Johnson, 'How Walmart convinced critics it can sell more stuff and save the world', *Financial Times*, 13 October 2022.
15 Y Fan, 'Ethical Branding and Corporate Reputation' in *Corporate Communications: An International Journal*, vol. 10, no. 4, pp. 341–50.
16 Polly Hemming, 'How the government supports greenwashing', *The Saturday Paper*, 29 October 2022.
17 Adam Morton, 'Australia's carbon credits system a failure on global scale, study finds', *The Guardian*, 27 March 2024.
18 Polly Hemming, 'How the government supports greenwashing', *The Saturday Paper*, 29 October 2022.
19 Ibid.
20 Priya Elan, 'Renting clothes is "less green than throwing them away"', *The Guardian*, 6 July 2021.
21 Michael Sainsbury, '"Not many airlines do such a dumb thing": how outsourcing took Qantas from soaring to sore', *Crikey*, 15 September 2023.
22 Alan Joyce, 'Election 2016: Qantas boss Alan Joyce backs Turnbull's big picture', *The Daily Telegraph*, 23 June 2016.
23 'Qantas will continue to campaign on social justice issues', AAP, 9 May 2019.
24 Joe Aston, 'Alan Joyce's lines aren't landing any more', *Australian Financial Review*, 27 August 2023.
25 S Homroy and S Gangopaddhyay, 'Strategic CEO Activism in polarised markets', *Journal of Financial and Quantitative Analysis*, January 2024.
26 Ryan Erskine, 'What is a brand really worth?', *Forbes*, 12 August 2017.
27 Neil Bedwell, 'Why employee stakeholders are the secret to your organization's transformative success', *Forbes*, 5 November 2018.
28 Shirin Ghaffary, 'How angry Apple employees' petition led to a controversial new hire's departure', *Vox*, 14 May 2021.
29 Zoë Schiffer, Casey Newton, and Elizabeth Lopatto, 'Apple employees

circulate petition demanding investigation into "misogynistic" new hire', *The Verge*, 13 May 2021.
30 Eric Johnson, 'Boeing communications chief resigns over decades-oil article on women in combat', *Reuters*, 3 July 2020.
31 US Department of Justice press release, 'Boeing Charged with 737 Max fraud conspiracy and agrees to pay over $2.5 Billion', 7 January 2021.

Chapter Five: A Festival of Hypocrisy

1 Jacob Mchangama, 'People want free speech—for themselves', *Foreign Policy*, June 2021.
2 Alice Terlikowski, 'Institute of Public Affairs runs ad in *The Australian* campaigning for freedom of speech', *Mumbrella*, 5 October 2011.
3 Paul Mason, *Postcapitalism: a guide to the future*, Penguin, 2016, p. 161.
4 Adam Serwer, 'Elon Musk's free-speech charade is over', *The Atlantic*, 12 April 2023.
5 Pat McGrath, Kevin Nguyen, and Michael Workman, 'Voice to Parliament referendum "prime target" for foreign interference on Elon Musk's X, former executive warns', *ABC News online*, 30 September 2023.
6 Jeannette Cox, 'A chill around the water cooler: First Amendment in the workplace', *Insights on Law and Society* 15 (Winter 2015), American Bar Association.
7 Lange v Australian Broadcasting Corporation (1997) 145 ALR 96 at 112.
8 James Ley, 'Godwin is Dead', *Sydney Review of Books*, reviewing Jeff Sparrow, *Trigger Warnings*, Scribe, 2018.
9 Hannah Giorgis, 'The Harper's letter is a weak defense of free speech', *The Atlantic*, 13 July 2020.
10 Michael Hobbes, 'Don't fall for the "cancel culture" scam', *The Huffington Post*, 11 July 2020.

11 Kate Manne and Jason Stanley, 'When free speech becomes a political weapon', *The Chronicle of Higher Education*, 13 November 2015.
12 Anne Appelbaum, 'The new Puritans', *The Atlantic*, October 2021.
13 James Button, 'Cancel Culture: it's complicated', *The Age*, 19 November 2021.
14 Conor Friedersdorf, 'Book-industry activists should be careful what they wish for', *The Atlantic*, 9 November 2022.
15 Ibid.
16 Dan Zak and Roxanne Roberts, 'Anthony Fauci is up against more than a virus', *The Washington Post*, 27 January 2022.
17 Jonathan Haidt, 'Yes, social media really is undermining democracy', *The Atlantic*, 28 July 2022.
18 Masha Gessen, 'How George Orwell predicted the challenge of writing today', *The New Yorker*, 10 June 2018.
19 Ryan Lizza, 'Americans tune in to "cancel culture"— and don't like what they see', *Politico*, 22 July 2020.
20 Adam Serwer, 'The myth that *Roe* broke America', *The Atlantic*, 18 May 2022.

Chapter Six: Academic Freedom and the University Brand
1 Bill Louden and Emma Rowe, 'FactCheck: does the Safe Schools program contain "highly explicit material"?', *The Conversation*, 22 November 2017.
2 Bridget Davies, 'Former Safe Schools manager faces backlash on flag comment', *Herald Sun*, 29 May 2016.
3 Chris Graham, 'Latrobe Suspends Safe Schools co-founder and academic Roz Ward for criticising "racist" Australian flag', *New Matilda*, 1 June 2016.
4 Henrietta Cook and Education Editor, 'Guard of honour greets Safe Schools founder Roz Ward as she returns to work', *The Age*, 6 June 2016.

5   Jeannie Suk Gersen, 'Unpopular Speech in a Cold Climate', *The New Yorker*, 14 March 2019.
6   Kate Taylor, 'Harvard's first black faculty deans let go amid uproar over Harvey Weinstein defense', *The New York Times*, 11 May 2019.
7   Philip G Altbach, 'Academic freedom: a realistic appraisal', *International Higher Education*, March 2015.
8   Hannah Forsyth, 'Universities and government need to rethink their relationship with each other before it's too late', *The Conversation*, 15 June 2020.
9   United Nations Educational, Scientific and Cultural Organization (UNESCO), *Recommendation Concerning the Status of Higher Education Teaching Personnel*, UNESCO, portal.unesco.org.
10 Jason Stanley, 'A university or a billionaires' toy', *Yale Daily News*, 10 October 2021.
11 Robert French, *Report of the Independent Review of freedom of speech in Australian higher education providers*, Department of Education and Training, 27 March 2019.
12 Glenn Altschuler and David Wippman, 'Florida is trying to roll back a century of gains for academic freedom', *The Washington Post*, 6 February 2023.
13 Hannah Forsyth, 'Universities and government', *The Conversation*, 15 June 2020.
14 Sweezy v New Hampshire (1957), 354 U.S. 234.
15 Sweezy v New Hampshire, 354 U.S. 234 at 263.
16 Jan Currie, 'Globalisation practices and the Professoriate in Anglo-Pacific and North American universities', *Comparative Education Review*, vol. 42, no. 1, February 1998, pp. 15–29.
17 Janes Guthrie and Adam Lucas, 'It's time for a royal commission into the restructuring of higher education', *Pearls and Irritations*, 3 August 2022.
18 Thomas Klikauer, 'What is managerialism?', *Critical Sociology*, vol. 41,

Issue 7–8, 1 November 2013.

19 Alison Wolf, 'The university admissions system doesn't make the grade', *Prospect Magazine*, 4 September 2019.

20 Ian Pearman, 'The power and practice of branding', *Times Higher Education*, 1 January 1990.

21 Alisa Percy, Michele Scoufis, Sharron Parry, Allan Goody, and Margaret Hicks, 'The RED Report, Recognition—Enhancement—Development: the contribution of sessional teachers to higher education', June 2008, p. 4.

22 Anna Fazackerley, '"My students never knew": the lecturer who lived in a tent', *The Guardian*, 30 October 2021.

23 Colleen Flaherty, 'Barely Getting By', *Insider Higher Education*, 19 April 2020.

24 Russell Marks, 'The managerial destruction of academic freedom', *Overland*, 17 June 2016.

25 Carolyn Evans and Adrienne Stone, *Open Minds: academic freedom and freedom of speech in Australia*, Latrobe University Press, 2021, p. 97.

26 Robert French, *Report of the Independent Review of Freedom of Speech in Australian Higher Education Providers,* Department of Education and Training, 27 March 2019.

27 James Cook University v Ridd (2020) 278 FCR 566 at 86.

28 From High Court case Ridd v James Cook University (2021) HCA 32, quoting JS Mill at para 64.

29 Louise Milligan, 'Cash cows', *Four Corners*, 6 May 2019.

30 Christopher Knaus, 'Fifty top professors condemn Murdoch University for suing whistleblower', *The Guardian*, 22 October 2019.

31 'Murdoch University abandons claim against respected academic whistleblower Gerd Schroeder-Turk', *Mirage News*, quoting press release of Maurice Blackburn lawyers, 13 January 2020.

32 Conor Friedersforf, 'Professors need the power to fire diversity bureaucrats', *The Atlantic*, 13 June 2022.

33 Jason Stanley, *How Fascism Works: the politics of them and us*, Penguin Random House, 2018, p. 43.
34 Yascha Mounk, 'Cancel Culture cuts both ways', *The Atlantic*, 8 November 2023.
35 Greg Lukianoff, 'The latest victims of the free-speech crisis, *The Atlantic*, 28 November 2023.
36 Ehud Barak, 'Israel must oust its failed government before it sinks into the moral abyss', *Haaretz*, 13 June 2024.
37 Joint ILO–UNESCO Committee of Experts on the Application of the Recommendations concerning Teaching Personnel 1 (Geneva, 4–8 October 2021).

Chapter Seven: The Journalism Paradox

1 Michael Schudson, 'The Vital Role of Journalism in a Liberal Democracy', *The MIT Press Reader*, 5 October 2020.
2 Eric Ting, 'An interview with Emily Wilder, recent Stanford grad fired from AP job over criticisms of Israel', *SFGATE*, 20 May 2021.
3 David Goldman, 'AP explains why it fired Emily Wilder for pro-Palestinian tweets', *CNN*, 30 May 2021.
4 Zoe Samios, 'Elizabeth Farrelly departs *The Sydney Morning Herald*', *Sydney Morning Herald*, 12 December 2021.
5 Adolph Ochs, 'Without fear or favour', *The New York Times*. Originally published 18 August 1896, republished 19 August 1996.
6 'About the Post', *The Washington Post*, 1 January 2021.
7 Brent Cunningham, 'Re-thinking objectivity', *Columbia Journalism Review*, July–August 2003.
8 Ibid.
9 James Fallows, 'The media learned nothing from 2016', *The Atlantic*, 15 September 2020.
10 Wesley Lowery, 'A reckoning over objectivity, led by Black journalists', *The New York Times*, 23 June 2020.

11 Ivor Shapiro, 'Skepticism, not objectivity, is what makes journalism matter', *The Conversation*, 18 April 2021.

12 Roger Sollenberger, 'James Murdoch says his family media empire legitimizes disinformation and obscures facts', *Salon*, 13 October 2021.

13 Gabriel Snyder, '*New York Times* public editor: the anatomy of the Wolfe scandal', *Columbia Journalism Review*, 27 January 2021.

14 Robert Zaretsky, 'Lost in Trumpslation: an interview with Bérengère Viennot', *Los Angeles Review of Books*, 16 January 2017.

15 Jon Allsop and Pete Vernon, 'How the press covered the last four years of Trump', *Columbia Journalism Review*, 23 October 2020.

16 Rachel Abrams, '*Washington Post* suspends a reporter after her tweets on Kobe Bryant', *The New York Times*, 27 January 2020.

17 'How objectivity in journalism became a matter of opinion', *he Economist*, 16 July 2020.

18 Melissa Koenig, 'More than 750 reporters sign letter condemning "Israel's killing of journalists in Gaza" as death toll rises', *New York Post*, 10 November 2023.

19 Sam Buckingham-Jones, 'Guardian warns over open letters and social posts amid Israel row', *Australian Financial Review*, 4 December 2023.

20 Antoinette Lattouf and Cam Wilson, 'Viral footage showed protesters chanting "Gas the Jews". Nobody can verify it', *Crikey*, 13 December 2023.

21 'BBC staff can attend Pride parades, director general Tim Davie says', *BBC online*, 31 October 2020.

22 Mike Berry, 'Hard evidence: how biased is the BBC?', *The Conversation*, 23 August 2023.

23 Chris Uhlmann, 'Once journos backed free speech', *The Australian*, 20 February 2016.

24 Emily Maitlis, 'When an agent of the Tory party decides the BBC's "bias", it's a huge problem', *The Guardian*, 25 August 2022.

Chapter Eight: Consensual Sex and Work

1. Jude Sheerin, '"Fatty" Arbuckle and Hollywood's first scandal', *BBC online*, 4 September 2011.
2. Patrick Dougherty, 'Hollywood's first scandal: the tainted legacy of Fatty Arbuckle', *MovieWeb*, 27 April 2022.
3. Amanda Harmon Cooley, Marka B. Fleming, and Gwendolyn McFadden-Wade, 'Morality and money: contractual morals clauses as fiscal and reputational safeguards', *Journal of Legal Studies in Business* 2008, vol. 14, 1 at p. 6.
4. Todd J Clark, 'An inherent contradiction: corporate discretion in morals clause enforcement', *Lousiana Law Review* (2017), vol. 78 at p. 17.
5. Ibid.
6. Michael Sandel, *What Money Can't Buy: the moral limits of markets*, Penguin, 2013, p. 22–23.
7. Claire Armitstead, 'Morality clauses: are publishers right to police writers?', *The Guardian*, 14 June 2018.
8. Vicki Schultz, 'The sanitized workplace', *Yale Law Journal*, June 2003.
9. Caitlin Flanagan, 'The problem with HR', *The Atlantic*, July 2019.
10. Lucy Hooker, 'Investment giant BlackRock cracks down on romance outside work', *BBC online*, 23 September 2020.
11. '"Apologists for rape": French actress Deneuve slammed for attack on #MeToo', *SBS online*, 11 January 2018.
12. David Crowe, '"How could he have been so stupid": Turnbull, Joyce and the "bonk ban" debacle', *Sydney Morning Herald*, 17 April 2020.
13. Julie Szego, 'Forget Barnaby, the real error of judgment was Turnbull's', *The Age*, 19 February 2018.
14. Monica Lewinsky, 'Emerging from "the House of Gaslight" in the Age of #MeToo', *Vanity Fair*, 25 February 2018.
15. Michael Warner, *The Boys' Club*, Hachette, 2021, p. 267.
16. Gay Alcorn, 'This is what the AFL calls respecting women? Looks like

patronising moralism to me', *The Guardian*, 17 July 2017.
17 Kim Kozlowski, 'University of Michigan board fires President Mark Schlissel', *The Detroit News*, 15 January 2022.

Chapter Nine: The Battle to Democratise Economic Power

1 Jack London, 'The Scab', *The Atlantic*, January 1904.
2 Construction, Forestry, Mining and Energy Union v BHP Coal Pty Ltd [2014] 253 CLR 243.
3 Senate Standing Committees on Economics, 'Systemic, sustained and shameful', Commonwealth of Australia, March 2022.
4 Celine McNicholas, Margaret Poydock, Julia Wolfe, Ben Zipperer, Gordon Lafer, and Lola Loustaunau, 'Unlawful', Economic Policy Institute, 11 December 2019.
5 Stephen Greenhouse, '"Old-school union busting": how US corporations are quashing the new wave of organizing', *The Guardian*, 26 February 2023.
6 Lee Fang, 'The evolution of union busting, *The Intercept*, 7 June 2022.
7 Jonathan Watts, 'Richest 1% account for more carbon emissions than poorest 66%, report says', *The Guardian*, 20 November 2023.
8 Carl Rhodes, 'Woke Capitalism: how corporate morality is sabotaging democracy', Bristol University Press, 2022, p. 71.
9 Matt Levine, 'Money Stuff: The Companies Are in Charge Now', Bloomberg, 18 January 2019.
10 Peter Overby, 'Obama bans DNC from taking lobbyists' money', NPR, 6 June 2008.
11 George Monbiot, 'How Big Tobacco's lobbyists get what they want from the media', *The Guardian*, 18 March 2014.
12 Josephine Rozelle, 'House Democrat presses oil CEOs for details of Trump's fundraising dinner at Mar-a-Lago', *CNBC*, 14 May 2024.
13 Eric Levitz, 'Democracy dies when labor unions do', *Intelligencer*, 18 September 2019.

14 Nick Bonyhady, 'BP worker wins after Hitler meme case goes all the way to Federal Court', *Sydney Morning Herald*, 22 May 2024.
15 Steven Greenhouse, 'Even if it enrages your boss, social net speech is protected', *The New York Times*, 21 January 2013.
16 Robert Reich, *Supercapitalism: the transformation of business, democracy, and everyday life*, Knopf, 2007, p. 216.
17 David Marchese, 'Thomas Piketty thinks America is primed for wealth redistribution', *The New York Times Magazine*, 1 April 2022.
18 Van Badham, 'Rightwing culture has Alex Jones-style craziness to energise it. What does the left have?', *The Guardian*, 3 March 2023.
19 William Yeomans, 'How the right packed the court', *The Nation*, 13 September 2012.